SUPERMAN'S NOT COMING

SUPERMAN'S NOT COMING

Our National Water Crisis and What **We the People** Can Do About It

Erin Brockovich

with Suzanne Boothby

R A N D O M   H O U S E
L A R G E   P R I N T

Published in the United States of America by
Random House Large Print in association with Pantheon
Books, a division of Penguin Random House LLC,
New York, and distributed in Canada by Penguin
Random House Canada Limited, Toronto.

Cover photograph by Leonello Calvetti /
Science Photo Library / Getty Images
Cover design by Kelly Blair

The Library of Congress has established a
Cataloging-in-Publication record for this title.

ISBN: 978-0-593-29547-2

www.penguinrandomhouse.com/large-print-format-books

FIRST LARGE PRINT EDITION

Printed in the United States of America

10 9 8 7 6 5 4 3 2 1

This Large Print edition published in accord
with the standards of the N.A.V.H.

To my grandchildren: Grace Bailey, Molly Berlin,
Charles Asher, and Clay Jorge

May we create a more sustainable world
for them with clean water for all.

CONTENTS

PART THREE: THE FINAL CALL

INTRODUCTION

Someone once asked me, what would your epitaph be?

My answer: Someone who gave a damn.

Let me be the first to tell you that life takes an interesting turn when your name becomes a verb. Well, first my name became a movie and then it became a verb. To "Erin Brockovich something" has become synonymous with investigating and then advocating for a cause without giving up.

My name is also used to describe other people. There's an Erin Brockovich of China. She's found more than four hundred villages in her home country where the children have been sickened by their water supply. There's an Erin Brockovich of Kenya, who is fighting lead poisoning, demanding compensation and cleanup from the government and companies whose factories have dumped toxins. There's an Erin Brockovich of food, whose youngest child had a severe allergic reaction to scrambled eggs and now advocates for reducing chemicals in our food system.

But before the movie and before I became a name people recognize, you should know that I was raised in Kansas—the land of sprawling wheat fields and bright yellow sunflowers. Lawrence, to be exact, which is the sixth largest city in the state, nestled between the banks of the Kansas and Wakarusa Rivers. It's a vibrant college town today with a population of fewer than 100,000 people. Like many parts of my home state, we had hot, humid summers and cold, dry winters. The American poet Langston Hughes spent his boyhood in Lawrence, and he based his first novel **Not Without Laughter**, published in 1930, on his experiences growing up in small-town Kansas, tornados and all.

I was born in the summer of 1960 when Chubby Checker's dance hit "The Twist" was playing on every radio and life in America seemed rosy and bright. Little did anyone suspect that the 1960s would be marked by such upheaval and that by the end of the decade, it would feel more like our great country was falling apart. Rachel Carson's book **Silent Spring** was published in August of 1962, calling out the chemical industry and launching an environmental movement. The Cuyahoga River in Cleveland, Ohio, burst into flames in 1969. Images really can tell a thousand words and the dramatic photos made headlines through-out the country. How did a body of water ignite into flames? A **Time** magazine article described the river as so saturated with industrial waste and sewage that it "oozed rather than flowed." That sight sparked major reforms and a newfound need for environmental action, which included the passage of the Clean Water Act and the creation of state and federal environmental protection agencies.

When I was a little girl, my father would sing songs to me all the time about water. Sometimes, we would be playing down at the creeks and he would make up little tunes. "See that lovely water, trickling down the stream, don't take it for granted, someday it might not be seen," he would sing.

My dad was a star college football player at Kansas University. He served stateside in the U.S. Naval Air Force during World War II. He went on to work for many years as an engineer for Texaco and later for the Department of Transportation. He was a genuine hardworking American who loved his family. He and my mom were married for sixty-five years. If that's not a testament to love, then I don't know what is! They both instilled so many of their values about persistence and drive in me. Not to mention that my mom was a journalism and sociology major, which I think helped fuel my snooping instincts.

Before he died, my dad promised that in my lifetime water would become a commodity more valuable than oil or gold, because there would be so little of it. I believe he was right and that time has come.

My dad had good instincts. He was the kind of father who was always there for me, and he shared his wisdom. He once said, "When I'm not here to save you, it's important for me to know that you can save yourself."

I was the youngest of four children, but my parents didn't baby me. They always told me that there's no single way to do something. If you can't make it work, you find another way. They taught me to fight for what I wanted in my life, and for that I am forever grateful. Despite my love of learning, I struggled in school and was eventually diagnosed with dyslexia, which meant I had trouble with reading comprehension. I was smart, but my grades didn't reflect it.

I had a teacher in high school named Kathy Borseff, who recognized that I knew all the answers in class, but I would flunk my written tests. One day she did an experiment and let me stay after class to take the test orally. I got an A+. She changed my life with that experiment. Experts knew so little about dyslexia at that time, and I hated people labeling me inferior and putting me in a box as a slow learner. Dyslexics typically have high IQs, but they are misunderstood. We think and learn differently. Thankfully, my parents protected me from losing my self-esteem too. They were constantly reminding me that I didn't have to choose to see myself as "slow," and I was thankful for the reminders.

I would frequently come home from school feeling so frustrated from the hurdles of the day, and one time my mom said, "Erin, you've gotta have some stick-to-itiveness." I rolled my eyes because I didn't think it was a real word. But not a few minutes later my mom came back with a **Webster's Dictionary** in her hand, and I was shocked to see it on the page. The definition: a propensity to follow through in a determined manner; dogged persistence born of obligation and stubbornness.

What a word! I was captivated by this concept and it gave me a lot of hope. Even if I had challenges, I didn't have to give up on the dreams I had for my life. In fact, I'd argue that these early challenges helped shape me into the woman I am today. Perhaps some of the challenges you are working with right now are shaping you too.

I still use this word as a reminder that I can't give up, even when the going gets tough. If you know my work, you've seen what I'm talking about. I'm not one to give up easily. One of my favorite parts about stick-to-itiveness is that it's not a skill you are born with. It's something you cultivate. Anyone out there can develop the ability to follow through, regardless of the stumbling blocks. In fact, dyslexia helped me in my work because I tend to think backward. When I study any water contamination case and see the levels of pollution, I go back in time. If the levels are high today, what did they look like five, ten, or even twenty-five years ago? You would be surprised by the levels of pollution you can find by taking a little trip in time.

All said, my parents offered me this great set of commonsense skills to work with that saved me and continue to influence my work today. Throughout this book, I will share those same tools with you.

———

Our water has become so toxic that towns are issuing emergency boil notices and shipping in

In the restroom at the Cannon House Office Building, the oldest congressional office building, in 2016

bottled water to their residents. As I started gathering research for this book in 2016, members of our very own U.S. Congress had their water shut down in Washington thanks to unsafe lead levels.

Erin with Dan Kildee, the U.S. representative for Michigan's 5th Congressional District since 2013. Kildee was born and raised and still resides in Flint, Michigan.

In response, Congressman Dan Kildee, who represents Flint, Michigan, a city now famous for its drinking water problems, said in a statement, "Every American deserves to have access to safe drinking water. America is the richest and most prosperous country in the world—we can afford to provide safe drinking water to our citizens."

Kamala Harris, U.S. senator from California, has tweeted, "I've said this many times & will say it again: everyone has a fundamental right to drink clean water. The Administration should take steps to protect Americans from these chemicals that are already impacting the water supplies of millions of Americans." This tweet was in regard to news that the Environmental Protection Agency (EPA) is still not setting drinking water limits for two toxic chemicals, PFOA and PFOS, which are contaminating millions of Americans' tap water at this very moment (and which you will read extensively about in this book). You will also learn a lot about chemicals going unregulated, even when the science shows they are linked to cancer and other major health issues.

As if poisoned water wasn't a big enough issue, the last six years (2013–2019) have been the hottest years on record. As our climate changes, and we experience more droughts, floods, superstorms, melting glaciers, and rising sea levels, we are seeing greater strains on our water supplies, infrastructure, and economy.

For years, I've been teaching one very simple concept: Superman is not coming. If you are waiting for someone to come save you and clean up your water, I'm here to tell you: No one is coming to save you. We can't survive without access to clean water (or water at all) and yet we are losing access to our most precious resource. Without water, it is literally GAME OVER for all of us. The time has come for us to save ourselves.

We are amid a major water crisis that is beyond anything you can imagine. Pollution problems persist and toxins are everywhere, stemming from the hazardous wastes of industry and agriculture. We've got more than forty thousand chemicals on the market today with only a few hundred being regulated. We've had industrial byproducts discarded into the ground and into our water supply for years. The companies who dump these toxins know it. They have always known it. The government knows it too. These issues affect everyone—rich or poor, black or white, Republican or Democrat. Large and small communities everywhere think they are safe when they are not.

Each water system is unique, but some of the most toxic offenders that I will talk about in this book include hexavalent chromium (an anticorrosive agent), perfluorinated chemicals (PFCs)—which include perfluorooctanoic acid (PFOA, used to make Teflon pans) and perfluorooctanesulfonic acid (PFOS, a key ingredient in Scotchgard), trichloroethylene (TCE, used in dry cleaning and refrigeration)—lead, fracking chemicals, chloramines (a water disinfectant), and more. Many of these chemicals are undetectable for those drinking the water. Hexavalent chromium is an exception, as it typically turns the water green at high doses and water heavily treated with chloramines usually has an odor. But like a blood test for disease, you can only find what you test for. If you don't order a specific test for one of these chemicals, you won't know it's there. And you can't treat water, unless you know what's in it. Many of these substances cause irreversible health problems when ingested and people in communities throughout the country are dealing with these repercussions. This book will highlight just a few of the thousands of stories. Some cases have good outcomes, some are still in process, and many are still struggling.

Now, I know what you might be thinking. What about the EPA, Erin? What about corporate remediation departments? Aren't the experts handling it?

The short answer is no.

These issues start with tiny little seeds of deception that add up over months and years to become major problems. Our resources are exhausted. Corruption is rampant. Officials are trying to cover their tracks. People are either completely missing the mark or not putting all the pieces together when it comes to the severity of this crisis. I've got senators and doctors calling me, asking me what to do.

But before you put this book down in deep despair, I want to urge you to muster up your own stick-to-itiveness and keep reading. I want to remind you that we are in this together. No one person must—or can—fix it alone. Not one senator, one community member, CEO, mom, or dad. It's up to all of us. We've got to work together.

Even in the movie that shares my name, we had a team working around the clock. I went door-to-door to talk with residents who had concerns and were asking good questions. We hosted community meetings. We worked with some of the best legal teams, researchers, and academics in the state of California. It was not a one-woman or one-man job. We fought together.

I've noticed over the years that when I visit towns and work with people, the number one thing everyone seems to need is permission. They are looking for someone to tell them that it's okay to move forward. Empowerment is a process that happens as we give ourselves authority to act on what feels right, what we know is right. But sometimes people get stuck. We are afraid to act out, and believe it or not, I can relate to that. It's not always easy to speak up or out of turn. Since we were young girls and boys, we learned to ask for permission—whether it was permission to leave the dinner table or to use the bathroom during class. As we get older, we must get permits to build an extra addition onto the house. We sign permission slips for our kids to go on field trips. It becomes a habit to think we need permission to act. We request time off from work—we don't just take a vacation. We text people instead of calling them. All these little acts add up and then we think: Who am I to stand up at a city council meeting and ask a question? I don't know all the answers. I'm not a water expert. What does everyone else think about the water? Is it really a problem or am I overreacting? We all have these doubts and questions. In the end, I think that the permission we are seeking is more about support. We want to know if we take action, it will be successful in some way and that our community will not shun us for these actions.

Let this book stand as your personal permission slip. Yes, you have permission to ask questions. Yes, you have permission to scrutinize your water professionals and find out if they have the right credentials. Yes, you have permission to start a Facebook group to make more people aware of your cause. You have permission to stick up for yourself when it comes to your health, your family, your life. The world needs all of us to get involved now more than ever.

The first action that you can take is to become part of what I hope will be the first-ever national self-reporting registry at www.communityhealthbook.com. (We do have state registries but many people aren't reporting.) This crowd-sourced map is my legacy project and it allows individuals and community groups to report and review health issues (cancer being the most prevalent) and community environmental issues by geographic area and by health topic. This self-reported research provides missing data points coming from the people that local, state, and federal agencies cannot or will not talk to and will not communicate to each other about. The research is intended to connect the dots between clusters of illness and environmental hazards in specific communities and regions of the country. If you or someone you know is sick or suffering, please report it. I will talk more about the map in chapter 3, and throughout this book.

None of us need a Ph.D. or a science degree, or need to be a politician or a lawyer to be aware and to protect our right to clean water. I'll take you step by step through how to take these actions to save your family and community. We have the power together to fight for better enforcement of the laws on the books, to push for new legislation, and to storm our city halls until our voices are heard and the water is safe for everyone to drink.

PART ONE

THE SCARY TRUTH

Man's attitude toward nature is today critically important simply because we have now acquired a fateful power to alter and destroy nature. But man is a part of nature, and his war against nature is inevitably a war against himself. . . . We're challenged as mankind has never been challenged before to prove our maturity and our mastery, not of nature, but of ourselves.

—Rachel Carson, writer and conservationist, in 1963, a year before her death from breast cancer

1

HOW DID WE GET HERE?

Let's get one thing straight. I'm not a troublemaker; I'm an advocate. I've shown up to community after community across the country for more than twenty years because the people who live in these towns invite me. I get hundreds of emails every single day, and what they say boils down to two little words: HELP ME.

People across this country (and the world) are scared. They have concerns about what's happening with their water. The color has changed. It smells awful. Their animals are acting weird. Their kids are dealing with strange health symptoms. I get a lot of emails about cancer—fourteen children on one street with cancer or multiple adults in one neighborhood dealing with the same kind of rare tumor. People who have reconnected through Facebook and discovered that tens upon tens of classmates from the same high school all have cancer. They don't know who to turn to for help. And thanks to a movie that bears my name, starring an Oscar-winning actress, people write to me. They trust me. Imagine that! A foul-mouthed, short-skirted blonde woman from Kansas.

Many of these people have tried other channels. They've tried contacting their local representatives, the EPA, the Department of Natural Resources, the Centers for Disease Control (CDC), or their local water authority, but most of the time their letters and inquiries get lost in the bureaucracy of these agencies. In many cases their concerns are intentionally not addressed. And so people ask me for help.

Thankfully, I have Bob Bowcock, my go-to partner in water investigations. Bob is a water treatment professional, and he's been a licensed California Grade V water treatment operator since 1985, which is a big deal since we have fewer than two hundred of them in the state. He started his career reading meters and worked his way up as a water treatment operator. Bob managed several Southern California utility districts and worked as a U.S. Army civil affairs leader, designing and constructing water treatment and distribution systems for federal governments in Southeast Asia and South America. He now runs his own consulting firm that provides practical, problem-solving techniques to water-related issues. He's an expert in emerging technologies related to water and wastewater conveyance, treatment, and disposal, and environmental compliance and remediation.

Bob and I met in court shortly after the movie came out, and I wasn't sure if he was an attorney, a whistleblower, or just a weirdo stalking me, but once I got to know him and his credentials, we started working together. These days, he's a good friend and the first person I'll send out to a community that has written to me. Once he gets to town, he will tour the treatment facility, write a report outlining exactly what is needed to fix the problem, and work with local officials, water treatment operators, and community members on solutions.

In March 2017, Bob and I were coaching Julie and Marie, two women from Columbia, Missouri, who have created a coalition in their town to fight for cleaner water. Since 1995, Columbia has been dumping its sewage right next to where the water wells pump into the drinking water system. These two women have dealt with health issues for both themselves and their kids.

They were telling us about a small setback. The local radio station dedicated a full hour to talk about the town's water issues and didn't give them any air time. Not only were they not invited to be on the show, but they weren't even allowed to speak when they called in. They were frustrated, and I understood their frustration all too well. It's what I've been up against throughout my career.

Bob Bowcock, Erin's water advisor, whose more than thirty-six years of experience have helped communities achieve top water quality, speaking at a community meeting

For years, people have told me I have no right to comment on water. I'm not a scientist or a doctor or a lawyer, and I don't have the research to back up my claims. How can I comment on the water in the absence of a peer-reviewed study? Here's what I told these women to say to those who dismiss them, and what I say all the time: I may not have the science, but neither do you.

In the absence of a peer-reviewed study, how can you say that the water is safe?

And that's a BIG problem in America today.

It's amazing to me how little most people really know about what's going on. We've got failing laws and polluters still dumping with little reprimand. It's time to understand how we got here so we can get clearer about what we want our future to look like.

BIRTHING OUR WATER LAWS & THE EPA

The Federal Water Pollution Control Act of 1948 was the first law created to address water pollution in this country, but it was virtually rewritten in 1972 and is now commonly referred to as the Clean Water Act (CWA). President Gerald Ford signed the act (which was proposed by Richard Nixon) into law on December 16, 1974, amid media reports and television documentaries warning that the quality of U.S. drinking water was declining.

Here's some of what was written in a 1975 EPA press release:

> Potential cancer-causing chemicals have been found in trace quantities in New Orleans' and Pittsburgh's drinking water. In Boston, lead from water supply pipes has been found in water drawn from the tap. Viral or bacteriological contamination of drinking water has resulted in communication of disease, often in smaller, more rural communities where treatment works are outdated or modern techniques are not available.

In other cities and towns, foul odors and tastes make the water unpalatable. While the overall quality of this nation's drinking water is well above that supplied in any other country, professional waterworks operators, government, and citizens all agree that a much better job must be done in guarding our supplies.

That was in 1975! It was during the Republican administration of former president Richard Nixon that we officially created the Environmental Protection Agency (EPA), a fact that conservatives today may have forgotten. In fact, in Nixon's 1970 State of the Union address he made remarks that today might characterize someone as a liberal environmentalist:

We can no longer afford to consider air and water common property, free to be abused by anyone without regard to the consequences. Instead, we should begin now to treat them as scarce resources, which we are no more free to contaminate than we are free to throw garbage into our neighbor's yard.

This requires comprehensive new regulations. It also requires that, to the extent possible, the price of goods should be made to include the costs of producing and disposing of them without damage to the environment.

We have been too tolerant of our surroundings and too willing to leave it to others to clean up our environment. It is time for those who make massive demands on society to make some minimal demands on themselves. Each of us must resolve that each day he will leave his home, his property, the public places of the city or town a little cleaner, a little better, a little more pleasant for himself and those around him. . . .

With the help of people we can do anything, and without their help, we can do nothing. In this spirit, together, we can reclaim our land for ours and generations to come.

Nixon made these remarks in response to years of widespread and visible pollution. He had bipartisan support for increasing measures to protect the environment, which is hard to imagine in today's political climate. He set up an Environmental Quality Council along with a Citizens' Advisory Committee on Environmental Quality. At the same time, Congress sent a bill to his desk called the National Environmental Policy Act (NEPA). The purpose of the act was

- to set a national policy to encourage "productive and enjoyable harmony between man and his environment."
- to promote efforts to prevent or eliminate damage to the environment and biosphere and stimulate the health and welfare of man.
- to enrich our understanding of the ecological systems and natural resources.

The act called for the formation of a Council on Environmental Quality (CEQ) to offer expert advice on environmental matters to Nixon and to review newly enacted Environmental Impact Statements, a requirement for all federal agencies planning projects with major environmental effects. This led to the creation of the Environmental Protection Agency, a new federal regulatory agency whose purpose was to protect human health and the environment. The agency brought together tens of thousands of well-meaning, intelligent scientists, engineers, lawyers, and administrators.

Since its inception, the agency has worked with the best available science in its efforts to reduce environmental risks to public health and help enforce federal laws aimed to protect human health and the environment. When Congress writes environmental laws, the EPA implements them by working to ensure that all U.S. companies understand how to comply with national regulations and by following up on any violations.

The Clean Water Act was created to protect large bodies of water such as streams, rivers, and bays from being destroyed by things like sewage, biological and radioactive waste, and industrial and agricultural waste. We needed it then and we need it now.

Originally, it was a strong law that helped establish structure for regulating water pollution. It gave the EPA authority to set water quality standards and implement pollution control programs, funded the construction of more sewage treatment plants, and even recognized the need to address nonpoint source pollution from agricultural sources like fertilizers and pesticides along with urban runoff. The law called for polluters to disclose the toxins they dumped into waterways and gave regulators the power to go after offenders with fines or jail time.

Good laws can be written, but they can be hard to follow. If we are not setting standards for what's safe, then anything goes. Since the 1970s, pollution has only increased, and violations of the law have continued to rise. Between 2004 and 2009, the Clean Water Act was violated more than half a million times, and most of the big polluters evaded any kind of punishment. As you can imagine, without much recourse the violations keep piling up.

But isn't the law meant to protect us? How can these violations continue?

Sadly, the courts left us hanging for many years. Specifically, a Supreme Court ruling from 2006 was just confusing. In **Rapanos v. United States,** the Court failed to clearly define which waterways qualify for federal oversight. The ambiguity has played out for years and ultimately left too much legal room for disputes, allowing polluters to dump carcinogenic chemicals and more without much worry about federal enforcement.

In 2015, President Barack Obama (with help from the EPA and the U.S. Army Corps of Engineers) finalized the Clean Water Rule to help clear up the confusion about which bodies of water the federal government could regulate. It clarified that smaller and more isolated waters like streams and lands could fall under federal authority. However, the rule never really went into effect because of a lawsuit still in progress. The current Trump administration has vowed to promote clean water, while at the same time expressing a desire to roll back regulations and restrictions by narrowing the scope of the Clean Water Rule. In February 2017, the president signed an executive order instructing the EPA and the Army Corps of Engineers to review and rewrite the Clean Water Rule and reassess whether the rule is consistent with promoting economic growth and minimizing regulations. The order wasn't enough to reverse the law. However, on October 22, 2019, the EPA and the Department of the Army published a final rule repealing the 2015 Clean Water Rule and restoring the prior regulatory text. As of this writing, the final rule is set to go into effect on December 23, 2019, but not without a fight from environmentalists. Jon Devine, director of federal water policy at the Natural Resources Defense Council said, "This unsubstantiated action is illegal and will certainly be challenged in court."

The CWA does not directly address groundwater contamination, so the government also created the Safe Drinking Water Act (SDWA) in 1974 to look specifically at waters designed for drinking use, including aboveground and underground sources. This law governs our tap water and makes the EPA responsible for setting safety standards for what we drink. It also requires all owners or operators of public water systems to comply with these standards. A 1996 amendment introduced the idea of the EPA creating detailed risk and cost assessments and peer-reviewed science to help develop those standards. Again, this sounds like a great way to protect us, but it has some downfalls that have recently come to light.

First, you need to know that the SDWA gives the EPA authority to identify contaminants and regulate their levels in drinking water to protect public health. The agency sets regulatory limits for more than ninety contaminants.

The EPA has three criteria, according to the law, when determining what to regulate:

- a contaminant may have an adverse health effect on people
- a contaminant is known to occur or there is a high chance that the contaminant will occur in public water systems often enough and at levels of public health concern
- regulation of the contaminant will result in a meaningful opportunity for health risk reductions for people served by public water systems

If the EPA establishes a regulation for a contaminant, then public water systems need to comply with it. But if the EPA decides **not** to regulate a contaminant, then it may issue a health advisory, which is a non-enforceable federal limit that serves as technical guidance for federal, state, and local officials.

Let's take a moment to get clear: we have enforceable and non-enforceable regulations.

Of the enforceable regulations, we have what are called maximum contaminant levels (MCLs). An MCL is the legal threshold limit on the amount of a substance allowed in public water systems according to the SDWA. The limit is usually expressed in a concentration of milligrams or micrograms per liter of water. These standards are set by the EPA for our drinking water quality. In order to set an MCL, the EPA first looks at what levels of a contaminant can be present with no adverse health issues. That level is called the maximum contaminant level goal, which is a non-enforceable goal. The MCL is set as close as possible to the goal, but this system is not perfect. Sometimes, the EPA will establish a treatment technique (TT) instead of an MCL, which is a procedure that must be followed to treat water for a contaminant. It's enforceable and it's not a perfect regulation either for reasons I'll point out soon. Both MCLs and TTs are known as primary standards in EPA-speak.

Science takes time. The EPA sets standards based on the science available. Maybe they know studies are coming out soon saying that a contaminant could cause cancer, so they set a goal or a health advisory, not an MCL. In other cases, they may have animal studies but not human ones. They can't set standards when they don't know the full impact for us. They can't create regulations without enough data. It's a slow dance of completing the studies we need to create the right rules and regulations.

Both perfluorooctanoic acid (PFOA) and

perfluorooctanesulfonic acid (PFOS) are byproducts of industry—chemicals used to make carpets,
clothing, fabric protectors, paper packaging, and
nonstick cookware. In 2009, the EPA published
provisional health advisories for PFOA and PFOS
based on the scientific evidence available at that
time, which was considered "inconclusive." In
those days, the MCL was 400 parts per trillion
(ppt) for PFOA and 200 ppt for PFOS.

By May 2016, the EPA had significantly lowered
the "safe levels" for these pollutants in our water
supply, based on standards that assume **lifetime**
exposure rather than drinking these chemicals
for only a few weeks or months. The new health
advisory for PFOA and PFOS is 70 ppt. These
new standards created instant water contamination crises for many cities and towns—fourteen
systems exceeded the federal threshold for PFOA
and forty systems were above the limit for PFOS.

This advisory came years and years after the
agency was first alerted to PFOA contamination in the drinking water near DuPont's Teflon
plant in West Virginia, and more communities
continue to come forward. People were exposed
for years at this higher level before a new advisory
was issued and it's still not an enforceable one.

Information continues to surface that the companies that made these substances knew about their
health impacts decades ago. In 2010, the Minnesota

attorney general and the Minnesota Department of Natural Resources filed a $5 billion lawsuit against 3M, headquartered in Maplewood, for damages to the environment. The lawsuit claimed that 3M released its perfluorochemicals (PFOS and PFOA) into the nearby groundwater and in 2004 the chemicals were detected in the drinking water of sixty-seven thousand people in Lake Elmo, Oakdale, Woodbury, and Cottage Grove. While the company tried to argue that no health effect to humans had ever been proven, documents released in the case showed that 3M researchers knew these chemicals could bioaccumulate in fish and that the compounds were toxic. 3M settled the suit for $850 million in 2018, and afterward the Minnesota attorney general's office released many internal documents including studies, memos, emails, and research reports, showing how much 3M really knew about these chemicals and their harm to both people and the environment.

The Agency for Toxic Substances and Disease Registry released a draft report in June 2018 discussing how people are exposed to these chemicals and the health risks they pose. The agency found that these chemicals are particularly damaging to vulnerable populations, such as infants and breast-feeding mothers, at levels lower than what the EPA deemed safe in the 2016 health advisory.

PFOA alone pollutes the blood of almost all

Americans and can even pass from mother to unborn child in the womb. It builds up in our bodies, and studies have linked even tiny exposure to PFOA to kidney and testicular cancers, birth defects, damage to the immune system, heart and thyroid disease, complications during pregnancy, and other serious conditions.

That's one example. These laws and regulatory agencies are meant to protect us, but the rules get muddy. Is it really too much to ask for clean, safe drinking water? We've got to find a way to get the laws and the science to sync up. I imagine it starts with more funding and more resources, and potentially taking a more cautious approach with so many of these chemicals. But it's important to remember that we wouldn't need so much regulation if polluters were cleaning up their own messes or not creating them in the first place.

Here's another question for you: Do you know what the MCL for lead is in this country?

You know lead—a nervous-system toxin that according to our own regulatory agency (the EPA) has no safe level of exposure. Lead in drinking water can cause everything from stomach pains to permanent brain damage.

It's a trick question. We don't have an MCL, and that's another big problem. We have a TT—a "treatment technique" regulation better known as the Lead and Copper Rule.

In Flint, Michigan, lead was leaching into the water supply for almost two years and public officials said everything was fine. Former Flint mayor Dayne Walling went as far as to drink the contaminated water on local TV to assure residents it was safe to drink. Since early 2019, thirteen state and local officials have been criminally charged in connection to the water disaster in Flint, some facing forty or more years in prison with more charges possible.

While school safety continues to be a huge issue in the aftermath of many mass shootings, school after school is finding toxic levels of lead in their water. More than 80 percent of New York City schools tested positive for elevated lead levels in April 2017, and the testing protocol came under fire after experts revealed that the city had been running water pipes the night before testing in 2016, a process called flushing that can make the water appear cleaner when tested. The problem has gotten so bad that states like California are starting to introduce legislation that would make it mandatory to test the drinking water for lead contamination in all school districts and colleges, which is a step in the right direction. I'm still wondering how that TT is going. . . .

The bill's author, assemblywoman Lorena Gonzalez Fletcher (D-San Diego), told a local radio station, "The lead crisis in Flint, Michigan, was a wake-up call. We've had this mentality of putting our heads in the sand and not really asking the questions we need to ask."

That's right, Lorena! It's time to get our heads out of the sand and start holding our officials accountable.

The bill would require schools to shut off any source of drinking water if lead contamination is discovered, and to inform staff and parents about the potential exposure. Do you realize that we weren't testing all these years or that government and industry employees were messing with the standards set for testing? Even low levels of lead in children's blood can create permanent damage, including decreased IQ and hyperactivity.

Here's another example of a law that protects industry, not people. The Energy Policy Act of 2005, which includes the infamous "Halliburton loophole," has helped create the mess that we all know as fracking. Hydraulic fracturing, an advanced extraction method used by oil and gas companies, requires millions of gallons of water, sand, and chemicals to break apart rock and release gas. The law allows fracking companies to hide the contents of the toxic chemical solutions that they pump into the ground. Thanks to the Halliburton loophole, these fracking fluids are protected under law, and so doctors responding to health complaints can't access the data showing what chemicals their patients have been exposed to.

How could such a law have been passed? Do you think money might have played a part? A big part. Corporations look at their bottom line first and foremost, hiring lobbyists and, as we'll see, contriving science to get what they want done.

Millions of Americans live within one mile of a fracking well and studies have found that the toxic chemicals from fracking, natural gas processing sites, and storage facilities are present in high concentrations in the bodies of people living or working near these sites. Now tell me how those who wrote this law can sleep at night.

THE GROWING HEALTH CRISIS

It is devastating that in our quest to become a supergiant, industrialized country, everyday people have been secretly robbed of our most basic human right—our health. Huge corporations and government agencies have been missing the mark, making grievous mistakes, or in many cases intentionally polluting our water for their own profit. And, not surprisingly, it's making millions of people sick.

Every community meeting that I attend about water turns into a meeting about the health crisis in a community, and that's not okay.

The reason that I get invited to these meetings is because my name has become synonymous with hope. It's become synonymous with fighting. And what many of you may not realize is that I never stopped. I became known for my work fighting for people in one town, but the fight is still going strong. The problems portrayed in that film have only gotten worse.

This isn't my story; it's everyone's story.

Once you know the truth and can see it, the question becomes what are you going to do about it?

This is a book dedicated to telling the truth. And sadly, it's a dirty truth. We can no longer take for granted the simple act of filling up a glass of clean water from our kitchen sink.

I want to help expose what's going on in this country; help make you aware of these problems, which are not going to fix themselves; and show you how to take actions that can reverse water toxicity in your town, city, and region.

It is hard to believe, but the average American uses nearly a hundred gallons of water each day for everything from drinking to cooking to bathing. We all need access to clean water.

Yet for years, reports and testing across the country show that the drinking water is not as safe or sound as we would like. Our water treatment systems are antiquated and regularly in violation of the laws we've established, containing highly concentrated levels of arsenic, lead, bacteria, and more. Unsupervised industry pollution combined with failing infrastructure is a recipe for disaster. To add insult to injury, the more polluted the water becomes, the more chemicals we need to treat it.

Water treatment facilities throughout the country are changing the way they handle our drinking water at alarming rates. Many are switching from chlorine, the primary disinfectant used in drinking water systems for more than a hundred years, to an alternative disinfectant chloramine, which is a mixture of chlorine and ammonia. Some estimates show that about one in five Americans drink water disinfected with chloramine.

One of the main reasons for this switch is to provide increased protection from bacterial contamination and more. But using chloramines is literally one of the cheapest options available and it's not as effective at controlling taste and odors in the water. Chlorine evaporates into the air relatively quickly, while chloramine is more stable and will last longer in the water system. Research has shown that chloramine causes deterioration of the municipal infrastructure thanks to changes in the water chemistry. In water systems that still use lead pipes or lead components, this reaction causes the lead and other heavy metals to leach into drinking water and out of faucets and showerheads.

Instead of spending the money to fix old pipes and update our systems, money-crunched municipalities are adding chemicals like ammonia to drinking water as a quick fix, which only causes more issues.

We know contaminants are in the water, and we know these contaminants are linked to illnesses and health issues, especially cancer.

Here are some numbers for you to consider:

- 1,735,350. That's the estimated number of new cases of cancer diagnosed in the United States in 2018.
- 15 million U.S. households (or 45 million people) obtain their drinking water from private wells, which are not covered by the EPA regulations that protect public drinking water systems. The presence of contaminants in this water can lead to health issues like gastrointestinal illness, reproductive issues, and neurological disorders.
- Half of all children in the U.S. are dealing with chronic health conditions. HALF. I can't say all those health conditions are coming from the water, but it certainly is contributing.
- **Legionella** outbreaks have quadrupled in the last fifteen years. **Legionella** is a type of bacteria found naturally in freshwater

like lakes and streams, but it has become more widespread in man-made water systems like showers, faucets, and plumbing systems. In 2016, about five thousand Americans were diagnosed with this severe (and sometimes fatal) form of pneumonia, called Legionnaire's disease, which people contract from breathing small droplets of water contaminated with the bacteria. How do they contract it? When they are in the shower.

I'm working with hundreds of communities now (and thousands more are reporting in), and these numbers represent just a small sample of what we are dealing with.

If you think getting involved isn't for you or that you're not a leader, I've got some news for you. We're all leaders. We can't afford to sit on the sidelines anymore—none of us can. You, your kids, your grandkids, and your neighbors need a better world now and a legacy to leave for future generations.

If you can answer yes to any of the following questions, then you have what it takes to effectively lead yourself and others. It's that simple.

- Did you get out of bed this morning and make breakfast?

- Did you drive your kids to school?
- Did you show up to a work meeting or organize a friend's birthday party?

The problems we face today are too big for any one person, even me. I need your help. I want to leave a legacy for my grandchildren and yours. We can either use our power to turn the state of our water around or leave our grandchildren with polluted water everywhere and not a drop to drink.

This is your wake-up call, America. Are you ready to act?

PASSING THE TORCH

When I had the honor of carrying the Olympic flame through Pasadena, California, during the 2002 Salt Lake City torch relay, I was scared. No one had given me instructions and I wondered, what am I doing here? But when the person before me handed me that flame, I took off confidently. I suddenly knew exactly what to do. Every time I meet with community members who are organizing for cleaner water in their town, I see the same thing happen. I ask a few questions and offer a few suggestions, and then they take off running with their ideas for change. They know what works best in their community.

I'm counting on you now to do the same. Consider this book your invitation to get involved. I'm here to show you how, and once you've got the basics, you'll have everything you need to save yourselves. It's time to wake up the hero within you, and now is the time to start. Ultimately, it's we, the people, who will save the day.

The 2002 Winter Olympics torch relay was a sixty-five-day run throughout the United States that led to the opening ceremony of the games in Salt Lake City, Utah. Erin carried the flame in Pasadena, California, on January 16.

UNDERSTANDING MEASUREMENTS

You will see me using different measurements throughout the book, such as parts per million (ppm), parts per billion (ppb), or parts per trillion (ppt), as they are the most common terms used to describe small amounts of substances found in water. They represent a measure of concentration. For example, a ppm means that in a million units of water exists one unit of that chemical. Scientists uses these measurements to show the amount of a toxic chemical found in a drinking water supply or body of water. It's wild when you think about how a small dose of a chemical can inflict so much damage.

You can easily convert these numbers too, if needed.

1 ppm = 1,000 ppb = 1,000,000 ppt

DEFINING TOXIC SUBSTANCES & THEIR IMPACT

You will also see me use the terms **toxic substance, toxic chemical,** or **poison** throughout this book. Let's define it as any substance that on ingestion, inhalation, absorption, or exposure within the body, even in relatively small amounts, can cause disorder or harm. Any chemical can be toxic or harmful under the right conditions. Many factors will impact how harmful a substance can be, including how much and by what means a person is exposed and how sensitive that person may be to a substance. Each person is different in terms of constitution, immunity, and more, which is why people display different health problems and issues from the same substance. Some people may not show any signs for years, or ever, after exposure to a toxin, while others may become sick more quickly.

2

IT BEGAN IN HINKLEY . . . AND IT'S EVERYWHERE NOW

Everything for me started in Hinkley, California, a tiny Southern California community located in the Mojave Desert. I was thirty-one years old, a single mom with three little kids. I'm now fifty-eight and have four grandchildren!

In 1991, I was working as a legal clerk and discovered that a carcinogen called hexavalent chromium (also known as chromium-6) had contaminated the water in the town—leading to a years-long environmental investigation and lawsuit. I started my work with the idea that one person can make a difference, and as I went along, I decided that person could be me.

By 2016, a report from the Environmental Working Group (EWG) found that about two-thirds of the American population—218 million people—are drinking water contaminated with potentially unsafe levels of that same chemical, chromium-6. To say that I'm furious is an understatement. Hinkley was one small town with a giant electric company that thought they could pollute the water and get away with it. Today, Hinkley is everywhere, and I'll tell you exactly how it's happened.

But first let's get back to these roots. Hinkley is really a kind of barren town, but there's a beauty to it and that's why people live there. Not everyone wants to live in the big city around congested streets and honking horns. People move to places like Hinkley for wide open spaces and to see the stars at night. It had sprawling alfalfa fields and farms filled with dairy cows. It's the kind of place that's supposed to be safe to live and raise kids in.

A big part of my fascination with what happened in Hinkley came from my parents and from growing up in Kansas. In the Midwest, we know that the greatest gift we have isn't how much money we have in the bank—it's our water, it's our land, it's the air we breathe, it's our health, and it's our family.

I was doing my best to uncover what the heck was happening out there. Originally, the law firm I worked for had taken on a real estate case from a woman who didn't want to sell her house to Pacific Gas and Electric (PG&E), the largest public utility company in the world at that time. When I went to visit the town and hear her story, it was obvious something more was brewing.

The first thing I noticed was that the water was

lime green. I thought, "Okay, we're definitely not in Kansas anymore." I had never seen green water like that. Then I noticed frogs with two heads, and others just lying lifeless at the surface of the water. The trees were dying. Wildlife was missing. People would tell me bizarre stories about their animals too, and how they would run in circles and knock their heads against trees. The cattle had hundreds of visible tumors all over their bodies—something I had certainly never seen before. The stories from people who lived out there centered around sickness. People had everything from constant nosebleeds to multiple miscarriages to cancer. The town was rural. It was supposed to be a serene, peaceful environment, but something was affecting the people, the wildlife, and the plants. It didn't make sense.

I kept pondering everything I had seen in the town. What's the one thing that trees, animals, and people all rely on? What's something that brings them all together? It's the water. Water is the source of life and it takes life too, and that's what set me on my journey.

On the three-hour drive from Hinkley back to my home in Los Angeles, I was constantly wondering what the hell I was doing. I made very little money. I never saw my kids, who were all under the age of ten. Everyone thought I was crazy and that I had no business researching a toxic case, or at least that's what they told me.

Yet this little nagging thought from my dad kept me going. He taught me that deception is the root of all problems. In Hinkley, and everywhere since, the problems I work on start with a lie—something we are all taught about as kids growing up. In high school, I lied to my dad once about being at school when I really had skipped that day to go to my friend's lake house. The one thing you couldn't do was lie to my dad. He grounded me for an entire school semester, which meant no phone privileges, no dating, and no social activities after school, and I missed a trip to Chicago I had scheduled with friends. The day after "my sentence," he flew out of town on a business trip, and before he left, he wrote me a letter that I have kept all these years. I want to share the most important paragraph from it with you.

I know last night tore you up—it did me too! But we are dealing here with a very basic principle and you are old enough to understand it. That is, if you, your brothers and sister, your Mother and I cannot freely and honestly communicate with each other and believe what we are saying and hearing then we have lost everything! To do otherwise tears up the very fabric of our family, which until you start your own, is the finest possession you will have on this Earth.

My dad was right, and in today's world we have lost the most basic principle of open, honest communication and trust. It doesn't matter how much money you have in the bank or if you are a liberal or conservative, no one should be poisoned or lied to about it. Ever.

I kept following my instincts in Hinkley. I kept talking to the people who lived there. It seemed obvious to me that when people drink a poison, it's going to make them sick. But I wasn't a doctor or a scientist, a lawyer or a government employee. I didn't study mass torts. What business did I have out there? One time I was talking to a PG&E expert, telling him about some of my findings, and he said, "Oh, we see that out here all the time."

I don't think so! Green water and two-headed frogs are **not** normal.

Lesson: Use your senses. If you've noticed something strange in your community, don't let other people's opinions get in the way of one of the most basic scientific skills—trusting your observation.

In fact, people ask me all the time how I got started in Hinkley and wonder what tools I used during that case. I tell them about three very simple concepts: logic, leverage, and loyalty. Let me explain.

LEARN THE THREE L'S: LOGIC, LEVERAGE & LOYALTY

Logic. It's all about common sense. If you see a tornado coming your way, you are not going to take the time to go look at the Weather Channel and find out the category of the storm. Your instinct tells you to run and get to safety as quickly as possible. You can use those same kinds of observation skills when it comes to your water. Something smells funny? That's a good observation. A lot of common sense came into play in my work in Hinkley, because I didn't have a precedent for what was happening at the time. You can use this tool in your own community too. Did you get a water violation notice in the mail? Don't just throw it in the junk pile. That's a big clue that something is wrong with your water and that more investigation is needed. Use your logic and pay attention to what's happening around you.

Leverage. That's all about gathering and building community. It involves talking to your neighbors and friends, which I know sounds like a strange concept in our digital world. Start fact-finding and asking questions together. Use the power of different perspectives to your advantage. Don't be afraid to speak up and check in with one another. It's not always easy because people may have different opinions, but this step can be a real game changer. Think about the impact of one person going to a city council meeting versus one hundred people showing up. We have strength in numbers, and if each person commits to talking to a neighbor or posting on their social media page, you can easily grow your impact. In Hinkley, we held community meetings and I personally went door-to-door talking with many people about what was happening. It was the first step in organizing and educating them about the issues at stake.

Loyalty. This step is about not giving up and about staying committed to your cause. When you stick with a cause, you will get somewhere. You may have setbacks, but you keep going. People may try to throw you off your game, and you need to remember that drinking brown water (or whatever it is for you) is not normal. Follow that hunch. Loyalty to my cause is what helped me get through long nights of research, talking to hundreds of experts, and keeping at it for years until the case was settled.

Whatever your cause, you need nothing more than your eyes, ears, nose, and a little common sense to see an environmental catastrophe in the making. You see, officials, government regulators, and corporate minions all have one thing in common: they are just ordinary people doing their jobs, and many of them are out to lunch.

I'm not foolish enough to think that we don't enjoy a certain standard of life thanks to business and industry. We need jobs and commerce. People need cars to get around town and electricity to read books at night. I'm not suggesting we turn away from modern life. We **do** need to learn to work together. Business can't make people sick or destroy the water we all need to live. It's not sustainable. We need purpose-driven corporations that are willing to clean up their messes and to work with communities to support us all.

We have a real opportunity right now to create change. Think about some of the biggest companies in the world, such as Google or Uber. These companies were created by looking at how to solve problems. Google's original mission statement was "to organize the world's information and make it universally accessible and useful." Uber wanted to solve the question of how to get a ride at the push of a button. We need more people working on solutions to our water issues, and that means both entrepreneurs who want to create companies and employees working inside companies to help solve these big problems.

Hinkley was just a microcosm of what's happening throughout the world today. I'm here to sound the alarm for you. The EPA isn't going to save us, and neither are our politicians. We need to rally ourselves.

You might be thinking: I'm not an activist. I don't understand the science of these chemicals or hold a degree in toxicology. Heck, I'm just trying to keep my family afloat and do the best I can.

I hear you. At the risk of sounding overly confident in your abilities, I don't think you need to be anything other than a compassionate, caring individual with integrity, respect, and appreciation for this world. It's really all you need to get involved. It could mean looking around to notice any patterns, or smelling the air, or sometimes it requires getting very quiet. I find many things in the field simply by being silent. If you are quiet enough, you can hear nature speaking to you. Many times, I just listen.

ACTION STEP: Identify the Problem

Science is not just people in white lab coats or Einstein's equations scribbled in a notebook. It's an observation leading to a hypothesis—a possible theory. It's truly a process of discovery that requires asking questions about the natural world and looking for answers.

The first step in the scientific method is simply asking a question based on something you observe. You know the basic questions: Who, What, When,

Where, Why, or How? Start with these basic questions and from there you can start researching.

Many times, as I go along in my investigation, I also use the concept of Occam's razor, which is just a fancy way of saying "keep it simple." Usually, the simplest solution is also the correct one. If the water looks or smells funny, most likely something in the water is making it look or smell that way. Plain and simple. If someone was dumping a substance into the water, and now you notice changes, then most likely the culprit is that substance.

Here are a few good questions to ask:

- What has changed in the surrounding area?
- Has the source of drinking water changed?
- Are changes happening in the way we treat our water?
- Is it possible someone has been discharging substances into our water?
- Are there any new businesses in town or old ones moving out?

These small changes have a big impact on our water systems.

I'll never forget the day I was standing in the hot sun collecting samples of water and doing field research when a PG&E lackey came up to me and said, "You're not a doctor. Do you even have a college degree? You have no right to comment on green water."

I realized at that moment how much intimidation is used in these kinds of cases. The more I kept pursuing leads and talking to people, the more clues I found. The closer I got to the truth, the more PG&E tried to bully me. Companies may try to bully you too. The "big guys" don't want you to discover the truth, so they will try to make you feel small, bad, or wrong. I looked right back at him and told him, "I didn't know I needed all that to be a human."

For me, dealing with dyslexia throughout my life has made me indignant when people tell me I can't do something, and I hate when people tell me that what I see isn't real. Many people in the communities I have worked with experience these same frustrations too. It makes sense to be upset when you are told the water is fine, especially when you know it's not. No one wants to be labeled as irrational or unwise. It upsets our natural instincts, which is the first way we can begin to help ourselves.

I'm here to tell you nothing is wrong with you. Don't let anyone convince you that brown water is good to drink. Your most basic right is to protect your health and well-being. In some indigenous languages the word for water means "lifeblood," because it is literally that essential to all life on earth. Many of the issues we face today have huge implications for both our bodies and our environment. You're not too small to stand up to these challenges. You are much mightier than you can imagine.

This guy from PG&E was using a kind of argument called an "appeal to authority," which is a logical fallacy. In plain English, it means if an argument comes from someone who lacks certain credentials, then it can't be true. Authority figures use this tactic to keep the upper hand all the time. But having a leg up does not mean that you are speaking the truth. In fact, using this kind of argument usually does the exact opposite—it helps hide the truth.

When it comes to my work in Hinkley, the research stands and continues to grow stronger. A Goliath energy company knowingly polluted the town's water and many, many people became sick and died because of careless actions. At one time, Hinkley was a thriving farm community; today it's a ghost town. The pollution drove the life right out of there. Even after all these years of legal actions and follow-up, the pollution is still there. If it can happen to Hinkley, it can happen anywhere. I may not have had all the fancy letters after my name, but I sure as heck knew that what was happening was wrong and it needed to be addressed. It's like the slogan from our own

Department of Homeland Security: "If you see something, say something."

In Hinkley, chromium-6 seeped into the groundwater from a PG&E gas compressor station. It was originally used at the facility to stop rust from forming in cooling towers and pipes, and then later discharged into unlined holding ponds during the 1950s and '60s, eventually leaching into the soil and contaminating the aquifer that supplied the town's drinking water. Groundwater in Hinkley tested as high as 580 ppb in the '90s when, really, almost **no** level is acceptable. So, you can see why the people there might have been feeling those effects. It's so sad to think that one chemical, one company, and so much negligence could cause this much damage. It's estimated that it will take at least 150 years to clean up the mess.

The class-action lawsuit against PG&E was filed in 1993, alleging that the company knew that harmful chemicals—especially hexavalent chromium used in production—were seeping into the groundwater and contaminating the water supply. Ultimately, that case resulted in the largest medical settlement lawsuit in history and put my life on a whole new trajectory. I helped more than 650 plaintiffs. Right after Hinkley, we discovered other towns nearby in California with similar issues related to hexavalent chromium, causing health problems and wreaking havoc on more lives. In

2006, PG&E paid another $335 million to settle a series of lawsuits for chromium-6-contaminated water, affecting about 1,100 people in Kings, Riverside, and San Bernardino Counties.

As I continued my work, I discovered that hexavalent chromium was used everywhere. It was an industry standard, used nationwide by giant corporations such as Lockheed Martin and Boeing and found seeping into water supplies near coal ash dump sites across the country. In fact, chromium-6 was the single most common corrosive inhibitor used in cooling towers in the United States until the 1990s. Millions of gallons of this toxic chemical were used everywhere from schools to hospitals to courthouses to food-processing plants to refrigerated warehouses. The cooling towers became filled with massive doses of chromium-6 and then as the water in the towers began to cloud up with minerals, the water would get discharged into the wastewater system, which was little more than unlined lagoons. The lagoons were designed to percolate the wastewater into the earth for "treatment," but sadly that contaminant went right into our drinking water. I can always tell when a community is dealing with this chemical because the water turns yellow-green.

For years, I couldn't understand why PG&E was so ruffled by one woman and one community bringing this issue to light. But when you know the dangers of this chemical and you know it's everywhere, at some point you will have more serious repercussions to deal with. At stake in Hinkley, and in many similar cases, was whether the science could prove that a chemical caused cancer and/or other health problems. Industry officials want us all to believe that these concerns are inflated and that no regulations are needed, because otherwise they must pay. They put profits above public health. The irony is that companies like PG&E have the resources, the technology, and the manpower to clean up their own mess, and yet they choose to lie, cheat, sue, intimidate, falsify documents, and outright bully anyone trying to protect the rights of drinking-water consumers.

FAKING THE SCIENCE

PG&E went to great lengths to cover up their misdeeds and influence the regulatory process. The company was not pleased when the **Erin Brockovich** movie came out exposing the dangers of chromium-6. A spokesperson from the company tried to downplay the movie's implications, saying, "Our general response with respect to the movie is just that we recognize it's a dramatization. It's an entertainment vehicle." PG&E also sent an internal memo to its employees that said, " 'based on a true story' doesn't mean that everything in the story is true." PG&E also wanted to make sure that all the media attention was not going to influence chromium regulations. In fact, the company created its own action plan stating they did not want the public swayed by a popular yet fictionalized movie.

Sound science is the basis for all legislation and policy decisions to protect public health, but large companies can influence the scientific process and conceal their own studies to avoid or postpone regulations. We've seen this dynamic play out with both the tobacco and the pharmaceutical industries for decades, and it's happening with chemicals that are polluting our water. For years, the Chrome Coalition, an industry group made up of both chrome producers and consumers, has worked quietly to minimize the health effects of exposure to chromium-6 by infiltrating the scientific literature.

"Between 1996 and 2008, Industrial Health Foundation, the legal arm of the Chrome Coalition . . . hired third parties to produce at least 18 epidemiological studies or reviews of the safety of chromium, all of which minimized the risk of disease related to chromium exposure," according to an article from the Union of Concerned Scientists (UCS).

Environmental pollution is not easy to detect

or prove. It's part of why regulating industry can be so difficult. It takes years to build a scientific case to prove the harmful effects certain chemicals have on our health. Asbestos was used to insulate houses for decades before we finally banned it. One of the biggest hurdles in the Hinkley litigation was establishing whether or not ingestion and skin exposure to chromium-6 could cause harm to residents. PG&E hired ChemRisk, a scientific consulting firm used by many companies dealing with regulatory issues. Dennis Paustenbach, a San Francisco scientist with a track record of product defense for companies like ExxonMobil and Dow Chemical, was CEO of the company at that time. Dennis, along with board-certified toxicologists Brent Finley and Brent Kerger, had the task of proving that chromium-6 didn't harm humans when ingested or from skin exposure. They decided to conduct original research that would add human studies to the record.

The scientists sat in a hot tub filled with chromium-6 contaminated water for hours smoking cigars and then took urine and blood samples for their study. Sounds like hard work, right? They found increases in total chromium concentrations in both their blood and urine samples, indicating that the chemical may have penetrated their skin, but the levels were not sustained for the five-day testing period, so they concluded that the exposure "was not expected to result in systemic uptake of measurable amounts of chromium-6." They also drank jugs of water contaminated with the chemical and ran more tests, coming to the same conclusion, that oral exposure was not dangerous. These studies were published in the **Journal of Toxicology and Environmental Health** without disclosing that these scientists were paid by PG&E. This work was not peer-reviewed or independently vetted by other scientists; it slipped through the back door into a major scientific publication. ChemRisk earned $1.5 million for consulting on the Hinkley case. While funding is typically disclosed in scientific journals today, more than 60 percent of research and development in science

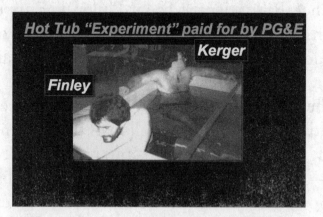

Scientists in a hot tub filled with chromium-6-contaminated water for three hours in an attempt to prove the chemical did not harm humans. The results were published per litigation and were bought and paid for by PG&E.

is still conducted by industry, 20 percent comes from universities and 10 percent from government, according to the Organisation for Economic Co-operation and Development (OECD).

I spoke recently to my friend Gary Praglin, one of the attorneys in the case, and he said all the lawyers at the time were mocking the research, calling it "three men in a tub." They couldn't believe these scientists were paid top dollar to sit in a hot tub.

"They put it on with a straight face and they acted like people were crazy to think that chromium-6 was anything other than an inhalation carcinogen because there were no published studies that said that it was—except for one," Gary said. I'll get to that study in a moment, because it played a key role in the case.

ChemRisk scientist Brent Finley also appeared on an ABC News segment in 1996 with Cynthia McFadden, drinking the green chromium-tainted water.

She responded by saying, "There are those who would say you drinking a gallon of this chromium-laced water doesn't prove anything except that you—in some people's minds—may be foolish."

How many times will we be duped by an expert on TV who drinks the water as "proof" that it's safe for consumption? You will see this trick used again when I discuss the Flint, Michigan, water crisis, which is another reason why I tell people to trust their own instincts rather than the opinions of the so-called experts.

Even after PG&E lost the Hinkley case, they did not back off their pursuit to downplay the effects of hexavalent chromium. It's very difficult to remove this chemical from the water and meet stricter standards, so it was worth both their time and resources to find science to ensure they wouldn't have to get involved with its cleanup. They took it a step further by trying to reverse the only study that showed just how dangerous chromium-6 could be for humans.

Let's look at the work of Dr. Zhang JianDong, who published a study in 1987 about people dying of cancer in a rural northeastern Chinese area at rates higher than other nearby villages. He spent twenty years studying this region and treating the residents with health issues. Like Hinkley, the area had massive chromium waste contamination in the groundwater—as much as 300,000 tons of chromium-6. He received a Chinese national award for his research, which U.S. scientists translated into English. We cited the study in court as evidence that chromium-6 might cause cancer when ingested. This study was the **one** study that showed exactly what PG&E did not want anyone to know.

But in 1997 (while PG&E was dealing with another lawsuit in Kettleman City, California), Dr. Zhang, now retired, appeared to retract his life's work, when a "clarification and further analysis" got published with his name as the author. The article, which appeared in a reputable U.S. medical journal, essentially claimed the cancer link to chromium in the rural villages did not exist. The article became evidence for U.S. regulatory agencies, including the EPA, to say that ingesting chromium-6 did not pose a cancer risk.

The later study didn't deny the high cancer rates, but it did say factors like lifestyle and other environmental issues were the likely cause, which Dr. Zhang adamantly disputed. Still, he and a Chinese colleague appeared as the sole authors of the "updated" report, even though it did not have a Chinese translation and the two doctors did not speak English.

Of course, Dr. Zhang did not write that article. Court papers later revealed that the second study was "conceived, drafted, edited, and submitted to medical journals by science consultants working for the lawsuit's defendant, a utility company being sued for alleged chromium pollution." The consultants were from ChemRisk, the company founded by Dennis Paustenbach. **The Wall Street Journal** reported the company "helped save industry hundreds of millions of dollars in cleanup costs for chromium pollution in New Jersey."

Instead of owning up to their mistakes, PG&E went out and hired scientific consultants to track down some of the only evidence about the dangers of this chemical and essentially muddy the research. They made it look like Zhang had revised his finding after taking a closer look at the original data. The **Journal of Occupational and Environmental Medicine** retracted the paper in 2006. So for nine years the research delayed regulations, compromised public health, and even influenced media.

John Stossel from Fox Business and **20/20**, who has interviewed me several times, wrote in his 2004 book **Give Me a Break**, "It was never established that the power company made anyone sick. The power company looked guilty because it did what companies usually do— escaped the lawyers by settling, paying some $300 million. . . . Hexavalent chromium is a carcinogen if inhaled at high levels, but the EPA says no data suggests that drinking chromium causes cancer."

Can you see how important the science becomes in these cases? Corporations have deep pockets and go to great lengths to create scientific doubt or bury information to protect their own financial interests.

A 2012 UCS report outlines the main ways corporations manipulate and control the scientific process and scientists in general:

Terminating and suppressing research. Companies have controlled the dissemination of scientific information by ending or withholding results of research that they sponsor that would threaten their bottom line.

Intimidating or coercing scientists. Corporations bury scientific information by harassing scientists and their institutions into silence. Scientists have been threatened with litigation and the loss of their jobs, have had their research defunded, have been refused promotion or tenure, and have been transferred to non-research positions, all of which leads to self-censorship and changes in research direction.

Manipulating study designs and research protocols. Corporations have employed flawed methodologies in testing and research that are biased toward predetermined results, such as changing the questions scientists are asking.

Ghostwriting scientific articles. Corporations corrupt the integrity of scientific journals by planting ghostwritten articles about their products. Rather than submitting articles directly, companies recruit scientists or contract with research organizations to publish articles that obscure the sponsors' involvement.

Publication bias. Corporations selectively publish positive results while underreporting negative results. While not directly corrupting science itself, these publishing and reporting biases skew the body of evidence.

But that's not all. PG&E also infiltrated a

blue-ribbon panel. Shortly after the movie came out in 2000, former California governor Gray Davis came to my boss Ed Masry and me and said, "We need a blue-ribbon panel for hexavalent chromium."

Despite PG&E's efforts to downplay the movie, it did bring attention to chromium pollution and its effects on human health. The California legislature passed a law requiring levels of chromium-6 to be more closely monitored in drinking water, and the California Environmental Protection Agency's Office of Environmental Health Hazard Assessment (OEHHA) announced that it wanted to establish an MCL for the contaminant. They needed a panel to review the scientific literature. A blue-ribbon panel brings together a group of experts to investigate and analyze a given question. They must be independent and use their expertise to study the issues and report their findings or recommendations to those with decision-making power.

Academics from the University of California organized the panel, then called the Chromate Toxicity Review Committee. The committee was supposed to provide guidance in identifying the optimum drinking-water level, or public health goal (PHG), for chromium-6 in drinking water. By September 2001, they finished their research and forwarded a report to OEHHA.

They reported, "We found no basis in either the epidemiological or animal data published in the literature for concluding that orally ingested Cr (VI) [chromium-6] is a carcinogen."

How did they come to this conclusion? PG&E hacked the panel! Paid industry scientists were appointed to the panel to downplay the effects of hexavalent chromium and influence the recommendations in another case of corporate-manipulated science. In addition, they had paid litigation experts presenting evidence to the panel and PG&E covered up facts in relation to the panel and the science that it relied upon.

In response to the panel's report, OEHHA withdrew its recommendation for a PHG for total chromium of 2.5 parts per billion and 0.2 parts per billion for chromium-6. PG&E, which had had a case pending with the people in Kettleman City for seven years, came to court and told the judge everything had changed.

Gary and I both testified at a hearing of the California Senate Health and Human Services Committee in February 2003, and Gary spoke specifically about how this research influenced the case.

"They were waving the blue-ribbon panel report—like a flag," he said in his testimony. "They said to the judge, The State of California has spoken. It has said that chromium-6 does not cause cancer by ingestion, and they wanted to amend their paperwork, their motions, their declarations, and move to dismiss our case. And they got that permission to do that. They amended all their paperwork, and we were given permission to take discovery—to take depositions, issue subpoenas—and we have obtained thousands of pages of documents in connection with the blue-ribbon panel process."

In my testimony at that same meeting, I talked about how the blue-ribbon panel was "created for a noble and lofty purpose, but it became corrupt, skewed, and biased for self-interest." The process was flawed.

"If we allow this panel—the chromium blue-ribbon panel—to control and manipulate science, they will be endangering tens of thousands of innocent people," I said. "The general public's health is now at stake."

Under state law, the first step to establish a limit for any chemical in the drinking water is to know what level would pose a health risk. If the expert panel can't find the appropriate data, they can't know the risk and then the state can't set a standard. You can see for yourself how good laws can go bad.

The panel cited a 1968 German study where mice were fed large doses of chromium-6-contaminated water and developed stomach tumors. After reviewing the study, the chromate committee concluded that a virus that hit the mice might have caused lesions that German researchers mistook for chromium-induced tumors.

Thankfully, Gary helped to break the story and expose that the panel had two paid PG&E consultants on it. One of those consultants was none other than Dennis Paustenbach and the other was Dr. Marc Schenker. Both were paid to advocate PG&E's position that chromium-6 does not cause cancer when ingested, during litigation against the company. Not only were these consultants paid millions by PG&E for their work, but they lifted two chapters of the panel report straight from their previous work. Sounds like a conflict of interest to me! Eventually, the panel report was thrown out due to all this controversy.

"The caution I'd give anybody involved in public health is that when you look at science, you have to ask who wrote and funded the studies being used. If it's all being written by industry hired guns, they are out to save a buck for the companies," Gary said in a 2004 article. When I spoke with him recently, he said this statement is still true today.

Flash forward almost twenty-five years from when I started my work in Hinkley.

In July 2014, California became the first state

in the nation to regulate this substance and establish a maximum contaminant level (MCL) for chromium-6 in drinking water. The MCL was 10 ppb for this industrial byproduct. For reference, the rest of the country uses a federal standard of 100 ppb for total chromium, including other types like chromium-3, which is nontoxic. Those federal standards were created at a time when hexavalent chromium was not linked to cancer, but subsequent studies have shown a direct correlation.

One piece of research that helped set the standards in California was from the National Institutes of Health. The National Toxicology Program essentially re-created the animal studies from Germany.

The National Toxicology Program studies (from 2007) found that:

> sodium dichromate dihydrate, a compound containing hexavalent chromium, causes cancer in laboratory animals following oral ingestion. Researchers found significant increases in tumors at sites where tumors are rarely seen in laboratory animals. Male and female rats had malignant tumors in the oral cavity. The studies conducted in mice found increases in the number of benign and malignant tumors in the small

intestine, which increased with dose in both males and females.

In September 2017, California dropped its MCL. The Superior Court of Sacramento County invalidated the standard, saying that "the state failed to properly consider the economic feasibility of complying with the MCL." The Safe Drinking Water Act does require the state to determine that the cost of treatment offsets the public health benefits. In this case, the court did not rule on whether the MCL was economically feasible or that it adequately protected public health, it simply found that the department did not adequately document whether the MCL was cost-effective.

The challenge came from the Solano County Taxpayers Association and the California Manufacturers & Technology Association, a trade group whose mission is to improve and enhance a strong business climate for California's thirty thousand manufacturing, processing, and technology-based companies. The city of Vacaville, California, estimated that the standard would cost about $7.5 million.

"As if the current challenges we're facing with the water supply in California aren't bad enough, along comes this unnecessary regulation, which will place steep cost burdens on taxpayers without a benefit to public health," Ourania Riddle of the taxpayers' association said in 2016.

While the MCL is no longer in effect, the state water board is in the process of adopting a new one rather than appealing the court's decision. I truly hope that the research available today will help determine a new MCL that is in the best interest of public health and safety.

Frankly, no level is safe in my opinion, but if these are the cards we are dealt then we need some measured level of safety. We need a national standard too. If California created one at the state level, then it's possible for the rest of the country to follow suit.

Incidentally, it's been common knowledge in the scientific community for years that people who inhale hexavalent chromium can contract lung cancer. Is it really so surprising that swallowing it also leads to cancer?

Ultimately, the Hinkley case taught me that pollution happens, that it affects us all, and that corporations try to cover it up. Little did I know that my work in Hinkley was the tip of the iceberg. As I worked to bring these issues to light, I found a rabbit hole bigger than anyone can imagine. When I began, I thought I had discovered a one-off situation, but I've come to realize that such issues are in all our backyards. They may already be happening in yours right now. Systematic failures,

corruption, and pollution are not stopping, and
we need to be informed.

FIRST STEPS

Notice the water coming out of your tap and
ask yourself some questions. Get as specific as
you can.

- How does it taste?
- How does it look?
- How does it smell?
- Does the water affect your body? Does it make
  your skin feel dry, itchy, or "off" in any way?
- Have you noticed any changes in your water
  quality in the last year?

News You Can Use

It's time to start fact-finding, observing, and
understanding the issues at hand. Stay informed
about your local water issues. Look for articles
in your local newspaper or on TV about water
contamination or problems in your town. Sign
up for newsletters of local water or environmental groups. Start paying attention to any stories
about your water source and treatment facility,
including boil advisories or chemicals that have
been detected above legal limits. Pay careful
attention to any companies in your area cited
for illegal dumping of their waste, especially into

waterways. Look for stories about Superfund sites and their cleanup.

Learn how to separate facts from fiction. Always try to find the original source of a story. "Fake news" was the 2017 word of the year, and it means false, often sensational information disseminated under the guise of news reporting. Real news stories will typically have three or more sources to comment on the story; they portray both sides, and they provide the who, what, when, why, and how. Ideally, news stories are objective, present facts, and report information from witnesses or experts. If an expert or scientist is quoted, do your own research and find out what other work they have published. Are they an industry supporter or are they an independent source? A blog post or an opinion piece is usually one person's view of a topic, which is very different from a news-based article. Watch out for persuasive language or opinions that try to influence your thinking. Get the facts and then make up your mind about how you want to proceed.

Build Your Confidence

No one feels confident in the beginning of a water struggle, but I want to encourage you to push past those initial fears. Don't believe the thoughts that say "I'm too young," "I'm too old," "I don't have enough experience," or "I don't have influence or power." Now is not the time to let those fears take over. I've seen people of all ages and backgrounds fight for what they feel is right and win. Take the attention away from yourself and put it on your message. You deserve access to clean water. Think of each and every person in your community that you can help. Remember you just need enough confidence to take that first step in the right direction.

3

CONNECTING THE DOTS & BUILDING A MAP

Hinkley resident Roberta Walker is the original water warrior of her town and the first in a long line of women that I have come to know and admire in my work. She is the person responsible for putting her town on the map, but the people of Hinkley were not seeking fame. She and her husband, Greg, had bought their home on ten acres of land for $25,000 in 1976. Greg was raised in the 3,500-person town of Hinkley, and his parents lived across the street. They were raising their two daughters, kept horses, and had a swimming pool—a great relief during those dry, hot summers in Hinkley. Roberta could see Pacific Gas and Electric's pumping station from her yard. PG&E was the largest employer in town, and she considered them a good neighbor.

In December 1987 during a routine environmental assessment, the company found that chromium had leaked into the town's groundwater supply and reported the issue to the regional water board, which promptly ordered the utility company to clean it up. In the meantime, they offered Roberta and her family, along with many others who lived near the facility, bottled water. Most of the homes in Hinkley had private wells, which were drawing directly from the contaminated water supply. But Roberta and others in town didn't question the company. She said officials from PG&E assured her on many occasions that there was nothing wrong with the water, telling her it was still safe to drink, cook, and bathe in it. She assumed that they were the experts and handling any problems with the water, and she was happy to receive the free bottled water.

But Roberta got more suspicious as the years went on. She started to play a game, asking for more and more water. Originally, the company delivered five gallons of bottled water to her home each week. She gradually asked them to increase the water to ten gallons a week to twenty gallons to thirty gallons. She eventually was receiving 150 bottles of water each week. At one point, she even asked the company if she could drain her fifteen-thousand-gallon pool and refill it with bottled water. The response? Sure, no problem.

The company started buying people's homes in town in the early 1990s. When PG&E officials made an offer on Roberta's home, she told them she was not interested and that she and her family didn't want to leave their home. She says the company gave her different reasons for the buyout, at one point suggesting that they wanted to build a freeway through the property. They initially offered her $50,000—double what her house was worth. She said no and a week later they came back with an offer of $60,000. The bids kept coming and kept going up and up, but she and her husband repeatedly said no. Other neighbors started to take the offers and sell their homes. Roberta noticed that after PG&E bought a house, they would demolish the property and burn any trace of what was left there. It looked like the company was essentially evacuating the area. She and her husband just wanted to be left alone so she finally gave them an outrageous offer—a quarter of a million dollars—or ten times the property value of her home. She thought she would never hear from them again, but two weeks later they were ready to accept her offer.

Roberta told me she originally thought it was too much of a good thing—that the chromium-3 levels were too high, which was what PG&E had told the locals. You see, there are two types of chromium—3 and 6. Chromium-3 is a trace mineral that the body can use to regulate insulin activity; it can be found in multivitamins. Chromium-6 is toxic. Roberta discovered the difference when she checked out a book on chromium from the local

ACTION STEP

Get Curious: What's Really Happening? What Can You Do?

Science is not just for experts. It's a process anyone can engage in. You start by asking questions and then looking for the answers. An important part of science is making observations, and I think we all need to bring that kind of science back into our lives. Get curious! Notice what's happening around you and don't assume someone is taking care of it. If your water smells funny, that's a valid observation. If it looks dirty, that's another good observation. Roberta Walker noticed many issues in her community, as do many other people who write to me. They observe changes in their water or in their own health or that of their families, and those observations add up.

library. She called PG&E to confirm what type of chromium was in her water. The man on the phone pulled up her record and said, "Chromium-6." Roberta just about passed out when he told her this news. But she decided to do a little more research at the Lahontan Water Board. She said a little old lady worked at the front desk and allowed her to go to the back to search all the records. She couldn't believe what she found—an entire file on her family with photos of her house. She saw files on her neighbors too. She said it was surreal and she couldn't understand why she was being "spied on." She started making copies of all the files and contacting lawyers. She had approached about 150 attorneys across the state who were too afraid to take on PG&E before she found Ed Masry and me. She's even more fiery than me, which makes me smile, because in each town I visit I always find another woman who is willing to roll out her fieriness.

Every case I've seen starts with someone just like Roberta. It only takes one person who is willing to speak up and stand up. The Hinkley case began with Roberta and her family. Eight plaintiffs eventually grew to 650 people in Hinkley. Almost every community with a water problem has a community leader, and nine times out of ten, it's a mom at the forefront of the fight. Mothers have the passion, the gumption, and the fortitude. They are the keepers of their backyards and their neighborhoods. Moms notice when their kids are acting strange or have weird health issues. They keep tabs on their kids, their friends, and their pets. I've seen so many of these women start with the title of mom, one of the hardest jobs on the planet, but come out of these cases with new titles like scientist, politician, and/or activist.

Environmental pollution exists all over the world. I've seen communities that have been exposed to varying levels of chemicals for prolonged periods of time. It takes time to see the effects of toxins on people. Many of these chemicals have latency periods of ten, twenty, or thirty-plus years. In some cases, like Flint, Michigan, it's only a few months before the symptoms show up. But we can learn from each person who reports their story and start making changes so that others don't have to suffer the same fate. We have enough evidence and information from the cases already out there to prevent more harm. The solution isn't to leave more people exposed and we can't wait for someone to come save us. We, the people, need to save ourselves.

We've got to look at the big picture. It's not just one small community here or there with water problems. The problems are everywhere, and I know this because I am the one receiving the calls and emails from the people who feel the most hopeless and helpless. I respond to requests for help in contamination complaints in all fifty states and in other countries. These people make up whole communities that are witnessing first-hand the harmful health effects that exposure to toxic chemicals has on them and their families.

Part of the missing puzzle has been that there's no agency on the ground going door-to-door talking to and identifying residents who may be affected by contamination in their area. As a result, many people have lost faith in the federal government to investigate what's making people sick in their communities, and that's why they turn to me. No one has access to the kind of general census information that I do, not the EPA, the FDA, or the CDC. They aren't collecting it! Agencies don't report to each other either. We have some state registries that track cancer, but even those numbers don't do much. I have become a kind of reporting agency for suspected disease clusters and environmental issues around the country. Thousands of Americans contact me every month asking for help and telling me about unexplained diseases in their neighborhood or on their streets. So, I started to put together a map of people reaching out to me for help. This map demonstrates that we need to do a better job of listening and responding to these communities, including the ones I haven't heard from. Without anyone to see the big picture, people are being left in the dark.

I often feel like Bill Paxton from that dramatic scene in **Twister** when they say the tornado is coming and he says, "It's already here." When you see issues in one community here or there, it looks bad. But when you line these communities up side by side and see the devastation, it's a storm the likes of which we've never seen before. The catalyst for former marine biologist turned author Rachel Carson to write her groundbreaking book, **Silent Spring,** was a letter she received from a concerned citizen about the mass death of birds from DDT spraying. Let's just say I'm getting that times ten thousand and then some. And just to quash any naysayers, I don't think thousands upon thousands of people email me because they have nothing better to do with their time than send me fan mail or write me outlandish stories. People write to me when they have serious issues. They are frustrated and need help.

Let's travel back to 2000 so you can see how the map developed. The movie was an instant hit with audiences and Julia Roberts won the Oscar, bringing even more attention to the film. I started getting stopped in bathrooms by people telling me that I looked like "Erin Brockovich." I was not prepared for the landslide of communications that came my way. I was getting 100,000 emails a month from people telling me their health and environmental woes. Emails were coming in from 126 countries and territories, and they are still coming today. Water problems exist all over—in Australia, Canada, France, Ireland, Italy, Greece, South Africa, along with every state in our country. I eventually set up ErinBrockovich.com, which is the hub of my work today. I don't go out looking for problems to solve: communities come to me.

The first step in fixing any problem is realizing you have one, and these emails served as the first sign of trouble. One thing I learned from my friend Trevor Schaefer, who survived a brain cancer diagnosis at the age of thirteen, is that so many of us are walking around with blinders on. I'm not blaming anyone, because I know we all lead busy lives. As a single mom for years, I know how hectic life can get. But until a health tragedy happens to you or your family, you don't see what's going on. The emails were a big wake-up call, even for me.

At first, I would get emails and respond to them as best I could. But dealing with dyslexia makes me more of visual person, and in 2008 I decided to start mapping out these emails. For example, if I got an email from Duncan, Oklahoma, I would put a dot on a map. Paw Paw, Michigan: add a dot. Tyler, Texas: add a dot. Kingston, Tennessee: add a dot. Charleston, West Virginia: add a dot. Wedron, Illinois: add a dot. You get my point. Guess what happened after a while to my "arts and crafts" project? That map got covered in ink.

The map is more than just a visual tool; it also helps me to recognize patterns and search my inbox. I would get an email from someone in Indiana—a single mom whose child was dealing with glioblastoma, a very aggressive form of brain cancer. I would think, "That's awful, but I'm not sure what to do with that." Then I'd get another email from the same town a week later, and I'd think, "That's odd. Didn't I see someone last week reporting about that? And I'd go back and check and realize, Okay, now I have two." A month could pass and then I'd get another email. And I'd

have six people from the same town unbeknownst
to each other. I started to plot each person's story
on the map. And a few months later I would look
at that map and see I had three hundred dots.
And that's when I thought "Holy Toledo, WTF
is going on?"

People wouldn't just send me their stories, but
they would send me pictures of their drinking
water too. The colors coming out of those faucets ranged from yellow to green to black. Now,
that's when I would think, "Houston, we have a
problem." A big problem. It seriously frightened
me, and I realized I needed to make this project
accessible to more people, because 99 percent of
Americans have no idea what's really happening,
including our elected officials. Most lawyers won't
touch these cases, and senators and representatives
don't generally respond either. People turn to me
when they have no one else to turn to.

I thought, what could I do with this information? It's a huge obligation to have so many
people writing to me. I wanted to be responsible
and do my best to help as many people as possible. So, I started plotting all the information
on a map with the hope that as more people
reported their stories, I could help shed light on
these issues. I've worked to digitize the process
so it's not just me and a bunch of dots. We now
have the technology to report these issues and get

to the bottom of what's really happening in real time with tons of data.

Today, the map runs on sophisticated software that anyone can access online at www.community healthbook.com. The software is called MIP (Mobile Investigation Platform) and it combines mobile data collection and geographic information system (GIS) capabilities for a much more user-friendly and efficient system. It's great for a one-woman operation like me. Now, anyone who wants to report to me can join the Community Healthbook and log their environmental concerns. The software administrators review each report that comes in to keep it organized and on topic. I can use that data to help people in the community whether it's by raising more awareness, starting litigation, or taking data to Congress. The map also enables people to find others reporting about the same issue—so communities can share resources and help one another too.

Community Healthbook launched in March 2017 and already has more than tens of thousands of people reporting. As more people add their information, we can start to see patterns. People can report information about what they think the source of contamination is—whether they've learned this from articles in their local paper or if they know about a chemical that got dumped from an old industrial site nearby. On the back end, the software is loaded with public data, containing relevant information such as EPA violations, water quality reports, and locations of toxic spills and fracking areas. Each person who reports helps to share a larger story of what's happening in our country and how these pollutants are affecting all of us.

The concept of the map is similar to **America's Most Wanted**. Remember that show? Instead of local law enforcement trying to find the location of a criminal, they could leverage the power of communities to help solve the crime, and I'd like to see a lot more of that happening when it comes to contamination. The map is built on a system that allows public health and federal officials to access the data in a protected way so that they can expeditiously investigate root causes and determine any further action. My hope is that this information can help us get new laws passed or get stricter enforcement of the laws already in place to protect those who are most vulnerable and in need of help.

Part of the problem with tracking diseases and clusters of disease is the law. For those who aren't familiar with it, former president Bill Clinton signed H.R. 3013 in 1996, the Health Insurance Portability and Accountability Act (HIPAA), which was intended to protect patient privacy guidelines. But a sad side effect of HIPAA is that it may have prevented a national reporting database. We simply don't know what we don't know, and that's one way we see water problems and pollution issues as isolated incidents rather than systemic failures. When people report to my map, the system is HIPAA-compliant. If someone reports their health issues on their own, we can track that data and then go back to them later and ask permission to use it, if for example an agency wanted to do a case study. Creating a big picture that helps connect the dots is a huge step forward in solving these issues on a larger scale.

I believe we are in an age of self-reporting. Right now, if people report to their state, it goes into an abyss. We're not doing anything with the information, and I want to change that. We can use the self-reported data in Community Healthbook as general information to see the larger picture, or if we want to take an issue to Capitol Hill, I can email everyone in a community and ask permission to share their data, and let the experts take it from there.

I've learned the value and impact of the power of numbers firsthand by going out in communities and knocking on doors for many years, and more recently by posting on Facebook to connect with even more people. Numbers are important when it comes to these cases. In math, $1 + 1 = 2$. But when it comes to principle and leverage,

$1 + 1 = 1,000$. Let me tell you what I mean by that. One or two people coming down with cancer is sad, but not necessarily cause for concern. But when it becomes hundreds or more people in a small town who are all dealing with a similar kind of cancer, it raises a big red flag. Every community that I've worked with that has been exposed to chromium-6, for example, exhibits similar health problems. The people experience chronic nosebleeds, headaches, colon, kidney, and heart issues, bone deterioration, cancers, infertility, and more.

I can almost spot the chemical by the symptoms people describe to me or by the color of the water. Bright green is always chromium-6, which is now found at unsafe levels in the drinking water of more than two-thirds of Americans. The dirty yellow and brown water images from Flint were from corroded pipes. When water stinks of bleach, it means that chemical compounds have built up in the water. These kinds of changes in your water are cause for concern. It's time to take notice and speak up. Be aware, be informed, be vigilant, be proactive: that's the best way to protect your health and welfare if you are uncertain about your water condition.

Ultimately, I keep doing this work because I am looking to find the truth. Plain and simple. Seeing is believing and that's why my map is so important.

CANCER CLUSTERS & TREVOR'S LAW

Let's look more closely at the issue of cancer clusters. In general, we see about 1,685,210 new cases of cancer each year in the U.S. alone, and each year almost 600,000 people will die from the disease. Communities throughout the country are experiencing unexpected increases in cancer. Here's a small sample of emails about cancer and disease straight from my inbox that show the stories beyond the statistics:

From Tremont, Mississippi:

Everyone has cancer in our little town. I lost a brother and sister in their 40s and my husband lost two sisters in their 50s. My dad also died of pancreatic cancer. We live in an area where Weyerhaeuser Timber Company sprayed all the hardwood to kill it (for years) and planted pine trees. I would like to find out if all this spraying has caused the high cancer rates in our area.

From Melbourne, Florida:

I grew up in Sayreville, New Jersey. For unknown reasons, many people in my town have died from different forms of cancer ranging in all ages. Dupont Factory and Hercules were located in the town. It is a large cluster of cancer in Sayreville.

From Grand Junction, Colorado:

I am 4 years out from breast cancer treatment. I had stage 2 invasive ductal carcinoma. While lying awake at night thinking about the high number of cancer patients in Grand Junction, I realized that the lady I bought my house from in 1997 died from breast cancer in 2000. The lady that bought my house from me in 2003 is going through breast cancer now. There were old mill tailings that subdivisions, city structures, etc., are built on. I am concerned for the residents in this valley. We have the highest rate of cancer in the state of Colorado.

From Gilbert, Arizona:

My good friend has a rare, aggressive form of sarcoma. His condition was diagnosed a little over two years ago when he was turning 31. He endured 6 tours of Iraq and Afghanistan only to come home to be diagnosed with this disease. I asked his wife permission to contact you as there must be something linked to his childhood that may have contributed to this. He grew up in Bolingbrook, Illinois. Interestingly, 5 other people that he grew up with had aggressive forms of cancer in the same age group and he is the only one still alive. I know you have a lot more resources and may be able to shed some light on what may be causing it. There could be a larger number of people affected that may be unknown. I can help get you in touch with people to provide more details.

From Waycross, Georgia:

This isn't my story, but a story about our community. We live in Southeast Georgia, where cancer rates are high. It's gotten so bad that my family and those around us are afraid to drink the water because we don't know what is causing the cancer. It's finally making local news, but as you probably know, the government is slow to react. From what I understand, the CDC actually used a local group's research as their own, suggesting that individuals stop smoking. My husband suggested I write to you. He has been more affected by cancer than I have. His nephew (age 15) and grandmother both died of cancer. His sister and sister-in-law have both survived cancer. Just use Google and search "Waycross Cancer" to read about our community issues. Thanks for your time and your contribution to helping those who don't know how.

From Clinton, Maryland:

I had a son who died at the age of 21 of colorectal cancer. I live in a cul-de-sac where there are 6 houses. Four of the 6 houses have a member of the family that got cancer and 3 of them including my son has died. The other two were older gentlemen and the other survivor is a man in his 50s. I think there has to be a connection. I just don't know where to start looking. My son was a healthy active athlete that played basketball in high school and college, watched what he ate, and exercised constantly. For him to die from cancer is just inconceivable. Several others on a cross street to mine have also died of cancer that I know about, but there could be more that I am not aware of.

From Newburgh, Indiana:

I am a 63-year-old female. I was diagnosed with the Sarcoidosis Disease in 1998. I lived in a rural area named Lyles Station Indiana for many years. This area is very close to the power plant located in Mt. Carmel, Illinois. What concerns me is that the population is very small and there are at least 4 other people that I personally know who have the same diagnosis. One passed away a few years ago due to complications. Since this is such a rare disease it concerns me that something may be causing this condition. I contacted the CDC and got no response. I also know you have some concerns about the quality of drinking water in the Evansville, Indiana area. This is the area I have lived and worked in for the past 15-plus years. Again, I am close to the Alcoa Plant in Newburgh, Indiana. I have followed your story, so I know if there is a reason for me to be concerned, you will know how to assist me.

These are real people asking good questions and making good observations. It's time for someone to provide them with answers.

When it comes to a cancer, it's easy to say that genetics or lifestyle play a part, but then we have the issue of children. Cancer is the second leading cause of death among children, exceeded only by accidents. They don't smoke, drink alcohol, or work stressful jobs. Yet, forty-six American children are diagnosed daily with cancers unrelated to genetics or family history. We know that children can be more vulnerable to chemical toxins than adults because they have both faster metabolisms and less mature immune systems. These numbers say to me that we need more research to understand what's really going on.

One person who cares very deeply about this

issue is my friend Trevor from Boise, Idaho. In 2002, at the age of thirteen, he was diagnosed with medulloblastoma, a highly malignant form of brain cancer. And Trevor was not the only one. Despite living in a small, idyllic mountain town, four other kids were diagnosed with the same disease the same year as Trevor, and the town had an abnormally high number of cancer cases both prior to and after these diagnoses. His mom, Charlie Smith, was concerned and took this information to the Cancer Data Registry, but officials told her that even if her data proved to be true the town was too small to warrant a cancer cluster study. They were not statistically significant.

Trevor did not let that stop him. Not only did he endure invasive tests, an eight-hour surgery to remove a golf-ball-sized tumor from his brain, and fourteen months of radiation and chemotherapy, but he made a promise that if he survived, he would dedicate his time to helping other children with cancer. He turned to politics and took his promise to Washington, D.C. In 2011, the Strengthening Protections for Children and Communities from Disease Clusters Act, also known as Trevor's Law, was introduced by Senator Barbara Boxer (D-CA) and co-sponsored by Senator Mike Crapo (R-ID). This bipartisan bill was created to help communities determine a connection between "clusters" of cancer, birth defects, and other diseases, and contaminants in the surrounding environment.

In 2013, I joined Trevor on Capitol Hill to testify for his bill that would require the federal government to document and track childhood and adult cancer clusters, not just in Idaho but also across the country.

Here's part of my testimony:

As an advocate for the past twenty years, I have reached an undeniable conclusion: there are simply too many cancers in this country and not enough answers. And that's all these communities are trying to do—get answers to the most basic questions: why is my son, who was perfectly healthy just months ago, now sick with leukemia? Why does my daughter have two brain tumors at the age of six? And why is the same thing happening to my neighbors' kids? Mothers and fathers ask me these questions by the hundreds every week.

I am not here to play scientist, nor am I here to sling accusations or assign blame. This is not a partisan issue. Gathering the information necessary to take action protective of human health is a long and daunting task, and when it comes to the health of our children, we cannot afford to jump to conclusions. But it's time for us to stop turning away from these communities. How many childhood brain cancers is enough for us to start getting serious about investigating the potential causes of these illnesses? We need to be listening to community members' concerns when they raise their hand and say something is not right in their neighborhood.

You, members of this committee, carry the voice and the will of those who elected you to serve this country. I can tell you those voices are crying out for help. Some of your constituents are fearful, others are frustrated; they all need your help to stay united as a community that is trying to find answers.

This is the issue of our time—whether it is pollution in our water, our air, or products we use every day. The government must play a stronger, better role in helping all Americans. I understand this might not be a popular position in some circles but most of my life has been about taking unpopular stands against big polluters so I'm okay with that. Madam Chairman, Senator Crapo, I believe that your legislation "The Strengthening Protection for Children and Communities from Disease Clusters Act" will help Americans who desperately need it. And the bipartisan nature of Trevor's Law will send a very valuable message that clean air and clean water and healthy communities are not political issues—they are human issues. American issues. I will also remind the public that it was a Republican president—President Nixon—who created the Environmental Protection Agency.

It's also important that the federal government doesn't just come in, run some tests, and leave. Make no mistake—the federal government must play a key role in identifying and responding to disease clusters because federal agencies have the research, response, and enforcement capacity that states and localities often don't. But we can't lose sight of the most important part of any effort to identify and respond to a possible disease cluster—the people themselves.

I am an advocate for awareness and a person's right to know. Oftentimes, we don't think about or understand what is happening to someone else until it affects us personally. Cancer or some chronic disease has touched all of us. And disease does not recognize our political party affiliation. I am proud to support this bill and am proud that it has bipartisan support. The time has come for the federal government to step up and provide the expertise and resources only it can.

Trevor Schaefer survived a brain cancer diagnosis at
the age of thirteen. Erin with Trevor on Capitol Hill
in 2013 to testify for his bill requiring the federal
government to document and track childhood and
adult cancer clusters throughout the country

Trevor's Law passed in 2016 as part of a Toxic
Substances Control Act (TSCA) reform bill and
is exactly a testament to what one person can do.
Trevor and his mom have been determined and
committed to this amazing health law that has
the potential to impact so many people. The law
calls directly on the U.S. secretary of Health and
Human Services to develop criteria to monitor,
track, and respond to instances of potential cancer
clusters in the United States, creating a national

registry, which can study and document where clusters exist, why they exist, and who might be affected by them. It will work to improve communication and data sharing between local, state, and federal governments. But like most good laws on the books to protect our health, this one is still in limbo and has yet to be implemented.

"If we don't show up for work, we get fired, but in Washington, it's just business as usual," Trevor said to me in a recent conversation. "If they don't act on a bill for the betterment of this country and our children, nothing happens. I think it comes down to accountability. What happens to anyone in Washington if they don't follow through? Nothing. How do we change that? We need to hold them accountable."

Thankfully, Trevor is still on the case. He created a foundation, Trevor's Trek Foundation, dedicated to promoting the awareness of childhood cancer and cancer clusters that exist in America's communities as well as supporting the implementation of Trevor's Law through advocacy, collaboration, and coordination. Right now, they have a bigger role to play than he originally intended—mostly to stay on top of the federal government to do their job. He's still in constant communication with his home-state senator, Mike Crapo, working to get a coordinator appointed within Health and Human Services for Trevor's Law. He continues at the grassroots level to keep building awareness and researching these issues. If a young boy can beat cancer, stand up and use his voice, and keep fighting, so can you.

WANT TO GET INVOLVED?
Community Healthbook

Share your story! Go to the Community Health-book website, www.communityhealthbook.com, and start an account. Once registered, you can report an issue by choosing a questionnaire and topic that best describes the issues you're facing and provide the details. We will review your submission and learn more about your circumstances. If further investigation is needed, I may even visit you to see what's happening in your neighborhood. You can visit the Community Healthbook as often as needed to report an issue, see what's happening in your community, or participate in new questionnaires.

Trevor's Trek Foundation

Go to the Trevor's Trek Foundation website, www.trevorstrek.org, to donate your time or resources to this worthy cause. Ask your local officials how they are tracking cancer cases and demand that more resources go to research and understanding how toxic pollutants are impacting our children.

4

FLOATING IN A SEA OF CHEMICALS

When water flows out of your faucet into a glass of drinking water, it could be filled with any number of toxic chemicals, pharmaceuticals, herbicides, pesticides, and even toxic byproducts that come from disinfecting the water itself. Of course, water treatment systems are supposed to filter out these harmful and disgusting substances, yet reports from across the country show that a lot of unwanted substances are slipping through. Our water quality is declining every single day. How is it happening?

The first thing to understand is that more than 70 percent of the earth's surface is covered in water, and while that might sound like a lot, about 96 percent of it is saline—or saltwater found in the ocean. Less than 1 percent of the water on our planet is drinkable. We drink from two main sources: (1) surface water such as creeks, rivers, lakes, and wetlands, and (2) groundwater, which is water found under the earth's surface in cracks and spaces in soil, rock, or sand. All this water must be treated before we drink it.

Our waterways are impacted by many different contaminants, but you can put them into three main categories: organic, inorganic, and bacterial. Organic contaminants are substances that contain carbon and its derivatives, which is everything from dirt to petrochemicals to herbicides like atrazine. Inorganic contaminants are man-made industrial and agricultural chemicals such as chromium, lead, and trichloroethylene (TCE). Biological (or microbial) contaminants refer to organisms in the water, such as bacteria, viruses, and parasites. We've specifically seen a rise in bacteria like **Legionella**, which can be fatal. We're seeing a surge in outbreaks of Legionnaire's disease, a severe form of pneumonia caused by the waterborne bacterium **Legionella**, across the country—as well as brain-eating amoebas. The U.S. Water Quality & Health Council describes **Legionella** as "public health enemy number 1."

Since the Industrial Revolution, factories and manufacturers have used freshwater sources as a convenient spot to dump their waste. Add on top of that waste from agriculture, wastewater treatment plants, and stormwater runoff, and you can see why we've got so many substances floating around in our water systems. We add all these chemicals to the environment without knowing a whole lot about them.

For years, we've followed the adage that "the solution to pollution is dilution." But the toxins have only increased with time, and we have reached a point where even large bodies of water can't possibly dilute the constant barrage of toxins. We allow chemicals in the water first, making everyone who drinks the water guinea pigs, and then years later science finds that these chemicals cause cancer and other serious health problems. Meanwhile, we've been drinking it for more than twenty years. I think a better system is to know what a chemical is capable of before it goes into our water supply. I'd like to see more businesses being good neighbors, testing their own products for safety, acting with integrity, and working with substances that won't harm people or the environment.

We also have problems when it comes to treating the water. We have more than 151,000 public water systems in the U.S., and no two drinking water qualities are the same. No two systems treat the water the same way, and no two systems pump to your tap the same quality of water. Every single chemical aspect of your water supply impacts water treatment techniques. There's no one magic bullet for cleaning up our drinking water supplies. No one size fits all.

We continue to hear the lulling use of the phrase "Your drinking water is safe," which is misleading and false. The Safe Drinking Water Act (SDWA) does not define "safe"; it barely establishes federal standards for drinking water. My water quality treatment expert, Bob Bowcock, is the first to emphasize that water treatment professionals are trained to say, "This water meets or exceeds all federal and state safe drinking water requirements." Yes, the water might be "compliant" when they tested it one day, but is it safe drinking water? Even if drinking water meets federal standards, it might not be safe if it is contaminated with an unregulated substance or tainted with contamination through some other scenario (for example, contamination resulting from residential piping). Last amended in 1996, the SDWA proposed a scientific, risk-based process for identifying, assessing, and managing health risks from contaminants in drinking water. Since 1975, the EPA has only developed drinking water regulations addressing ninety-one contaminants.

Bob also says that water treatment is as much about waste management as it is about treatment. Water treatment operators are waste managers. The $64,000 question is how are we going to dispose of our waste? We need to figure out responsible ways to manage all this waste. To solve this massive problem, we also need to be connected to the bigger issue of toxins today.

We are living in a hyper-toxic time. We're aren't just dealing with the toxins themselves, but the fact that they have accumulated in the environment for long stretches of time. American children are growing up exposed to more chemicals than any other generation in history and it shows. Rates of chronic disease for children, especially those living in poverty, are on the rise. Nearly half of U.S. adults (or 117 million people) are living with one or more chronic health conditions. We assume watchdogs are in place and that regulatory agencies and government standards are keeping us safe. But our health records show a different story. Big businesses rule the roost, dumping their leftover chemicals wherever they like with little regard for our safety. These chemicals affect our water, our health, and our future, and we need more transparency and education.

We have more than eighty-five thousand chemicals in the Toxic Substances Control Act (TSCA) Inventory and more than forty thousand chemicals actively in use on the market today in all kinds of products from shampoos and baby lotions to cell phones and Tupperware. Each one of us interacts with these chemicals every day, but we are just beginning to uncover what this constant exposure means for our health. We have studied only about two hundred, or 1 percent, of them for safety. How much of any toxic substance can a human body ingest and still be well?

In 1975 John Quarles, then deputy administrator of the EPA, said that legislation to prevent the spread of dangerous chemicals in our environment was "one of our most urgently needed environmental laws" and that "existing federal laws fail to deal evenly and comprehensively with toxic substances problems." He also said that the Safe Drinking Water Act, then recently enacted, dealt with "the problem at a point when contaminants are very difficult to control."

He advocated requiring premarket notifications on all chemicals so that we would understand the risks new chemicals posed to human health and the environment. Back then, six hundred new chemicals were being introduced each year for commercial use. Today, about two thousand new chemicals are introduced each year, and we still don't know their impact on our health despite our widespread exposure to them. When it comes to protecting public health, we need to understand the general effects of these chemicals and the level of exposure that is considered hazardous to human health.

Congress passed the Toxic Substances Control Act (TSCA) in 1976. Before that we had no records of what chemicals were manufactured, used, or released into the environment and no means of regulating them. This law gave the EPA authority to help regulate new and existing chemicals with reporting, record-keeping, and testing requirements, and restrictions on chemical substances used commercially. It also gave the EPA authority to maintain a master list of chemicals and keep an inventory of them.

This law has been considered one of the **least** effective environmental laws we have. The EPA has little capacity to prevent a company from bringing chemicals to market. When the law was signed, more than sixty thousand chemicals already in use became grandfathered into the system with no toxicity testing. The TSCA also made the EPA responsible for gathering data on safety rather than the companies producing the chemicals. The agency had to demonstrate health or environmental risks before requiring companies to test these chemicals. It's basically an "innocent until proven guilty" approach, which is a huge burden for any agency, and especially an overworked and underfunded one. The EPA has not routinely assessed the risks of chemicals already in use. On the rare occasion that they do, it's a legal hassle that can take years. The law also contains provisions allowing certain chemical information to be protected as trade secrets, helping preserve competitive advantages for the manufacturers. It's just another way the law has fallen short—keeping companies thriving, while our health remains at risk.

The TSCA is a law with good intentions that has been virtually unenforceable. In 2009 testimony before the Senate's Committee on Environmental and Public Works, John Stephenson, director for

Natural Resources and Environment, simply said, "EPA lacks adequate scientific information on the toxicity of many chemicals. One major reason is that TSCA generally places the burden of obtaining data about existing chemicals on the EPA rather than on chemical companies."

Only six chemicals have been regulated under the TSCA: PCBs, asbestos, radon, lead, mercury, and formaldehyde. Meanwhile, the list of substances known to cause cancer in humans, also called carcinogens, is more than twenty, and when you meet the top toxins in your water, you will see overlap with this list, including chromium, TCE, and PCBs. Companies know these substances cause harm, they know they are in the water supply, and yet we don't fix the problem. P.S.: The list of suspected or anticipated carcinogens is much longer and the list of chemicals we simply don't have data on is even longer still.

In 2016, we attempted to reform the nation's outdated toxic chemical laws. After many years of initiatives in Congress, former president Barack Obama signed the Frank R. Lautenberg Chemical Safety for the 21st Century Act on June 22. I remember the date because it's also my birthday. The amendment was intended to help increase public health protections from toxic chemicals, but it was still too lenient on industry and didn't account for budgeting—in other words, how the

EPA can fund costs associated with new regulations. It also weakened the states' ability to pass their own, stricter legislation. The agency has promised a review of existing chemicals with ten of them listed as a priority, but we know that many thousands still need review. Even with updates to the law it could be decades before we see any major reviews of these toxins or changes that could positively impact our health and well-being. Bottom line: We should know what these chemicals do before we put them on the market.

Working on toxic legislation reform with New Jersey senator Frank Lautenberg, who died in 2013. The Frank R. Lautenberg Chemical Safety for the 21st Century Act (Lautenberg Chemical Safety Act) was signed into law on June 22, 2016.

While I was writing this book, the first study of plastic pollutants in our tap water came out, showing that 94 percent of thirty-three tap water samples from across the U.S. tested positive for the presence of plastic fibers. Those sample sites included the U.S. Capitol complex and the headquarters of the EPA in Washington, D.C. We produce more than 300 million tons of plastic in the world each year, and about half of all plastics are created for disposable items such as water bottles. We don't have any long-term studies about the effects of ingesting these tiny plastic fibers, which are essentially fragments of larger pieces of nonbiodegradable plastic. One thing we do know is that endocrine-disruptors like bisphenol A (BPA) and di-(2-ethylhexyl) phthalate (DEHP), two chemicals widely used in plastics, are now part of this new toxic mix in our water.

BPA is a chemical that highlights one of the major problems with evidence-based science and toxicity. In the 1930s, a British scientist discovered that BPA mimicked human estrogen, but this lab research didn't slow down production of this new technology and for generations BPA was the gold standard in plastics. In the 1990s, Stanford University researchers made a new discovery—that tiny amounts of BPA could leach out of plastic. The question then became whether those trace amounts of BPA could cause harm. Recent studies show that more than 90 percent of Americans tested have BPA in their system. Yet, we still don't have a regulation in place and the risks of BPA contamination are still in dispute. One reason is that studies have produced conflicting and/or inconclusive results, in part because alterations in the endocrine system can be subtle, take years to fully understand, and are generally hard to pinpoint. Academic scientists do not have clout with the regulators who ultimately must determine the kinds of studies that can help oversee these chemicals and their impact on human health.

The point is that we shouldn't be drinking polluted water. Period. We certainly should not be drinking plastics, and we don't have any safety standards in place to protect our health.

Another huge symptom of our toxic buildup is seen in the thousands of Superfund pollution and contamination cleanup sites across the country that are invading our homes, businesses, schools, daycare centers, nursing homes, you name it, every minute of every day with toxic vapors causing illness, and most of us have been told nothing. The EPA's Superfund program began in 1980 to help clean up some of the country's worst hazardous waste sites and to respond to local and national environmental emergencies. But since then, how many areas have been thoroughly cleaned? How many people are even aware that they exist?

A Superfund site is any land that has been contaminated by hazardous waste and identified by the EPA as a candidate for cleanup because it poses a risk to human health and/or the environment. Most of these sites are "discovered" when the presence of hazardous waste is made known to the EPA—meaning communities usually find them first because people get sick. These sites get placed on the National Priorities List (NPL). We have almost 33,000 Superfund sites in the U.S., and the number is growing. About 1,400 of these sites are on the NPL, they are full of asbestos, lead, radiation, and other hazardous materials, and they are not getting cleaned up fast enough.

I posted on Facebook in 2015 about a site near Torrance in Los Angeles County, where the EPA has been working for decades to clean up two adjacent Superfund sites: Del Amo Superfund and Montrose Chemical Superfund. Several large-scale industrial companies left a toxic footprint that is still being cleaned up today. The **Los Angeles Times** reported that the sites are two of the worst chemical dumps in the nation. The companies had dumped trichloroethylene (TCE), benzene, and chlorobenzene into open unlined pits, which subsequently leached into the groundwater and migrated into the environment.

The U.S. government owned the 280-acre Del Amo site during World War II, and it also hosted a synthetic rubber plant and manufacturers of styrene and butadiene. The land was sold to Shell Oil Co. in the 1950s. Goodyear Tire and Rubber Co., Dow Chemical Co., Shell, and others dumped their wastewater sludge into six unlined pits and three unlined evaporation ponds on a four-acre disposal site from 1943 to 1972, when the facility was shut down. At that point, any open pits and ponds were filled in with dirt. It was declared a Superfund site in 2002.

The neighboring Superfund site, spanning some thirteen acres, was the former home of a Montrose Chemical Corp. plant that manufactured the pesticide DDT from 1947 to 1982. Once closed, the company demolished the factory and paved everything over with asphalt. The property was declared a Superfund site in 1989. In addition to contaminating the local groundwater, the plant dumped chemicals into the ocean from the Palos Verdes Shelf.

By the 1990s, discoveries of bowling-bowl-size chunks of DDT led to tearing down sixty-three homes, according to the **Los Angeles Times**. Subsequent ongoing remediation measures to reduce contamination include capping waste areas and treating soil and water. Ongoing monitoring of sites and surrounding areas has detected disturbing growth in TCE concentrations underneath homes.

At least fourteen thousand people who live within a mile to the south and thirty-four thousand people within four miles drink from a deep aquifer there. It's just one example of these sites and one that's not far from my own backyard. About 53 million Americans live within three miles of a Superfund site, including 17 percent of all U.S. children under the age of five.

You can search for your community here: www.epa.gov/superfund/search-superfund-sites-where-you-live. I'm working to put this map right next to my own Community Healthbook and see how closely the disease clusters match these toxic areas.

When it comes to chemicals, we desperately need more testing for their safety, and we need to err on the side of caution when it comes to bringing them to the marketplace. I would like to see continued monitoring and testing of Superfund sites, both old and new. We also need to bring "polluter taxes" back to industry. Up until 1995, the Superfund program was funded mostly from taxes on crude oil, imported petroleum products, hazardous chemicals, and imported substances that use hazardous chemicals as a feedstock, and on corporate modified alternative minimum taxable income. Those taxes expired, and since 1996, oversight and cleanup of Superfund sites has been largely paid for with our tax dollars.

Ultimately, many of these toxins are making their way into our water. If there's a substance in my water that's a poison, then I'm concerned, and you should be too. When I work with communities, I help bridge the gap between the people who live there and what may be going on with any agencies or in politics. I don't like getting involved in politics because it doesn't matter what your party affiliation is, if you are rich or poor, or the color of your skin; we all need access to clean water. If there's one agenda across the board that I think everyone needs to be united on, it's making sure we all have safe drinking water. Period.

You need to know the facts about what's in your water, where to go, and who to turn to when you have concerns. You can't make good choices if you don't have the information. You deserve to know if your water is safe to drink. Does it meet state and federal drinking water standards? And what's the true cost of compliance? What's the true cost for you as the consumer buying a product from your municipal or public drinking water system? That's the real question. The next chapter will cover the top toxins that I have concerns about, so you can start to learn more.

I know it can seem daunting to get started so here are a few simple actions that will help you understand where your water comes from and what pollutants might be in it.

WHO IS CLEANING YOUR WATER?

Not sure who is responsible for cleaning your water? Find out. Unfortunately, there's not an app for it yet. But the EPA provides a map that will help you find your local water utility. Or ask a neighbor or elder in your community who might know. If you live in an apartment building, speak to your management company to find out who supplies water to your taps.

Find Your Water Report

Do you know what toxins are in your water? Knowledge is power. The first step is to get a copy of your Consumer Confidence Report (sometimes called a Water Quality Report) from your water company. This annual water report is provided to customers by July 1 each year and will give you details about contaminants that have been detected in your water system. It should come in the mail with your water bill. If you pay your bill online, you should be able to go directly to the water utility's website and get a copy or request a downloadable PDF.

Water Report Elements

Each report should list your water source— whether it's a lake, river, or public well. It will also list the contaminants found in your source water and tell you what levels have been detected. Contaminants found to have a higher level than what the EPA recommends should be listed. Be sure to take note of any violations—meaning the contaminant has been detected at a higher level than the EPA laws allow. If violations are listed, the report should also include how those contaminants may affect your health and how the water utility is working to address the problem.

Well Water

If your water comes from a private or community well rather than a municipality, then it's up to you to maintain the safety of your water. The EPA does help with information on how to maintain your well here: www.epa.gov/privatewells. If you can't find what you need, try contacting your local health or environmental department and request a list of the state-certified (licensed) laboratories in your area that test water. Get to know your watershed and be aware of the industrial and agricultural businesses located nearby that might pose risks to the quality of your well water.

Go DIY

You can get your water tested on your own and see what you find. The EPA has a Safe Drinking Water Hotline: 1-800-426-4791. Call and find a water testing agency in your area or ask friends and neighbors if they have recommendations. You can also use the Environmental Working Group's

Tap Water Database: www.ewg.org/tapwater. Plug in your zip code and the report will show which contaminants have been found in your city's water system that exceed federal or state regulations.

Research Toxins

A simple Google search of any contaminant will get you started on the journey to understanding the basics of a chemical substance. The next chapter outlines some of the top toxins I've dealt with and gives you details about where these contaminants come from, how they are regulated, and some of the health hazards they might pose.

Get Connected

You may already have a local community group or nonprofit working to improve the water quality in your neighborhood. Join them! Search for local groups or contact national organizations like the Clean Water Network, Waterkeeper Alliance, or Clean Water Action and ask how you can get involved and help. Let these groups know if there's a company you suspect might be polluting or tell them about local issues and see how they can help put pressure on the right organizations to follow laws and help make change happen.

Don't Contribute to the Problem

Think before you dump. Your sink and toilet are not safe places to deposit paints, chemical cleaners, used oil, unused pharmaceuticals, or other potential contaminants that can pollute the water supply. Contact your local sanitation, public works, or health department to get information about how to properly dispose of hazardous waste. Work to reduce the amount of single-use plastics in your life as best you can by buying more items in bulk and skipping plastic containers whenever you can.

5

THE TOP TOXINS

I want you to meet the top toxic chemicals found in our water and learn everything you can about how these chemicals got into our taps and our bodies, how we regulate them, and the potential health hazards they pose. This list is by no means all-inclusive, but these six pollutants are some of the worst offenders that are plaguing communities throughout the country.

Toxin #1: Hexavalent Chromium

Additional Names/Spellings: chromium-6, Cr6, chromium VI, Cr-VI

This substance is often referred to as the "Erin Brockovich chemical," but I assure you it was here long before me. I may have helped expose its dangers, but the real story is how this chemical came to be in every town across the country and how it has polluted our drinking water. A 2016 analysis of federal data from drinking water tests throughout the country shows that hexavalent chromium contaminates water supplies for more than 200 million Americans in all fifty states. But federal regulations only monitor general chromium in water, which includes the two most common forms: chromium-3, a naturally occurring metallic element, and chromium-6, the toxic version used by industry to make everything from motor vehicle bumpers to textile dyes, wood preservation and anticorrosion products, and more. We don't differentiate between the two at the federal level and that's a big problem.

The word "chromium" is derived from the Greek word **chroma**, which means "color." Even though chromium is an odorless metallic element found in nature, the man-made version—hexavalent chromium—creates a bright green or yellow color when you see too much of it in the water. In industry, chromium-6 was the gold standard for corrosion resistance, and it was added to paints, primers, plastics, stainless steel, and surface coatings to increase durability. Chromium was once valued for bringing bright shininess to car bumpers and aircraft engine components. It was also used in cooling towers for office buildings and manufacturing plants throughout the country, because hexavalent chromium is one of the most efficient and cheap corrosion inhibitors available. But it's highly toxic. In 1980, the National Toxicology Program and the Department of Health and Human Services published **The First Annual Report on Carcinogens**, listing chromium-6 as a human carcinogen, and in 1986 the California Air Resources Board identified it as a toxic air contaminant (TAC) that causes both acute and chronic problems such as yellow teeth, shortness of breath, coughing, wheezing, bronchitis, pneumonia, skin ulcers, dermatitis, and lung, nasal, and sinus cancer. It's not until more recently that research has also shown how dangerous it is when found in your drinking water.

National Regulations: MCL

The EPA has a national drinking water standard of 100 parts per billion (ppb) for total chromium, including chromium-6. This means that water systems are only required to test for chromium, which is a bit confusing since one type of chromium is a known carcinogen and one isn't. This MCL (maximum contaminant level) for total chromium was set in 1991 and based on the science available then. As I've mentioned, it's a slow process for the science to catch up to safety standards. In 2008, the National Toxicology Program published a two-year drinking water study of animals and found that hexavalent chromium is carcinogenic after oral exposure.

According to their website, the EPA regularly re-evaluates drinking water standards, and based on the science on chromium-6, it began a rigorous and comprehensive review of its health effects in 2008. Yet in 2018, it was still classified as an "emerging contaminant." Of the more than eighty emerging contaminants monitored, only perchlorate, an ingredient found in rocket fuel and explosives, has been recommended for regulation. When tap water from a public water system exceeds the federal standard for chromium, consumers are supposed to be notified. But even after all the hype around hexavalent chromium, I would guess that most people wouldn't know what to do if they received such a notice.

State Regulations: MCL + PHG

As I mentioned in chapter 2, the only state that had a regulation for hexavalent chromium was California and the MCL was set at 10 parts per billion, which is much lower than the federal standard and higher than the public health goal (PHG) of 0.02 parts per billion. The PHG was established by California's Office of Environmental Health Hazard Assessment (OEHHA) and was a first for both California and the country, but in 2017 that MCL was dismissed due to a court case and the state water board is working to create a new MCL.

The process to establish a PHG is quite detailed and thorough. Scientists compile all relevant information, including studies of the chemical's effect on animals and humans who have been exposed to it. With this data, scientists perform a health risk assessment to identify the level of chemical in the drinking water that would pose no significant health effects in people who drink the water every day for seventy years, and OEHHA assumes that adults drink two liters of water each day. They also take into consideration vulnerable populations, such as pregnant women, children, seniors, and those with pre-existing health conditions, before setting the final goal. PHGs, while not enforceable, do matter for public water systems that must provide information about contaminants in their annual Consumer Confidence Reports and tell customers about the health risks when they exceed the public health goal. P.S.: Reports must be sent to you by your water supplier each year by July 1. Let's make that fact more known!

How can the PHG be so much lower than the drinking water standard? MCLs account for the chemical's health risks along with other factors, such as their detectability, treatability, and the cost of treatment. A chemical's MCL is required to be as close to its PHG as is "technologically and economically feasible, placing primary emphasis on the protection of public health." The California

Department of Public Health estimated that the cost to meet the state's MCL was almost $20 million a year.

New Jersey and North Carolina have endorsed nonlegal limits for chromium-6 in tap water. Both states have been plagued with issues related to mismanagement of coal ash, a toxic byproduct of coal-burning power plants, making its way into water supplies. Coal ash contains a mix of hazardous heavy metals, including chromium-6, lead, arsenic, and mercury. In 2010, the Drinking Water Quality Institute, a New Jersey agency made up of scientists, utility officials, and citizens, recommended a health-based maximum contaminant level (similar to a public health goal) of 0.07 ppb. But environmental proponents say that state regulators have dragged their feet about putting any laws on the books. In North Carolina, residents living near Duke coal ash ponds received "do not drink" letters from state regulators in 2015, noting that their well water tested positive for unsafe levels of hexavalent chromium. But that standard was later overturned by political appointees at the North Carolina Department of Environmental Quality (DEQ) and the North Carolina Department of Health and Human Services (NCDHHS) who worked for then governor Pat McCrory, an employee of Duke Energy for twenty-eight years.

Health Concerns

Hexavalent chromium is a carcinogen and a reproductive toxicant for both males and females. It can also lead to eye and respiratory irritation, asthma, anemia, acute gastroenteritis, vertigo, gastrointestinal hemorrhage, convulsions, ulcers, and damage or failure of the liver and kidneys.

Toxin #2: Chloramines

Additional Names/Spellings: Secondary disinfection, monochloramine, chloramide, chloroazane

Chloramines are what I like to call the godfather of where we've gone wrong with our water. Municipal water districts are adding ammonia to chlorinated water—a process called chloramination—to help meet standards set by the EPA to lower levels of disinfection byproducts, which many in the industry call "unintended consequences." Several different types of chloramines exist, including monochloramine, dichloramine, trichloramine, and organic chloramines. Typically, monochloramine is used most commonly to treat drinking water, so for the purposes of this book I will use the term **chloramines** to refer this mixture.

To truly understand the problem with chloramines, you need a brief history of water treatment.

Drinking water comes from many natural water sources, such as lakes, rivers, and streams, and it generally contains organic matter—leaves, dirt, fish excrement, and so on. Adding chlorine to water, called chlorination, is one of the primary water treatment methods we've used for more than a hundred years, because it's highly effective at killing most potentially harmful organisms such as bacteria, viruses, and parasites. It's done a good job of preventing disease. In fact, before chlorination, typhoid, cholera, dysentery, and diarrhea outbreaks were common in cities across the world. Treating the water helped reduce these health problems, but with the advances came potential side effects.

In 1974, scientists discovered that chlorine (the disinfectant) itself could react with naturally occurring materials in the water to create what are called disinfection byproducts (DBPs). These are substances that form when the disinfectant reacts with natural compounds in the water. Many of these DBPs have been shown to cause cancer, including trihalomethanes (THMs), which are a group of chemical compounds. Today, we have more than a thousand cities with unsafe levels of total THMs (TTHMs) in their water. TTHMs is when four distinct chemicals, chloroform, bromodichloromethane, dibromochloromethane, and bromoform, are present. Any imbalance of THMs means the system is out of balance. These compounds occur when organic matter in the water reacts with chlorine, so essentially the system is not being chlorinated properly, meaning you have too much or not enough. But many cities don't get to the root of the problem by finding the source of the organic matter. When you know what's in the water, you can treat it more effectively instead of creating a chemical cocktail mix. In the last forty years, we have discovered more than six hundred other DBPs in chlorinated tap water, including haloacetic acids (HAAs). As you can imagine, the water has only become more polluted (with both organics and inorganics), creating more treatment headaches and violations.

The EPA has worked to regulate DBPs with the adoption of the EPA Stage 1 and Stage 2 Disinfectants and Disinfection Byproducts Rules (DBPRs). These rules help to tighten drinking water regulations, requiring water treatment systems to monitor and reduce DBPs so they can provide cleaner drinking water. They apply to both community water systems (public water systems that supply water to the same population year-round) and non-transient non-community systems (public water systems that supply water to at least twenty-five of the same people at least six months per year, such as schools, office buildings, and hospitals). They require these systems to add a disinfectant to the drinking water during any part of the treatment process. These laws strengthen protection against microbial contaminants and aim to reduce dangerous DBPs like TTHMs and HAAs. Under the Stage 2 DBPR, systems need to conduct an evaluation of their distribution systems to identify the areas with high disinfection byproduct concentrations. These locations are then used as the sampling sites for Stage 2 DBPR compliance monitoring. But from the get-go, utility companies have been concerned that the regulations were too expensive.

Then along came chloramines. This alternative disinfectant method is a mixture of chlorine and ammonia. Water treatment facilities have been switching at alarming rates from chlorine to chloramines, largely to help public water systems meet federal disinfection byproduct requirements. I would say it's a convenient fix, but not necessarily a safe or effective one.

Chloramine treatment is the cheapest way of meeting EPA regulations, but it's one of the most dangerous ways as well. For starters, chlorine evaporates into the air relatively quickly, but chloramine is more stable and will last longer in the water system. The goal is to provide increased protection from bacterial and viral contamination, and certainly chloramine does that. But it is also a known carcinogen and causes more rapid deterioration of the municipal infrastructure and degradation of water system valves and fittings. In systems that still use lead pipes or lead components (which means millions of homes and buildings), the chloramine causes lead and other metals to leach out of faucets and showerheads and into our drinking water. Studies indicate the formation of toxic byproducts in drinking water may be higher when utilities use chloramines. These studies also show that chloramine causes more dangerous byproducts than other treatment alternatives, such as ozone or chlorine dioxide.

One of the most famous cases of chloramines gone wrong was when Washington, D.C., switched to using chloramines in 2000, which led to major corrosion issues in the city's aging lead pipes. By 2001, lead levels were detected to be at least eighty times higher than the accepted safe limits. A congressional investigation and lawsuit followed.

In addition, many systems include chlorine burnouts in combination with chloramines to meet their standards. A burnout happens when the water treatment process changes from chloramines to free chlorine, which is a stronger, faster-acting disinfectant. They do this to clean the water pipes and essentially flush the entire system, so that they can test the water before a burnout and then test again after. They never test the water during a burnout, and they don't have to, as most plants are only required to report quarterly. Some burnouts can last up to ninety days. The regular use of chloramines doesn't remove all the harmful organics and dirt from the water supply, so the system gets "flushed" with chlorine, forming thousands of chemical combinations that could cause cancer and other health issues.

Let me give you an example from one of the towns I've worked with. In 2015, I wrote an open letter to the Tyler, Texas, city council. In it, I highlight the difference between what it means to be compliant with EPA regulations and what it means to have safe drinking water.

An Open Letter to the Tyler, Texas, City Council:

There appears to be some confusion in the press as to what exactly I mean when I talk about the "safety" of the drinking water. Obviously, I am not primarily concerned about an MCL violation for HAAs back in May and reported in late October. What I am most concerned about are the repeated calls to our offices about high levels of chlorine taste and odor in the drinking water in Tyler for months leading up to the TCEQ [Texas Commission on Environmental Quality] Violation reporting requirement of late October.

There has been a significant misinformation campaign about the water quality problem in Tyler; and quite frankly, I am further concerned it has been misdirected toward the "triggering event," the TCEQ Violation notice.

As elected officials in Tyler, you know the water quality complaints I am talking about far precede our stepping in and opening up our own investigation. We know there are areas where the problems are considered worse than others; we have spoken directly to scores of your consumers.

The problem in Tyler, Texas, is you are misusing chloramine (chlorine + ammonia) in your treatment process to control the formation of regulated disinfection byproducts. This misuse has led to the ultimate destruction of your distribution system. In 2014, you performed a one-month distribution system chlorine burnout. This year you were faced with a two-month system-wide burnout (August and September).

Your water distribution system is suffering from serious nitrification and biofilm re-growth. Because of the loss of residual disinfectant in tanks, reservoirs, and at endpoint pipelines, you are overdosing the system. Overdosing chloramine increases nitrification and thus biofouling. You are caught in a vicious circle of self-destruction.

At the same time, during chlorine burn-outs, you are exposing your consumers to dangerously high levels of HAAs and TTHMs. Ask your water treatment professionals what the disinfection byproduct levels were during the sixty days of the burn-out; we have. This is the gaping loophole in the regulation. You don't have to test for the presence of the toxins during a burnout. You get to plan ahead, game the system, and only report what you want, when you want. Just because you do not test doesn't mean the regulated chemicals are not there.

So, that is our problem when you burn-out the consumers . . . Let's talk for a minute about the other ten months of the year. Now that your ammonia is turned back on, does this make the water "safe"? No, it makes the water "compliant." These are two very different concepts. We prefer SAFE.

Chloramine at the dose you are feeding to fight the nitrification, biofilm, and depleting residual is causing immediate and short-term health effects. Chloramine at any dose is causing chronic long-term health effects. Toxicologists have figured out the disinfection byproducts formed by chloramine "not-yet-regulated" are far more toxic than free chlorine byproducts that are "regulated."

Chloramine is causing your water to be more corrosive thus exposing consumers to dangerous levels of lead and copper (brass water meters and plumbing fixtures are made with lead). Chloramine is causing property damage to your consumers' plumbing, water heaters, fixtures, and appliances. Chloramine is causing structural damage when the pipes develop those pinhole leaks you have all seen. Chloramine is destroying the city's distribution system. Chloramine is causing environmental damage. Where does all the flushed-out water with extremely high levels of chlorine and/or chloramine go?

1. May we please have the water quality data for all tests performed at the treatment plants and the distribution system from June 1, 2015, through the present?
2. May we please have copies of the water treatment plant operations logs from June 1, 2015, through the present?
3. May we please have the Scope of Work, name, and contact of the third-party investigator recently retained by the City of Tyler?

Thank you all very much for your time and assistance in obtaining the requested information in a timely manner.

As you can see from this letter, more problems were created when Tyler switched to using chloramines. Besides impacting the taste, odor, or color of the water, chloramines can react with the distribution system itself. As we saw in Tyler, it was a self-destructive process. Many municipalities that use chloramines report failure of rubber-made valves, gaskets, and fittings, which are key components in any water treatment system. Yes, it might be a cheap fix, but you get what you pay for.

The other interesting observation about chloramines is that people contact me saying their water smells like chlorine. Many times, it's happening because of these chlorine burnouts where the water utility is trying to meet its standards. It's a dirty practice that cheats the system. The levels of chlorine used in a burnout produce chloroform, which if inhaled in a hot shower or through medical devices (humidifiers, CPAPs, or nebulizers) can cause chemically induced asthma and pneumonia. It's important to know that chlorine in clean drinking water doesn't smell. When you smell what you think is chlorine in water, it's due to exceedingly high levels of toxic chemical compounds reacting with the chlorine. The utility has other options to clean the dirt out of your drinking water, but they won't use them without pressure from you, the consumers.

In another case in Harris County, Texas, one of the most populated metropolitan areas in the country, which includes Houston and its surrounding areas with a population of more than 4 million people, residents started writing to me in 2014 because their tap water had a strong chlorine smell, along with sediment and sludge showing up in it.

The water utility responded with the following statement:

> We are aware of the residents' concerns. The water has always been safe for human consumption and continues to meet the TCEQ requirements. We have been performing routine maintenance on the system which is required periodically when delivering surface water in large systems. The residents were notified of the routine maintenance through a message on their water bill and by signs posted throughout the district. As part of the process, we have switched disinfectants and have increased our flushing.

The "flushing" they are referring to is a chlorine burnout. The levels of chlorine used in a burnout produce chloroform, which is primarily what you smell. As noted in the open letter to the Tyler City Council, when this substance is inhaled in a hot shower or through medical devices (humidifiers, CPAPs, or nebulizers), it can cause chemically induced asthma and pneumonia. A better solution is to clean the dirt out of the drinking water and stop adding ammonia (chloramines) to mask the reactions that lead to the biofouling requiring the burnouts.

To put it simply, chloramine has absolutely no place in our drinking water.

Here are a few more reasons why:

1. Chloramine is an ineffective disinfectant. According to Hach, a global company in water quality testing, chloramine is twenty-five times less effective than chlorine in disinfection. When dosing and mixing are not precise, utilities effectively expose everyone in the system to raw water. In fact, chloramine is so ineffective that utilities that use it are required to annually revert back to chlorine only to clean out the bacteria that has become accustomed to ammonia.

2. Ammonia is a food source for bacteria, so when the chloramine breaks down, the ammonia feeds the bacteria it is supposed to stop. Further, a byproduct of this compound is nitrification. Nitrogen is released into the water, which causes more growth of bacteria. Nitrates can reduce hemoglobin in a newborn baby's blood,

resulting in blue baby syndrome, a fatal condition.

3. Genetic damage occurs as a result of exposure to chloramines, according to a study conducted by the University of Illinois at Urbana-Champaign. Further, chloramine is five times more damaging to patients with respiratory illnesses in hospitals where chloramine was routinely used to disinfect.

4. Chloramine is very corrosive, particularly with lead and copper. In Washington, D.C., chloramines were the cause of lead leaching into the water and causing learning disabilities in children under five years old. A related lawsuit was settled for $250 million.

5. The purpose of chloramine is to trick the system (and save some money) so the utility can meet current regulatory standards. It reduces the amount of DBPs by preventing the chlorine from reacting with organics. It also generates NDMA, or nitrosamines, a disinfection byproduct 10,000 times more carcinogenic than anything it purports to displace.

As I say to a lot of communities concerned about chloramines, you have choices. Get the facts and get into conversation with your water officials. We need to stop cutting corners when our health and safety are at stake.

National Regulations

The EPA does not by law tell water treatment professionals how to comply with Stage 1 and Stage 2 Disinfectants and Disinfection Byproducts Rules (DBPRs). It has never suggested, directed, or required the use of chloramines as either a primary or secondary disinfectant, and they do not tell water treatment professionals what method they should use. The maximum residual disinfectant level (MRDL) for chloramines is set at 4 parts per million, which means that this is the highest level of a disinfectant allowed in drinking water without causing the possibility of adverse health problems. This enforceable regulation means that if tap water exceeds these limits, the water utility must notify citizens of violations.

Health Concerns

Chloramines are known to be toxic to kidney dialysis patients and harmful to fish. While I don't have scientific research to show other health issues associated with chloramines, I have thousands of people who have reported health problems to me when their water system switched to using it. These symptoms include severe skin rashes, dry and scaling skin, skin outbreaks "like hives," swollen ears, extreme fatigue, hacking coughs, nasal congestion, itchy, burning, and swollen eyes, stomachaches, and yeast infections. We also have research on trihalomethanes, which are very dangerous to pregnant women. Studies have demonstrated that women exposed to drinking water with high levels of TTHMs have a greater risk for miscarriages in the first trimester and if exposed in their second trimester, are more likely to have babies with a low birth weight.

Toxin #3: Lead

Additional Names/Spellings:
Pb, atomic number 82

Lead is a heavy metal that's been used for centuries, most notably to construct ancient Rome's aqueducts that brought water from faraway sources to fountains, public baths, homes, farms, and gardens. The system supplied water for more than a million people at that time. Many historians believe those lead pipes could have contributed to the fall of the Roman Empire, but we developed amnesia at the turn of the twentieth century and started using lead again for water lines, pipes, and plumbing as well as in ammunition, ceramic glazes, and paints.

While lead is now banned in gasoline and paint, more than 6 million lead service lines are still providing drinking water across the country. The U.S. Agency for Toxic Substances and Disease Registry reported in 2007 that environmental levels of lead had increased more than a thousandfold during the past three centuries thanks to human activity, and particularly between 1950 and 2000 when the use of leaded gasoline was highest throughout the world.

Today, lead is known as a cumulative poison and one of the best-researched neurotoxins at the center of one of the greatest environmental crimes of our century. I'm not just talking about Flint, Michigan, but schools across the country. In 2017, more than 80 percent of New York City public school buildings in all five boroughs had elevated lead levels, and those numbers were exposed only because Governor Andrew Cuomo ordered stringent testing.

Parents in Portland, Oregon, called for the resignation of their superintendent when news broke that the state's largest public school system waited more than two months to notify them about elevated lead levels found at taps and drinking water fountains. New Jersey governor Chris Christie ordered the state to test its three thousand public schools after thirty schools in Newark found lead levels up to thirty-five times above the federal limit.

Lead is most toxic to the developing brain, so it's children ages six and under who bear the brunt of this toxic exposure. In Flint, Michigan, about ten thousand kids were exposed to drinking water with unsafe levels of lead. But the story of schools across the country is still unfolding. Schools and childcare facilities are not required under federal law to test their drinking water unless they have and/or operate their own public water system. Despite knowing how dangerous lead is for children, testing is voluntary for the estimated 98,000 public schools and 500,000 childcare facilities not regulated under federal law.

From a health perspective, it's important to know that there are no safe levels of lead consumption. Corrosion of lead plumbing is the major source of lead in our drinking water, which is only made worse when treatment methods like chloramines react with lead in the pipes, causing it to seep into the water. We need swift action to replace all lead pipes throughout the country, along with updates to the legislation that is meant to protect us.

National Regulations: Lead and Copper Rule

Lead in our drinking water supply is monitored under the Lead and Copper Rule (LCR) as part of the Safe Drinking Water Act. It's a treatment technique rule, which has seen many revisions since it was first enacted in 1991. Originally, LCR set a health-based maximum contaminant level goal of zero, requiring water systems to work with their customers to collect samples from the tap. The rule then established an action level for lead of 15 ppb. When more than 10 percent of customer samples exceed this action level, the system must work to control corrosion and notify the public when levels are too high. But how the rule gets enforced depends on the size of the system.

All water systems that serve more than fifty thousand people are required to install corrosion control treatment (CCT). CCT usually involves the addition of chemicals or adjusting the pH of the drinking water. Systems serving fewer than fifty thousand people are not required to install CCT if the system meets lead and copper action levels during two consecutive six-month monitoring periods. When smaller systems exceed the action level, they are required to work with their state to monitor water quality and work to install and maintain CCT. The LCR is the only national drinking water regulation that requires sampling drinking water at customers' taps in their homes, and often by the consumers themselves.

If it sounds complicated to you, imagine how complicated it is for those who must implement and enforce it. The EPA published a white paper in 2016, detailing revisions needed for the rule. The executive summary plainly states that "the regulation and its implementation are in urgent need of an overhaul. . . . There is a compelling need to modernize and strengthen implementation of the rule—to strengthen its public health protections and to clarify its implementation requirements to make it more effective and more readily enforceable." Key challenges outlined in the white paper include the rule's complexity and its limited focus on key areas of concern such as schools.

The complexity of LCR also allows room for corruption. A January 2016 investigation published in **The Guardian** revealed what many of us on the inside already know, which is how water authorities use questionable practices to downplay the amount of lead found in samples. The law is fuzzy, so I'm not saying anyone is violating EPA protocol, but many cities advise citizens to run their taps for several minutes to flush lead from the pipes before testing. This practice influences results and is not a true sampling of what's in the water.

A 2016 Reuters report found that almost three thousand areas had reported lead poisoning rates at least double the levels found in Flint. These areas, from Warren, Pennsylvania, to South Bend, Indiana, to Goat Island, Texas, are dealing with crumbling infrastructure and receiving little attention or funding to help. Another recent report from the American Water Works Association found that if water was tested directly from lead pipes (rather than at the tap), up to 96 million Americans could be drinking water with unsafe levels of lead.

While LCR has helped reduce our exposure to lead and copper, we clearly still have a long way to go. In 2017, Congressman Frank Pallone Jr. introduced the Safe Drinking Water Act Amendment (H.R. 1068), the first major update to SDWA in more than twenty years, to help develop stricter standards for lead, perfluorinated compounds, and algal toxins. It would also provide grants to help schools and communities replace lead service lines. The EPA announced the first major overhaul of the LCR in October 2019, working to protect children and at-risk communities. The proposed revisions keep the current action level of lead at 15 ppb but introduce a new trigger level of 10 ppb, which means that when a city's water hits this level it would be required to reevaluate its water treatment plan and possibly add corrosion control chemicals to the water. The proposal also calls for all water systems to develop and update lead service line (LSL) inventories and for water systems to notify customers within twenty-four hours if a sample collected in their home is above 15 ppb. Water systems must conduct regular outreach to the homeowners with LSLs. The proposal includes a new requirement for systems to annually test drinking water in 20 percent of schools and child-care centers in their service areas. Cities would be required to replace lead service lines when a home-owner replaces their portion of the line. However, cities would only be required to replace 3 percent of lead service lines each year, which is lower than the current requirement of 7 percent.

"The new LCR is an opportunity to build on decades of progress in reducing lead exposure. Despite setbacks like the Flint, Mich., experience, nationwide efforts to reduce exposure to lead from all sources—paint, gasoline, toys, soil and dust, drinking water—have resulted in a dramatic reduction in lead exposure in the United States over the past forty-five years," David LaFrance, CEO of the American Water Works Association (AWWA), said in a statement. "Still, important work remains. AWWA looks forward to working with EPA, states, and utilities to find safe and affordable approaches that achieve further risk reduction and improved confidence in drinking water."

State Regulations: New York & California

To fill gaps in federal legislation some states have started to implement stricter rules for lead, particularly in schools. In 2016, New York became the first state in the country to pass legislation that required all of its school districts to test their water systems for lead and develop remediation plans when necessary. New York schools are now required to report their lead test results to the state Department of Health through an electronic reporting system. But environmental groups such as the Natural Resources Defense Council say that the landmark law needs to add further protections for children and that much of the state's data is still incomplete.

California state assemblywoman Lorena Gonzalez Fletcher (D-San Diego) introduced Assembly Bill 746 to require all public schools from pre-kindergarten to community colleges and state universities to test the water for lead contamination. In October 2017, California governor Jerry Brown signed the bill, which will strengthen lead regulations in schools throughout the state. When elevated lead levels are detected, water sources are required to be shut off immediately and all staff and parents of students must be notified of their potential exposure to lead.

Health Concerns

Lead exposure can impact cognitive function and learning, decreasing IQ and academic performance. It is also associated with decreased attention, and increased impulsivity and hyperactivity in children. In adults, long-term lead exposure can cause increases in blood pressure and hypertension, leading to coronary heart disease and death from cardiovascular causes. It's also associated with a decrease in cognitive function, symptoms of depression and anxiety, and lowered immune function in adults.

Toxin #4: PFCs (perfluorinated chemicals)

Additional Names/Spellings: General:
Polyfluoroalkyl Substances (PFAS)

Perfluorooctanoic acid (PFOA), C8,
ammonium perfluorooctanoate

Perfluorooctanesulfonic acid
(PFOS), perfluorooctane sulfonate,
perfluorooctylsulfonic acid

GenX, perfluoro-2-propoxypropanoic
acid, or PFPrOPrA

PFCs (perfluorinated chemicals) are the contaminants of concern right now. Both PFOA and PFOS are byproducts of industry that have been used regularly since the 1940s and '50s. These man-made chemicals, found in everything from firefighting foams and stain-resistant sprays to nonstick cookware and water-resistant fabrics, have no business in our water supply. Not surprisingly, the highest levels of PFCs are found near facilities that made or used these substances, but they have made their way far beyond the factories.

Scientists have found PFOA and PFOS in the blood of nearly all the people they tested in the U.S. Researchers at Johns Hopkins University's Bloomberg School of Public Health also found that newborn babies are exposed to both PFOA and PFOS in the womb. They are very stable compounds not easily broken down in the environment or in the human body, which is why they have been nicknamed "forever" chemicals. PFCs accumulate in the body and stay in it for years, which is a huge health concern. These chemicals represent another example of corporate cover-up and industry knowing that their products were harmful but distributing them into the world anyway. In 2017, the Environmental Working Group and researchers at Northeastern University found PFC pollution in tap water supplies for 15 million Americans in twenty-seven states from more than four dozen industrial and military sources from Maine to California.

Perfluorooctanoic acid (PFOA) has helped sustain the success of one of the world's largest corporations—DuPont (and its spin-off the Chemours Company). "We earn our place as the world's most innovative science company by turning scientific breakthroughs into commercial breakouts," says the company's corporate website. PFOA is an essential component of Teflon, used to make their signature nonstick cookware. Chemours, spun out of DuPont in 2015, now owns and produces Teflon itself. Safety concerns about Teflon and other perfluorinated chemicals started to gain public attention more than a decade ago. In 2005, DuPont paid a $16.5 million settlement to the EPA, which accused the company of violating the Toxic Substances Control Act by concealing knowledge of PFOA's toxicity and its presence in the environment. It was the largest civil administrative penalty the EPA had obtained in its history at that time, yet the fine represented less than 2 percent of DuPont's profits from PFOA that year.

The EPA learned of the violations from a letter written by Rob Bilott, a corporate defense attorney turned environmental crusader, who represented a cattle farmer from Parkersburg, West Virginia, in a suit against the chemical company. The story was portrayed in the 2019 American legal thriller **Dark Waters**. Wilbur Tennant originally contacted Bilott because the cows on his farm were dying at alarming rates, and Tennant believed that the DuPont factory located in his town was responsible. As it turns out, sixty-six acres of Tennant's property had been sold in the 1980s to DuPont, which turned them into a landfill for waste from its factory, a common practice big companies employ in small towns. Tennant's brother had health issues and sold the land because he needed the money. DuPont named the plot of land the Dry Run Landfill, after the creek that ran through it—the same creek that flowed to a pasture where Tennant's cows grazed.

Before this case, Bilott represented big corporations; in fact, his specialty was defending chemical companies, which made him an expert in the EPA's regulatory guidelines. He knew how big companies worked and how to defend claims against them. He took on this case as a family favor and originally filed suit against DuPont in the summer of 1999. The company responded by commissioning a study of the property by three veterinarians chosen by DuPont and three chosen by the EPA. The report found that the animals' health was due to "poor nutrition, inadequate veterinary care, and lack of fly control."

As the trial came closer, Bilott made an important discovery that would change the course of the case. He found a letter DuPont had written to the EPA mentioning a substance at the landfill called PFOA. He then asked DuPont for all documentation related to the substance and the company refused to provide it. He then requested and was granted a court order, and he soon received more than 110,000 pages that included private internal correspondence, medical and health reports, and confidential studies from DuPont scientists. Bingo!

These documents revealed that the company had known for a long time about the harmful effects of PFOA, and they had dumped hundreds of thousands of pounds of this dangerous substance from the Parkersburg factory into the Ohio River. The company had also disposed of 7,100 tons of PFOA sludge into the Dry Ridge Landfill, where it seeped into the ground. They had tested the water there too, and it had exorbitantly high concentrations of PFOA. Yet, the company never told the Tennants or disclosed any of this information when the suit was filed. The company also knew that PFOA was in the local water table, which supplied drinking water to more than 100,000 people living in the area.

Bilott uncovered in those documents that DuPont had been running secret medical tests and studies on PFOA for more than four decades, finding that it caused adverse health effects in animals including damage to organs. By the 1990s, DuPont knew that PFOA caused tumors in lab animals. Tennant's case was eventually settled, but Bilott kept going. He spent months writing a 972-page public brief against the company, which in 2001 he sent to then EPA administrator Christie Whitman and U.S. Attorney General John Ashcroft. This same brief led to the EPA civil administrative penalty.

In 2006, eight major companies voluntarily agreed to phase out their global production of

PFOA and PFOA-related chemicals. By 2009, the EPA established a provisional health advisory for PFOA of 400 parts per trillion to help address short-term exposure to the chemical, but remember, a health advisory does not require local water authorities to tell customers if PFOA is in their water. In 2013, DuPont stopped production and use of PFOA. The five other companies that produce it are also working to phase it out of production. As of 2017, DuPont and Chemours Co. have settled more than 3,500 lawsuits related to the disposal of PFOA from its Parkersburg, West Virginia, plant and have agreed to pay $671 million in settlements.

Perfluorooctanesulfonic acid (PFOS) has a similar story. It was the key ingredient of Scotchgard, a fabric protector made by 3M, a global conglomerate headquartered in St. Paul, Minnesota, that reported $30 billion in sales in 2016. Scotchgard, introduced to the market in the 1950s, became the benchmark for protecting carpets from stains. But the PFOS contained in it has never been good for people's health. "PFOS is persistent, bio-accumulative, and toxic to mammalian species," according to a 2002 study by the environmental directorate of the Organisation for Economic Co-operation and Development (OECD). Persistent, accumulative, and toxic are not a good combination.

PFOS and PFOA were also used to make firefighting foams used at military bases throughout the country from the 1970s on. Again, when water supplies near these bases have been tested, widespread contamination has been found. The U.S. Department of Defense knew for decades that these foams had possible adverse environmental and health effects before the public was made aware of concerns. Communities near bases from Washington State to New York are pursuing lawsuits against 3M for PFOS contamination in their water supplies.

PFOS was voluntarily phased out of production in the U.S. by 3M between 2000 and 2002, and the EPA issued regulations to limit future manufacturing. Yet the damage to the environment and our health has persisted. In 2016, Harvard researchers found more than 6 million Americans have been drinking water with unsafe levels of these industrial chemicals and the highest levels have been found in watersheds near industrial sites, military bases, and wastewater treatment plants. The actual number of people exposed may be even higher, because government data for levels of these compounds in drinking water is lacking for almost a third of the U.S. population—or about 100 million people.

Interesting side note: 3M makes water filters that reduce "chlorine taste and odor, trihalomethane (THM), lead, sediment, cysts, arsenic, barium, cadmium, chromium (hex), chromium (tri), copper, fluoride, radium, selenium, turbidity, total dissolved solids (TDS), mercury, asbestos, chloramine, MTBE and volatile organic compounds (VOCs)." No PFCs are mentioned.

National Regulations: Lifetime Health Advisories for PFOA & PFOS

Currently, we have no enforceable national drinking water limits for PFCs. While communities continue to raise awareness about and call attention to the dangers of these chemicals, the EPA has been dragging its feet about regulating these chemicals beyond setting health advisories. Part of that hesitation could stem from the fact that hundreds of sites owned by the Department of Defense are contaminated with these chemicals and a national regulation could cost the federal government billions of dollars in legal fees.

In 2009, the EPA published provisional health advisories for PFOA and PFOS based on the scientific evidence available at that time, which was considered "inconclusive." The MCL was 400 parts per trillion for PFOA and 200 parts per trillion for PFOS.

In May 2016, the EPA significantly lowered the "safe levels" for these pollutants in our water supply, based on standards that assume lifetime exposure rather than drinking these chemicals for only a few weeks or months. The new health advisory for PFOA and PFOS is 70 parts per trillion. These new standards created instant water contamination crises for many cities and towns—fourteen systems exceeded the federal threshold for PFOA, and forty systems were above the limit for PFOS. My website almost crashed with all the people contacting me from Alabama, Arizona, North Carolina, Ohio, and many other places.

Only the systems that have tested for PFOS and PFOA can report their figures. Tens of thousands of drinking water systems across the country have never even tested for these contaminants. The current advisories come years after the EPA was first alerted to PFC contamination. In 2013, a Harvard School of Public Health study found that exposure limits set by the EPA then were up to one thousand times too high. People were exposed for years to these higher levels before a new advisory was issued, and that advisory is still not enforceable.

State Regulations

So far, the state with the strictest standard for these chemicals is New Jersey with a current guidance level of 40 ppt, which is stronger than the national health advisory of 70 ppt. The New Jersey Department of Environmental Protection wants to set an even lower maximum contaminant level (MCL) of 14 ppt for PFOA, which has been found in thirty-seven New Jersey public water systems. Fourteen other states, including Arkansas, Connecticut, Colorado, Delaware, Iowa, Maine, Michigan, Minnesota, Nevada, New Hampshire, North Carolina, Oregon, Texas, and Vermont, have standards or guidelines for PFAS in groundwater, drinking water, and/or wastewater.

Health Concerns

DuPont scientists have concluded that PFOA is linked to six illnesses, including kidney and testicular cancer, ulcerative colitis, thyroid disease, pregnancy-induced hypertension, and high cholesterol.

"Studies indicate that exposure to PFOA and PFOS over certain levels may result in adverse health effects, including developmental effects to fetuses during pregnancy or to breastfed infants (e.g., low birth weight, accelerated puberty, skeletal variations), cancer (e.g., testicular, kidney), liver effects (e.g., tissue damage), immune effects (e.g., antibody production and immunity), thyroid effects and other effects (e.g., cholesterol changes)," according to the EPA's own fact sheet for PFOA and PFOS. Their health advisories are based on peer-reviewed studies of the effects of these PFCs on lab animals but are also informed by epidemiological studies of human populations exposed to PFOA and PFOS. Research has linked PFOS exposure to immune suppression, thyroid disease, high cholesterol, reduced fertility, and possible cancers in the bladder, colon, and prostate.

GenX

As I was writing this book, my inbox was flooded with concerns from people living in Wilmington, North Carolina. Scientists found elevated levels of GenX, a new generation of chemical designed to be a safer alternative to PFOA, in the Cape Fear River, which supplies drinking water to about 80 percent of New Hanover County's more than 112,000 residents. The Fayetteville Works Plant, originally built by DuPont, and now owned by Chemours, has been dumping GenX into the Cape Fear River since 1980 from their plant located almost a hundred miles north in Fayetteville. While there are many unknowns about this emerging contaminant, North Carolina governor Roy Cooper did step into action (thanks to a vocal community) to block the company from continuing to dispose of this chemical in the water supply. Whether the company will comply with these regulations remains to be seen. Byproduct chemicals are rarely regulated, and many times they are not monitored or reported.

The EPA also issued a statement: "While EPA has not established a drinking water regulation, health advisory or health-based benchmark for GenX in drinking water, the agency is working closely with the states and public water systems to determine the appropriate next steps to ensure public health protection."

Health Concerns

We don't know the long-term health effects of GenX because we don't have the studies, but DuPont has short-term research that shows it causes tumors and reproductive problems in lab animals. Like its predecessors, GenX does not belong in our public drinking water systems. Pollution should not be a public experiment.

Toxin #5: Fracking Chemicals

Additional Names/Spellings: hydraulic fracturing, fracturing, hydrofracking

Economic growth and energy consumption are intrinsically linked. Hydraulic fracturing, or fracking, is a relatively new and advanced extraction method for getting previously hard-to-reach fossil fuels out of the ground. It's arguably one of the most important energy innovations of our time.

Beginning in the early 2000s, small independent oil companies slowly began to refine the practice that forces hydrocarbons from shale and sand deposits scattered throughout our country. Now, we are in the midst of what many call a "shale revolution," with companies like Halliburton, ExxonMobil, and BP injecting millions of gallons of water mixed with chemicals miles underground to release natural gas and/or oil. Fracking has helped increase U.S. production of oil and natural gas, leading to lower energy prices. But are those savings worth it?

The EPA estimates that twenty-five thousand to thirty thousand new wells were drilled and hydraulically fractured in the U.S. between 2011 and 2014, and U.S. oil production continues to boom with more than 2 million wells spread out from California to Pennsylvania. Many of these wells are located near or within drinking water sources. By 2013, almost four thousand public water systems serving more than 8.6 million people had at least one fracking well within one mile of their source.

I'm not against the practice itself. The right regulations exist to extract safely, but they are not being enforced. Fracking is exempt or excluded from many major federal environmental laws put in place to protect us and the environment. These laws include the Clean Air Act, Clean Water Act, Safe Drinking Water Act, National Environmental Policy Act, Resource Conservation and Recovery Act,

Emergency Planning and Community Right-to-Know Act, and the Comprehensive Environmental Response, Compensation, and Liability Act, or Superfund. Fracking creates billions of gallons of toxic waste each year and is exempt from all hazardous waste laws. Can you see a problem?

We've been told fracking helps create jobs and keeps America energy independent, but this dangerous practice is also one of the culprits of our escalating drinking water problems. When you pump a brew of substances containing man-made chemicals into the environment (through underground water aquifers), you can absolutely taint the water. The EPA reports that up to seven hundred different chemicals are used for this process in sites throughout the country. They include chemicals such as arsenic, benzene, cadmium, lead, formaldehyde, chlorine, and mercury, which are associated with developmental or reproductive toxicity. We have more than a thousand documented cases of water contamination from fracking operations—whether it's from toxic wastewater, well blowouts, or chemical spills. Wastewater from fracking may be more toxic than the fluids that go into it, so more research is needed to study the byproducts generated throughout the process.

Fracking is happening in residential areas, near homes, schools, and playgrounds. More than 17 million Americans live within a mile of an active oil or gas well. The EPA has studied the impact of fracking on drinking water and released a report in 2016 stating that "activities in the hydraulic fracturing water cycle can impact drinking water resources under some circumstances."

The following activities and factors can result in more frequent or more severe impacts:

- Water withdrawals for hydraulic fracturing in times or areas of low water availability, particularly in areas with limited or declining groundwater resources.
- Spills during the management of hydraulic fracturing fluids and chemicals or produced water that result in large volumes or high concentrations of chemicals reaching groundwater resources.
- Injection of hydraulic fracturing fluids into wells with inadequate mechanical integrity, allowing gases or liquids to move to groundwater resources.
- Injection of hydraulic fracturing fluids directly into groundwater resources.
- Discharge of inadequately treated hydraulic fracturing wastewater to surface water resources.
- Disposal or storage of hydraulic fracturing wastewater in unlined pits, resulting in contamination of groundwater resources.

National and State Regulations

Most fracking decisions are made at the state or federal level, even though local communities see the biggest impact from this practice. The Ohio Supreme Court overruled local drilling regulations. The Colorado Supreme Court also overturned voter-approved fracking bans in several Colorado cities. And those are just a few examples. Despite the dangers, the oil and gas industries have used their deep pockets and close government allies to aggressively push back against local communities that don't want fracking in their neighborhoods. Former North Carolina governor Pat McCrory legalized fracking in the state, rolling back state laws that have been in place since 1945. When the state's Mining and Energy Commission began holding hearings to determine whether or not to approve the practice in August 2014, a local paper reported that homeless men unfamiliar with fracking were bused from Winston-Salem to a state hearing to give the appearance of a pro-fracking turnout.

In March 2017, Maryland became the second state with gas reserves to ban fracking. New York banned drilling wells in 2012 and Vermont preventively banned fracking in 2012, even though it has no known frackable reserves. We need to urge state and federal leaders to reject attempts to limit local control of fracking.

I'm not an energy policy expert, but we all need to consider the energy we use and how we can use it more efficiently, and to continue to look at sources of energy that are clean and renewable, and have less impact on our environment. While natural gas is considered one bridge to get us to cleaner energy options, the unregulated extraction process comes with costs to both the environment and public health.

Health Concerns

People who live near fracking wells report numerous health issues such as nausea, headaches, sinus issues, and sleep disruptions. Researchers at Johns Hopkins University studied fracking communities in Pennsylvania and found that people living near wells were twice as likely to deal with migraines, fatigue, and sinusitis conditions. University of Colorado School of Public Health researchers found that people living within a half mile of gas-drilling operations had higher health risks, including cancer. Further research has found that the chemicals used in and produced by fracking can disrupt the functioning of the endocrine system and are known to cause cancer, birth defects, and other developmental disorders.

Toxin #6: TCE

Additional Names/Spellings:
Trichloroethylene, 1,2,3-Trichloroethylene,
trichlor, trike, and tri

TCE is a colorless, nonflammable liquid solvent used in both industrial and household items to make hydrofluorocarbon chemicals. While this chemical's name does not roll off the tongue, its widespread use in multiple industries means that most of us have been exposed to it. In 2011, total estimated commercial production of TCE in the U.S. was 270 million pounds. But as more information about this man-made chemical has come to light, we have seen production go down.

Starting in the early 1900s, it was used to remove grease and dirt from metal parts and was a favorite in the aircraft industry from the 1950s to 1980s. TCE was used as an industrial solvent in the rubber industry—in paints, varnishes, adhesives, and paint strippers—and to produce agricultural chemicals such as fungicides and insecticides. It was also used in the dry-cleaning industry and in spray fixatives for arts and crafts.

"From getting stains out of favorite shirts to baking cookies and everything in between, Whirlpool® appliances are there to help you keep the day moving" reads the company's website, another corporation as American as apple pie with more than $20 billion in annual sales. For

forty-five years, the Whirlpool refrigeration production facility was based in Fort Smith, Arkansas.
In 1967, they started using TCE as a degreaser and
discontinued its use in 1981. Yet, in 2001 the company became aware that a plume of TCE had been
found in the groundwater beyond its property
and underneath homes in a nearby neighborhood. TCE is known to have a latency period of
twenty years or more. When I worked with this
community, people reported brain tumors, throat
cancers, and nasopharyngeal cancer, and these
rare cancers always raise a red flag for me. The Fort
Smith plant closed in June 2012 and the company
has been working to clean up the contamination.

Most people get exposed to TCE by consum-
ing contaminated drinking water. The water is
contaminated from some combination of industry
discharge/spills and existing hazardous-waste sites.
TCE breaks down slowly and can move through
soil to find its way into drinking water sources.
It was added to the list of substances known to
cause cancer in the "14th Report on Carcinogens"
released by the U.S. Department of Health and
Human Services in November 2016.

TCE and its health effects made the cover of
Newsweek in 2014 because it was one of the top
pollutants at Camp Lejeune, a North Carolina
military base that is considered one of the worst
toxic sites in the U.S. TCE was found in the drinking water of the 240-square-mile base as part of

what was described as "a toxic cocktail of industrial solvents, dry-cleaning chemicals and gas." In the next section, I will talk more about Camp Lejeune and the efforts to fight for clean water there.

National Regulations

The maximum contaminant level goal for TCE is 0. The EPA set the MCL (an enforceable regulation) at 5 ppb. In December 2016 and January 2017, the EPA published two proposed rules under section 6(a) of the TSCA. One bans commercial use of TCE in vapor degreasing, and the other bans the use of TCE in commercial and consumer aerosol degreasing and as a spot cleaner in dry cleaning. These proposals aim to prohibit importing, manufacturing, processing, and distributing TCE for commercial purposes.

Health Concerns

Health problems associated with drinking water containing unsafe levels of TCE include liver issues and increased risk of cancer. In a toxicological review of TCE, the EPA found that it is "carcinogenic to humans by all routes of exposure" based on evidence of a causal association between TCE exposure and kidney cancer. Both human and animal data show this chemical can affect the kidney, liver, immune system, male reproductive system, and a developing fetus, according to the Agency for Toxic Substances and Disease Registry (ATSDR), and it's also associated with increased rates of childhood leukemia.

IN SUMMARY

When it comes to these chemicals and trying to figure out if your water is safe, remember the **precautionary principle**—in the absence of scientific information or consensus, the best possible action is to avoid exposure until more data can be collected. Of course, I have outlined the science as best we know it, and yet our own government is slow to respond to the research. Don't let your body be the guinea pig.

PART TWO

A HOPEFUL FUTURE

Water sustains all life. Her songs begin in the tiniest of raindrops, transform to flowing rivers, travel to majestic oceans and thundering clouds and back to earth again. When water is threatened, all living things are threatened.

—Indigenous Declaration on Water, 2001 (Ancient Hopi message)

6

THE COMMUNITIES RISING

Imagine if the nightly news reported that we had a bioterrorism threat that could affect millions of Americans. It would be mayhem! People would be in a panic, running for cover, and demanding that our elected officials help protect us all. Yet there is a threat affecting millions of Americans—drinking contaminated water in this country—and it is business as usual. Water pollution is one of the greatest risks to human health, and few of us realize the intensifying burdens on our country's water resources until these problems turn up at our door.

When most of us think of a water crisis, we think of what we saw in Flint, Michigan, but all communities are vulnerable to (and many are experiencing) all kinds of water crises. Ongoing infrastructure issues, lack of resources, misappropriated funds, and shortsighted decisions go right along with toxic contamination to impact our water supply each day. A water main breaks in the U.S. every 2.5 minutes or so, according to Casey

Dinges, senior managing director of the American Society of Civil Engineers. These breaks are caused by many factors, including changes in temperature, corrosion, and deterioration of old pipes. Repairing these breaks usually requires the water to be shut off, and during that time contaminants can enter the water supply.

LOSING WATER IN WEST VIRGINIA

It's easy to take clean water for granted until it's suddenly not there. Just ask any of the 300,000 residents in Charleston, West Virginia, who woke up one morning in January 2014 to a do-not-drink order on their tap water. They couldn't brush their teeth, brew a cup of coffee, or make oatmeal that morning thanks to an industrial chemical spill, and not a small one at that. About ten thousand gallons of an unregulated chemical, 4-methylcyclohexanemethanol (MCHM), leaked from a storage tank into the Elk River. The cause? Corrosion—in the form of a one-inch hole where chemicals seeped out and into the river. Records showed that the tank had not been inspected since 1991.

Do-not-drink orders like this one, along with boil advisories, are becoming more common in cities and towns throughout the nation. They are indicative of larger drinking water problems at play and show the gaps and failures in our infrastructure. From the calls and emails I receive, I could easily estimate that there are 1,500 boil-water advisories happening each month in the U.S., but no one is tracking them at the national level. Suddenly losing access to clean water or wondering whether the water is safe to drink is both a huge inconvenience and a health hazard. No one wants to receive this kind of wake-up call.

It's no secret that West Virginia is a global hub for the chemical industry with the presence of conglomerates like DuPont, Bayer, and Stockmeier Urethanes USA. A little-known fact is that such chemical storage containers are scattered along American waterways, often near critical infrastructure such as water treatment plants. In this case Freedom Industries, a company that processed and stored chemicals for the coal industry, owned the tank situated about a mile upstream from the West Virginia American Water treatment plant. Even with a robust carbon filtration system, the treatment facility, which supplies water to most of the households in the state capital, was overwhelmed as the chemical leaked downstream to its facility and released a pungent, licorice-like odor into the air. Many residents remained under a "do-not-use" advisory for more than a week. Hundreds were treated at local hospitals for a host of health problems including severe skin rashes and sores, dizziness, and vomiting. Scores of schools and businesses shut down as well. Sam's Club and every other retailer within a twenty-mile radius sold out of bottled water.

About five thousand people reached out to me in the days after the spill. Bob Bowcock and I worked with local organizers to host a town hall meeting at the Charleston Municipal Auditorium on extremely short notice. During the discussion, many community members voiced their frustration and said they felt helpless. People in times of crisis need leaders, yet local legislators let their phones ring rather than answering their constituents' questions, according to many residents' accounts. When these incidents happen, trust gets diluted. People wake up to how little they know about their water system and are left wondering who is helping protect them and their health.

Bob and I couldn't believe officials hadn't thought to inventory the chemical sitting in this tank or the thirteen others along the Elk River, as they clearly posed a threat to the water supply. If terrorists dumped unknown chemicals into a community, we would call it a chemical attack. But when it's American industry, we let the chips fall where they may. At the time, chemicals stored aboveground in West Virginia were not subject to regular environmental inspections, and the plant had no spill prevention or response plan in place. MCHM is one of the more than sixty thousand chemicals grandfathered as part of the Toxic Substances Control Act. While the use of this chemical was technically legal, officials in West Virginia, including chemists, toxicologists, and emergency responders, scrambled to find any information about it and its impact on people.

One of the most honest statements came from Jeff McIntyre, president of the West Virginia American Water company at that time, who said, "We don't know that the water is not safe, but I can't say it is safe. The only appropriate use for this water is toilet flushing."

Meanwhile, state officials contacted the Centers for Disease Control and Prevention (CDC) for advice on whether the water was safe to drink. The CDC didn't have a standard in place for MCHM, so they made one up relying on a small amount of data. The agency set a drinking water advisory of 1 ppm based on limited information they requested from the manufacturer, Eastman Chemical Company, which included one animal toxicology study.

"There are unknowns," acknowledged Karen Bowling, West Virginia's secretary of health and human resources at the time. "So, we have to rely on what's already known about [it] and what's [been] tested about this particular chemical."

Residents depended on these standards. They were also subject to the hemming and hawing of Gary Southern, then president of Freedom Industries, who drank bottled water during a press conference and dodged questions from local reporters.

On the day of the incident he said, "Look guys, it's been an extremely long day. I'm having a lot of trouble talking at the moment. I would appreciate it if we could wrap this thing up."

These comments are reminiscent of BP CEO Tony Hayward after the 2010 Gulf of Mexico spill, the worst in U.S. history, when he said, "There's no one who wants this over more than I do. I would like my life back."

They both speak about themselves, not the people suffering. They speak from a corporate culture of ducking responsibility, leaving the locals to handle the ramifications of their pollution. Days after the spill, Freedom Industries declared bankruptcy and closed shop. The damage had been done, and not just to residents who may have drunk contaminated water, but also to businesses that had to close, workers who lost wages, and even the city of Charleston, which reported losing more than $120,000 in tax revenue in the days after the disaster.

Dr. Rahul Gupta, director of the Kanawha-Charleston Health Department, said complaints about the contaminated water continued for months after the disaster and that people refused to drink the water. In April of that year, the health department conducted a survey, which found that fewer than 40 percent of respondents were drinking water from their taps and fewer than 10 percent felt that their water was safe.

Two years after the incident, a federal judge fined Freedom Industries $900,000 for violating the Clean Water Act, but it's unlikely that the already-bankrupt company will ever pay their criminal penalty. Southern did go to court and on February 17, 2016, he was sentenced to one month in federal prison, followed by a six-month term of supervised release, and a $20,000 fine for environmental crimes connected to the 2014 chemical spill. Five other former officials from the company were also prosecuted for federal crimes associated with the incident, but these fines and jail times are more like wrist slaps to these executives. Southern was later accused of trying to hide $6.5 million in his savings by transferring the money to an annuity account to protect it from creditors.

Booth Goodwin, the lead prosecutor in the case, described the spill as "completely preventable."

"If we don't want it to happen again, we need to make it crystal clear that those who engage in this kind of criminal behavior will be held accountable.

That's exactly what we have done through these prosecutions," he said in a statement.

About 225,000 residents and thousands of business owners filed a class-action lawsuit against Eastman Chemical and West Virginia American Water. The lawsuit alleges that the water company did not prepare for a leak of that kind near its facility. In 2017, the $151 million settlement offered the average household more than $500, while compensation for businesses ranged from $6,000 to $40,000 per claim.

Both companies issued statements not admitting fault:

West Virginia American Water said, "A resolution through a settlement allows us and our dedicated employees to serve our customers without the distractions of ongoing lawsuits."

Eastman said, "We worked with plaintiffs' counsel to negotiate a global settlement to resolve all litigation, and to provide benefits and closure to the community."

Nearly two months after the spill, the state House of Representatives and Senate passed legislation to help further regulate chemical storage. The House bill passed 95 to 0 and specified that the state Department of Environmental Protection (DEP) needed to conduct inventory and annual inspections of the 1,600 above-ground storage tanks located close to drinking water supplies. It also required public utilities to have a response plan in place for chemical spills. In April 2014, West Virginia governor Ray Tomblin signed into law the bill that is commonly referred to as the "storage tank law." The state completed all inspections in January 2015 and discovered that about 1,100 tanks did not meet the new requirements.

Several other states, including Virginia, Indiana, and Georgia, followed suit, passing similar legislation requiring inspections for these chemical tanks. Joe Manchin, U.S. senator from West Virginia, tried to take these rules nationwide, but so far lawmakers have not passed any federal mandates. Nationwide regulations would help prevent these kinds of spills and protect communities across state lines. The Elk River feeds into the Ohio River, and in 2015 scientists detected crude MCHM in Louisville, Kentucky—meaning that the chemical traveled hundreds of miles across state lines. We still don't know the impact to people in Kentucky and in other places that may have ingested trace amounts of this chemical. In the closing hours of the 2015 legislative session, West Virginia legislators passed a partial repeal of the 2014 law with industry lobbyists continuing to push for a total exemption.

The Elk River spill exposed not just industrial negligence but the delicate nature of our country's water infrastructure. One slipup can cause disaster for an entire town, and that's not considering the hundreds of billions of dollars in investment that our system desperately needs to stay afloat. In a January 2017 exit memo, EPA administrator Gina McCarthy said that our environmental infrastructure needs are significant and that more than $655 billion in investment is needed for drinking water and wastewater in the next twenty years—and that doesn't include replacing the country's lead service lines. The average American town maintains a water system that's at least fifty years old. More antiquated systems have water mains that are at least a century old. Jim Gebhardt, the director for EPA's Water Infrastructure and Resiliency Finance Center, wrote on the EPA's blog, "The implications of deteriorating infrastructure can be felt nationwide—each year our country experiences about 240,000 water main breaks, $2.6 billion is lost as our water mains leak trillions of gallons of treated drinking water, and billions of gallons of raw sewage are discharged into local surface waters from aging sewer overflows."

Aging water systems burdened with toxic buildup are exactly why this crisis has become so dire. We must properly fund our municipalities and water treatment plants so that we can reduce further harm. But it's a complicated problem that will take more than a fledgling EPA or a disconcerted administration. I'm here to help sound the alarm for all of us and share stories from those people working on the front lines for safer, cleaner water. These folks have seen pollution issues on their doorstep. They have faced incredible health challenges and have had their lives impacted by poisoned water. They have asked the biggest question of all: Why? They have gone searching for answers, helping to make change. It's my passionate hope that telling their stories will inspire you to join them. It's time to realize that change begins with each of us.

NOT A DROP TO DRINK

Perhaps no place better exemplifies how infrastructure fails people than Martin County, Kentucky, one of the poorest counties in the country. President Lyndon Johnson visited the tiny town of Inez, the county seat, in 1964 to garner support for his war on poverty. More than fifty years later, the poverty rate there hovers close to 40 percent, which is more than twice the national average. While some of the richest coal mines in the U.S. are located in Martin County, today many of them are closed and residents are unemployed.

Years of mismanagement and neglect have made water problems the norm in this rural Appalachian community. Pipes are cracked and leaking. A coal slurry spill in 2000 flooded local rivers with more than 300 million gallons of toxic sludge, contributing to concerns about water quality. Even today, residents' water bills include warnings about disinfection byproducts violating EPA standards in their water. Meanwhile, brown water is flowing from their taps when water is running, while many people contend with restricted water hours or have lost all access to water for days and weeks at a time. The aging water system has been failing residents for years, and the situation got so bad that a January 2018 video of an emergency Martin County Fiscal Court meeting to discuss the water went viral with footage of an angry citizen being choked by a police officer and dragged out of the meeting.

"I regret none of it because I was standing up for the people of Martin County," Gary Hunt, who was cited for disorderly conduct and escorted out of the meeting, told a local news station. "It's not just been this winter it's been an ongoing problem for five years."

Schools were closed for more than ten days in January 2018 alone because the water was turned off from 7 a.m. until 3 p.m. Without access to water, the schools can't open as the restrooms can't be used and food can't be served. School closures also mean that the more than 350 children in the community who rely on meals at school went hungry those days.

The Martin County Water District announced its plan to solve the problem by proposing an almost 50 percent increase in water rates. Most residents can't afford to pay their bills. More than one in ten households throughout the country can't afford their water bills either. If the new rates are approved, the average water bill will be more than $63 a month—making rates in Martin County the second highest of all water districts in the state.

"Two years after Flint, Michigan, called attention to the systemic water woes hitting our most vulnerable people and poorest communities, the epidemic of water poverty in this country shows no signs of abating," said Wenonah Hauter, executive director of Food & Water Watch, in a statement. "Now, Martin County urgently needs assistance to address the systemic failure of its water system. The entire community has had water outages for weeks and water quality problems have plagued the county for years."

Once again, having clean water in America is not a given. This Kentucky county needs a functioning water system. But every crisis has a silver lining, and this one did bring locals together to demand action. Consumers have played an important role in helping to spread awareness about this story. Two community groups, one called Concerned Citizens of Martin County and another online group called the Martin County Water Warriors, helped attract media attention and worked with their county to find solutions.

"We just want to help our water plant," Nina McCoy, a local organizer with Concerned Citizens, told a local news station. "I mean this is our water plant, we are not fighting our water plant."

After locals started reaching out to me, I sent my water expert Bob Bowcock in February 2018 to assess the problem and work with water officials to provide people there with answers. Bob found serious problems with their source water and an outdated treatment plant—designed for one town not an entire county. Trained professionals from other states are now on the ground fixing leaks and helping to train water operators there to fix systemic problems.

The community is on the right track, as the water board has new members who are receptive to new ideas and input and active community groups holding them accountable, along with local and national media coverage. The new board of directors has secured $4.7 million in funding for the county's infrastructure, including $3.4 million from the offices of Governor Matt Bevin and U.S. Representative Hal Rogers.

"Martin County presents an opportunity to demonstrate a community's resolve to everyone working together, digging themselves out of a really bad situation, and moving forward in a positive way," Bob told the local press. "I hope it sets an example to help other communities in Kentucky and across this country."

I don't claim to have all the answers when it comes to our water woes. I'm not afraid to admit that when I started my work in this field, I knew nothing about chromium-6 or water contamination in general. I was a broke, single mom with dyslexia trying to make ends meet. I was the least likely person to become anyone's hero, but I was willing to listen to people's stories and use my common sense to guide me. I would make phone calls to experts to get more information, which sometimes meant calling the same toxicologist multiple times in one day until I understood what needed to happen next. I was willing to do my part to put the pieces together to help a community. That's all it takes. You only need to make the commitment to ask one question, make one phone call, show up to one meeting, or talk to one neighbor. You don't have to know all the steps, you just need to be willing to take that first step and get started somewhere. As you read more of the stories of people I've worked with, you'll see that's exactly how they got started too.

My job title has morphed into being both a passionate advocate and a kind of "environmental superhero" with Bob as my trusty sidekick and science guy. He and I have traveled to all fifty states, each more than once, responding to and helping with water and other contamination cases. We were first responders at the BP oil spill in 2010. We were on the scene in Louisiana when three different communities discovered deadly brain-eating amoebas in their drinking water systems within weeks of one another. We've rallied next to military veterans and their families outside the steps of the Supreme Court when the justices were hearing arguments about the polluted drinking water at North Carolina's Marine Corps Base Camp Lejeune. We have helped organize and speak at countless town hall meetings held at universities, public libraries, and American Legion rooms in towns throughout the country. Our goal is to help communities better understand what's going on with their water and work together to create safe drinking water for everyone.

People think when I speak to a community that I'm coming in with an agenda, but my only role is to empower the people. Politics and party affiliation don't matter when it comes to clean water, and if there's one agenda across the board that everyone needs to be united on, it's making sure that we all have access to safe drinking water. The big message I share is about how to find your voice. Change happens when people are willing to speak up and put pressure on their politicians and agencies, who typically don't respond until they hear from people in the community. Once you have the facts and information and feel empowered to stand together, you can use your collective voice to ask your officials the necessary questions and garner more attention for these critical issues. That's the power of the people. Even just one person in a community who cares about the drinking water can quickly gain momentum. One can become two, two can become four, four become eight, and so on. I've seen it happen in many places, and I'm excited to share more of these stories, because let's face it, it's not always easy to stand up and speak out. It's scary! It takes courage and determination.

When it comes to drinking water contaminant exposure, toxicology, and health effects, concerned consumers are repeatedly laughed at and told that their water is perfectly safe to drink. Even the so-called experts don't always know the full scope of the problem as it's unfolding, and as I've mentioned we won't find chemicals that we don't test for. People are often told to talk with their medical doctors about their concerns with the water, but medical professionals usually know less about these issues than a random guy walking down the street. Who can you turn to for accurate information about your drinking water? You can start by trusting yourselves to get more involved.

MORE THAN A CHILDREN'S STORY

My work can get quite somber at times, and I'm always looking for ways to address water issues in a way that will rouse my audience. Enter the land of Oz. Yes, it's a fictional place and I'm sure you have seen the 1939 movie, **The Wizard of Oz**, on television. The movie is based on **The Wonderful Wizard of Oz**, the novel written by L. Frank Baum that was published in 1900 during the height of the Industrial Revolution and largely based on his experiences living on the drought-ridden plains of South Dakota.

Baum once said about his work, "I believe that dreams—day dreams, you know, with your eyes wide open and your brain machinery whizzing— are likely to lead to the betterment of the world. The imaginative child will become the imaginative man or woman most apt to create, to invent, and therefore to foster civilization."

While I was growing up in Kansas, Dorothy's story resonated deeply with me. When her family farm gets hit by a tornado, she is thrust into the sky and taken far from her family. She lands in a new, unfamiliar place—the land of Oz. Her mission becomes clear: to find her way home, because we all know there's no place like home. To get home, she must travel to the Emerald City, by way of the Yellow Brick Road. On the journey, she meets the Scarecrow, the Tin Man, and the Cowardly Lion. But this story and its characters are more than a fantastical childhood tale. I want to share a few interpretations, and why I think these lessons are still so important today.

One theory about the book is that Baum wrote the story to teach his four children the value of individualism, and the power of thinking for themselves in a world where increasingly everyone was being taught to think and work alike. At that time, the world was transitioning from an agrarian society to one of booming industry and manufacturing. Led by both the oil and steel industries, the U.S. quickly rose to become the world's leading producer of manufactured goods. People started finding more work in factories, and by 1913 Henry Ford had installed the first assembly line for the mass production of automobiles. At the same time, national wealth was increasing and men like John D. Rockefeller, Andrew Carnegie, and Commodore Vanderbilt were amassing their great fortunes, while 10 million Americans subsisted in poverty. Farmers were producing more than ever, but surpluses caused crop prices to plunge. From 1870 to 1897, wheat prices dropped from $1.06 a bushel to 63 cents a bushel, corn from 43 cents to 30 cents a bushel, and cotton from 15 cents to 6 cents per pound, according to the U.S. Department of Agriculture. Tensions grew between farmers and industry. These times tested the American Dream, which promised success and prosperity for all who were willing to work for it. Perhaps Baum was also reminding us not to leave behind the people who helped build our great country—the farmers, the factory workers, and the families.

Another interpretation of this children's story comes from Henry Littlefield, a high school history teacher, who proposed that the story of Oz was an allegory on populism, a political reform movement supporting the concerns and rights of the people. In an essay published in **American Quarterly** in 1964, Littlefield describes how each character in the book represented an interested party from that time. First, you have Dorothy, who exemplifies the everyday, hardworking people looking for a better life. He theorized that the Cowardly Lion was William Jennings Bryan, a politician from Nebraska who ran as a Populist and Democratic candidate for president in both 1896 and 1900. He was nicknamed "the Lion" because of his fiery rhetoric and was called cowardly for not supporting America's decision to go to war with Spain in 1898. The Scarecrow is the American farmer seen as uninformed and ignorant by the elite policymakers—"if they only had a brain." The Tin Man represents the industrial workers who had been exploited and worked as cogs in the machine for their rich and powerful employers.

The Yellow Brick Road is the gold standard, which was a debate at the time. Would the economy be based on a fixed amount of gold, which many rich businessmen supported, or would farmers and others who were in favor of the unlimited use of silver coins win out? In the original manuscript, Dorothy wore silver slippers representing the fact that farmers and laborers supported free silver. In the movie version, the slippers changed to a ruby-red color because producers thought the shoes would stand out more in Technicolor. And finally, there's the Wizard, who Littlefield said was any president of the United States. The people looked up to this position, but the president was merely subservient to the interest of the evil witches, who epitomized Wall Street and the interests of big business. Does any of this sound familiar? Today, we have industry lobbyists—perhaps the flying monkeys—along with many other problems associated with money in our political system. We all put power in our elected officials while wondering who is really holding their strings.

During my own journey on the Pacific Gas and Electric case, I decided I wanted to meet the Wizard. I wanted to peek behind the curtain at one of the largest natural gas and electric energy companies in the U.S. to see how things really worked. Do you know what I found? Just like Dorothy, I discovered that the Wizard is only as powerful as we let him be. The Wizard is nothing more than a power-hungry few at the top, who rule through fear and intimidation with a lot of flash. And you know what else I learned? I wasn't afraid of the Wicked Witch or her flying monkeys either. Those things scared the hell out of me as a kid! My journey has shown me that there is no Wizard or person out there who's going to give me the answers. The journey Dorothy takes home is one into her own heart and mind. It's a journey that leads her to understand, for the first time, that she could always get home, that she had the power to make that happen. I could say the same thing to industry—you have the power and you can use your power for good to clean up your mess and become a better neighbor.

To me, the characters in Oz also represent people who think they are missing what it takes to stand up to the powerful industrial forces. They think they don't have what it takes to fight pollution. But as we all walk down our own path, whether we are searching for more money, job security, justice, or better health, we must remember that we all have enough brains, heart, and courage to get the job done. You may go searching for the Emerald City, and go chasing the Wizard, hoping for someone to help make your life better and return you back home. I have learned through my journey that we already have the answers to bring ourselves home.

The problem is not what you don't have; it's what you don't know that you do have. Water is life. It's time for all of us to step up and save it.

Barbara Kingsolver, a novelist, once wrote, "Hope is a renewable option: If you run out of it at the end of the day, you get to start over in the morning." That's exactly what Bob and I do each day, along with the thousands of other people working on water issues today. I've learned to tune out the noisy thoughts that tell me I can't do it—that these problems are just too big. Instead, I show up each day with new hope. I love this planet and I know we can still save it. I show up because I love my family and I want them to live in a world with clean water. Love will see us through these struggles.

Action begins right at the local level—everyday people getting involved to fight for a better future and help their communities. That's what this book is all about—empowering you to make a difference. It's about becoming your own hero. Real change happens when people have the knowledge and tenacity to stand up and fight. When you see something wrong in your own backyard, you need to speak out. I'm a firm believer in the power of communities banding together to act. I hope these stories will inspire you to look at the issues in your town, talk to your neighbors, get involved in local politics, and be part of the movement in America to clean up our water.

RUNNING TYSON OUT OF TOWN

This tale takes place in Tonganoxie, Kansas—a town fifteen miles from where I was raised in Lawrence. In September 2017, mothers from "Tongie," as the locals call it, started emailing me asking for help to fight a massive Tyson Foods chicken-processing plant (also known as a slaughterhouse) coming to their town. Founded in 1931, Tyson is one the largest producers of meat and poultry in the world, employing more than ninety-five thousand people in its U.S. production facilities, but it's also one of the biggest polluters, responsible for dumping millions of pounds of toxic chemicals into America's waterways.

Chicken is big business in our country. Americans eat more chicken than any other country in the world, according to the National Chicken Council. Each year, the chicken industry (which consists of about thirty-five large companies) raises and slaughters almost 9 billion chickens for food. At the top of that chicken chain is Tyson, which processes and sells more than $11 billion worth of chickens each year and leads in the production of ready-to-cook poultry products. The company has a long record of criminal prosecutions for both pollution and labor practices. Tyson was the second-biggest polluter of our waterways from 2010 to 2014, according to the EPA's Toxic Release

Inventory, ranking only behind AK Steel and just above the U.S. Department of Defense. Tyson and its subsidiaries' processing plants dumped more than 104 million pounds of toxic pollutants into waterways during that time, more than Cargill, Koch Industries, and ExxonMobil combined. Think about that the next time you're shopping for chicken at your grocery store.

Thousands of animals living together in cramped facilities leads to big pollution problems. Commercial chicken farms and processing facilities produce large amounts of waste. Oftentimes, manure gets stored in massive piles near the facility that can leak into the water system. In addition, slaughterhouses use millions of gallons of water to flush away tons of chicken guts, heads, feathers, and blood. While facilities are required to treat the water before they release it, toxins still slip through.

The southeastern shores of Virginia, Delaware, and Maryland are often referred to as "chicken country" thanks to their abundance of big poultry farms and processing facilities. Back in 1998, Tyson paid a $4 million civil penalty, which was the largest fine ever imposed on a food-processing company in Maryland, for a plant they had bought and taken over in Berlin, Maryland, which discharged illegal amounts of phosphorus, nitrogen, and other toxins into a creek near the Chesapeake Bay, the largest estuary in the U.S. Although nitrogen and phosphorus are necessary nutrients to sustain plant and animal life, it's a delicate balance. In excess, these compounds become food for algae, causing it to grow out of control. These harmful algal blooms produce toxic effects on people, fish, and birds. By 1999, up to one-third of underground wells in this area did not meet EPA drinking water standards for nitrate, which is a compound of nitrogen that is concentrated in chicken waste.

Companies can legally dump their waste into our waterways; they just need an NPDES (National Pollutant Discharge Elimination System) permit. The Clean Water Act prohibits anyone from discharging pollutants (industrial, municipal, and agricultural waste) through a "point source" into a U.S. body of water—unless they have this permit. A "point source" includes pipes, ditches, channels, containers, and concentrated animal feeding operations. The permit specifies limits on what a company can discharge and comes with monitoring and reporting requirements that are intended to maintain both water quality and human health.

Companies like Tyson continue to violate the law. In 2003, Tyson pleaded guilty to twenty felony violations of the Clean Water Act at its Sedalia, Missouri, poultry plant, paying $7.5 million to the U.S. and the state of Missouri. Tyson admitted to having illegally discharged untreated wastewater from its poultry-processing plant into a tributary of the Lamine River. The plant processed about 1 million chickens per week, generating hundreds of thousands of gallons of wastewater each day. Between 1996 and 2001, Tyson repeatedly discharged untreated or inadequately treated wastewater from its plant. Despite several citations from the Missouri Department of Natural Resources, numerous warnings, administrative orders, two state court injunctions, and the execution of a federal search warrant at the Sedalia facility to stop its illegal discharges, Tyson continued to dump untreated wastewater through its storm drains.

Also in 2003, Tyson and five other poultry companies agreed to pay $7.5 million to settle a lawsuit in Tulsa, Oklahoma, where officials claimed the companies were responsible for 170 million pounds of chicken waste polluting Lake Eucha and Spavinaw watershed, which provides drinking water to the city's residents.

Tyson paid the maximum fine of $500,000 for violating worker safety regulations at its River Valley Animal Foods plant in Texarkana, Arkansas, in June 2009. A maintenance employee was overcome with hydrogen sulfide gas while repairing a leak at the facility and later died. Another employee and two emergency responders were hospitalized due to exposure during the rescue attempt, and two other employees were treated at the scene.

The Justice Department fined Tyson $2 million in August 2009 for dumping its waste into the Missouri River. Tyson paid another $5.2 million in February 2011 to settle allegations that the company had bribed Mexican officials to certify chicken products for export. In September of that same year, Tyson paid $32 million to settle a twelve-year litigation over whether the company should pay its hourly poultry-plant workers for the time it took them to change into and out of their work clothes and protective gear. The company settled a similar lawsuit in 2014, avoiding a trial by paying $7.75 million to workers at a Tyson Fresh Meats beef- and pork-processing plant in Goodlettsville, Tennessee. In 2016, Oxfam America released a report showing that Tyson poultry workers were denied bathroom breaks and that many wore diapers during their work shift to stay on the job all day.

Despite its previous lawbreaking ways, the company has publicized its commitment to sustainable food production and to expand efforts for a better workplace. "We believe sustainability is about continuous improvement and solutions that last, and this includes a healthier workplace," said Noel White, chief operations officer at Tyson Foods, in 2017. "We've always been committed to supporting our employees and have sound workplace practices in place, but also want to do better. That's why we're taking steps that include expanding training, improving workplace safety and compensation, increasing transparency and helping workers with life skills."

Back in Tonganoxie in September 2017, Tyson company officials announced plans to build a $320 million poultry complex by 2019, the first new plant for the company in twenty years. The Kansas governor was on board and excited to announce the estimated 1,600 new jobs it would create for the town, which is significant for a town of 5,300 people. But local moms were not happy about this news. They sent me photographs of their children playing and wrote to me pleading that they didn't want this giant corporation to ruin their small, beautiful town or endanger their kids' safety. The proposed site was just blocks from a local baseball field and a few miles from the local elementary and middle schools.

One woman explained, "We live on well water roughly 2.7 miles from town. My children and I play in the creek that runs on our property. We have a pond. Our community will be destroyed. Please help us. We need every voice we can get." Another woman wrote, "Americans need to start coming together coast to coast to propose a law that prevents bullies like Tyson picking on the little towns like us! Erin, how can we win this?"

I often struggle with how I can help communities

facing giant corporations and their hired guns, toting along paid-off politicians and offering promises of jobs. I have received pollution and environmental complaints about Tyson Foods for more than a decade, and I know that the company's record speaks for itself. When I posted an article about the Tyson plant on Facebook, it got thousands of shares and more than four hundred comments. Sometimes, a little media attention and recognition from me is all it takes to get a community going on their own. They created a nonprofit organization and launched a social media campaign, creating a Facebook group, which quickly grew to more than six thousand members. (Facebook

In 2017, mothers from Tonganoxie, Kansas, or "Tongie" as the locals call it, started emailing me asking for help to fight a massive Tyson Foods chicken-processing plant in their town. Organizers for "No Tyson in Tongie" made signs and showed up in droves to town meetings.

is still one of the fastest and easiest organizing tools for groups, despite the many controversies the company has faced in recent years.) Activists made white-and-red signs that said, "No Tyson in Tongie" to display on homeowners' lawns and T-shirts with the same slogan. Signs are a great way to raise awareness and get more people interested in these cases.

"The continued presence and involvement of area citizens in local politics and the community speaks volumes about the unity regarding planning for the best interests of our region in the future," said Jen Peak, one of the Tongie organizers, in a statement. "The fact that 'No Tyson in Tongie' signs are still on every street throughout town and all over the countryside is a testament to the strong, unified, and continued opposition to and vigilance regarding the proposed Tyson Project."

People in town also showed up in droves to a September 2017 rally organized by Kansas legislators, including Kansas Republican state representative Jim Karleskint, who lives near the town and said it was the largest gathering he's ever seen for a community of their size. And then the kicker: the county's board of commissioners, which had just approved $500 million in industrial revenue bonds for the Tyson facilities, revoked its decision five days later. Tyson soon announced its plans were on hold while it scouted for other plant locations. If companies want to do business with these small towns, they need to clean up their act and get off the list of our nation's biggest polluters. Tyson said they wanted to hold town meetings to address residents' questions, but then they never bothered to show up. The people have spoken, and they are ready for business that is environmentally sustainable. It's time to stop polluting for profit, and in our own backyards.

CLEANING UP CHROME-6

Justice doesn't come all at once; it usually comes in steps. No place exemplifies this idea more than Hinkley, California, where after more than twenty-five years and a $333 million settlement awarded to the people, pollution still exists today. National regulations for hexavalent chromium in drinking water remain unchanged since 1991, at a level of 100 ppb for total chromium. California regulations, which were set at a more stringent 10 ppb for chromium-6 in 2014, were revoked in 2017 due to a lawsuit alleging the state had not conducted an economic feasibility study. The people who live in Hinkley today are still dealing with pollution problems and have continued to push for Pacific Gas and Electric to do the right thing and clean up their mess. I wish there was better news to share with you about this town. We're finally starting to see some cleanup happen, but it's been a longer road than anyone could have anticipated. I can't believe that more than twenty years later I'm still talking about what happened in this small desert town, but this story represents so much of what the water crisis today is all about. This case is really the story of how corporations, like PG&E, pollute and get away with it.

Back in the '90s, Roberta Walker spearheaded the effort to get help for her town. She spent hours at the local water board looking at maps of her neighborhood and making copies of old files. She came to the law offices of Masry & Vititoe holding a huge box of documents—remember, those times were not as digital as today—and that's what jump-started my journey from a legal clerk to consumer advocate. Thanks to Roberta's persistence and stellar research along with community support, we won that lawsuit. I had sincerely hoped it would provide justice for the people of Hinkley and preserve life in that town, not to mention bring these important issues into the public eye. But the lawsuit and the movie were just another layer in this case.

In December of 2010 (about fourteen years after the lawsuit had been settled), Roberta had another Hinkley resident calling her all the time. When they finally met during a lunch break, Carmela presented her with documents that stunned Roberta. Carmela knew about the 1996 settlement though she had not been part of it, but when her horses stopped drinking the water at her Hinkley home, she became worried. It was no secret in town that PG&E was lagging on the cleanup, but she had proof that the original plume of contamination was in fact spreading. Again, action began with one person trusting their common sense that the water was still poisoned. Roberta had moved seven miles northeast of her original home in Hinkley to escape the pollution, thinking the contamination was limited to a certain area near the compressor station. Now, that same plume was only a mile from her new home and still growing.

Elaine Kearney moved into her dream home in Hinkley in 1995, near her sister's ten-acre property and right before the first case in town was settled. By 2010, one of her daughters had had five miscarriages and dealt with painful ovarian cysts, while another was in treatment for advanced cancer. Even the family dog was covered in tumors. Elaine herself had heart disease and strokes that kept her in and out of hospitals. She had seen houses throughout her neighborhood getting bulldozed after PG&E bought them. In a **New York Times** article, she talked about her property value and health issues, "We can't sell it," she said. "We can't walk away or we'll lose a chance at a settlement."

Once again, residents got into action. This time they put pressure on PG&E, raised awareness about the company's lingering and leisurely cleanup efforts, and demanded more accountability from the Lahontan Regional Water Quality Control Board, which was described by a **Times** article as "a chronically underfunded state agency that evaluates and enforces PG&E's cleanup plans." The water quality board was assessing PG&E's treatment of the plume. At the time, PG&E's plan involved injecting the tainted chromium-6 groundwater with ethanol, which is no great elixir, to help convert it to the less harmful chromium-3. But a feasibility study from the water board found that this method could take more than a hundred years to restore the area. And not long after learning all this information, Roberta got another knock on her door from PG&E, once again offering to buy her home and deliver clean bottled water to her family.

Roberta was not the only resident offered another buyout. Between 2010 and October 2014, PG&E purchased about three hundred more properties in Hinkley. By 2012, the company paid another $3.6 million fine to the town because of the spreading pollution. The company still admitted to no wrong-doing but promised to install new wells and help improve the drinking water quality at the local elementary school. As more residents left town, Hinkley's school shut down in 2013, after talks with PG&E to help subsidize it failed. The school, which originally opened in 1902, had taught many generations of Hinkley children. Not long afterward, the town's post office closed too.

By 2013, PG&E had spent more than $700 million on its cleanup efforts, but the contaminated water persisted. Sheryl Bilbrey, in charge of PG&E remediation efforts at that time, told PBS journalist Miles O'Brien on **NewsHour**, "It's a very complex project. We are highly regulated. There's a lot of interested parties. The other thing is, it's very important to us that we get it right." I was interviewed during this same segment, and I said that I thought the cleanup was under control, and so did the state and the community.

Reports from the water board clearly state that from July 2011 to July 2014, hexavalent chromium concentrations steadily increased from 9 to 19 ppb in one well near Acacia Street, and from 2013 and 2014 levels increased from 7.8 to 24 ppb in another well located southeast of Santa Fe Avenue and Mountain View Road. In 2015 the Lahontan board issued another new cleanup order combining outstanding requirements from previous orders and adding new requirements and deadlines for future cleanup and abatement actions.

I thought that after the lawsuit, and certainly after the movie, PG&E would clean up this pollution. They didn't. They stalled on cleanup for years, as the cover-up continued. It's hard to imagine that all this trouble and heartbreak was caused by a chemical that helped control rust in their gas cooling towers. When I think about the situation, I feel sad, disappointed, and even disgusted by PG&E's actions. It really brings up so many questions about such contamination cases and their subsequent cleanup. What would possibly make a company of this magnitude finally do the right thing? It's so frustrating for everyone who knows the people there and the town. It's a place where people live to experience a slower pace of life than in the city, where they can see the stars at night and enjoy riding horses in the open fields during the day. They don't deserve any of it.

Visiting Hinkley in 2015 I was appalled to see empty lots where so many houses used to stand. Many residents have simply left, seeking a better life for their families. Sadly, there's little life left in Hinkley beyond a few homes with plunging property values and acres of alfalfa plants still growing in the fields. We need to do better. Thousands of Hinkleys exist in this country—small farming communities where industry dumps their waste and thinks they can get away with it. My hope is that if more people know what's really going on, we can bring back life to many of these forgotten towns.

In April 2016, the Lahontan board issued another executive order allowing for more vigorous use of ethanol injection into the groundwater, and in November 2016 it approved a comprehensive cleanup order that allowed PG&E to continue with ethanol injections without needing regulatory approvals. The company also pumps the tainted water onto alfalfa fields, where the soil's bacteria can help convert the chemical back to chromium-3. PG&E's top environmental executives told California water regulators that at least half of the chromium-6 has been removed from the groundwater in Hinkley and that the plume was starting to retreat in April 2017.

Hinkley was just the beginning. Before that case settled, I began working on another case in 1994 with about 1,100 plaintiffs who also had illnesses related to chromium-6-contaminated groundwater near PG&E's Kettleman Hills compressor plant. Kettleman City is another farming community nestled between Los Angeles and San Francisco. Two of the longest streets in town are named General Petroleum Avenue and Standard Oil Avenue. Just like the Hinkley timeline, in the '50s and '60s runoff from PG&E's cooling towers seeped into the ground, contaminating the local water supply. When I drove into town to inspect the four big cooling towers, I didn't see any of the usual signs of contamination. So I got out of my car and started walking around, quietly observing, and that's when I spotted something. The needles on the tamarisk trees were coated with the same white powder that I had seen in Hinkley. I headed to the local water board to do a little more digging and discovered a 1964 letter from the U.S. Department of the Interior notifying PG&E of excessive chromium-6 in a well in town.

After I talked to residents, it became clear that the contaminated well was used for drinking and bathing. Once we gathered more evidence, we took this case to court, and it took ten years to settle. Take that in for a moment, because while the lawyers, scientists, and researchers were working to get this company to come clean, the families who lived in this town continued to deal with hospital visits, birth defects, and other health issues, while also needing to travel some thirty miles each week to the next largest town of Hanford to load up on bottled water. In 2002, PG&E spokesman Jon Tremayne declined to discuss the details of the Kettleman case with **SFGate**, but said the utility was ready for a fight. "We will definitely defend ourselves in court," he said.

The utility was already in the midst of its own crisis as this toxic case came to light. PG&E filed for Chapter 11 bankruptcy in April 2001 facing $9 billion in debt due to state-imposed deregulation laws, market manipulations spearheaded by Enron, and California's energy crisis, which led to sky-high wholesale power prices and rolling blackouts throughout the state. The bankruptcy, the largest in U.S. history for a utility at that time, kept the company afloat to continue providing power to millions of California residents while it worked to renegotiate its debts. But California's governor, Gray Davis, called the move "a real slap in the face to California." Consumer advocates called it a "a thinly-veiled effort to escape the California regulatory system."

Despite PG&E's financial problems, the Kettleman suit settled for $335 million in 2006. In a twenty-two-page decision, U.S. bankruptcy judge Dennis Montali wrote, "The chromium claims didn't cause this bankruptcy. Trial in state court should proceed as expeditiously as possible." Part of the settlement included an apology from PG&E to residents. "Clearly, this situation should never have happened, and we are sorry that it did. It is not the way we do business, and we believe it would not happen in our company today," according to a company statement. Despite the pretense, the executives and the board of directors remained intact. None of PG&E's leadership was ever reprimanded for these actions. They paid their fines and continued business as usual.

In 2016, a federal jury found PG&E guilty again—this time for violating safety regulations that led to a gas pipeline explosion in the San Francisco Bay Area that killed eight people and destroyed thirty-eight homes in San Bruno. The utility was convicted not just for the blast but for misleading federal investigators about how they identified high-risk pipelines. They systematically worked to misclassify pipelines and save money rather than apply the appropriate testing and regulations for them. Once again, no one in upper management faced prison time. Ultimately, PG&E was convicted of six felony charges and fined the maximum penalty of $3 million, which is in addition to the $1.6 billion fine the company received from California regulators. The court also prohibited the company from passing down any of these costs to its ratepayers.

In January 2019, the investor-owned utility filed for Chapter 11 bankruptcy **again**, as it faced massive liability claims—up to $30 billion—for the devastating and deadly wildfire seasons in Northern California. This was after the company spent $1.7 million in 2018 lobbying state lawmakers to release them from legal liability associated with wildfire property damages. Hot summers and high winds certainly contributed to the fires, but huge safety failures connected to PG&E's power lines and faulty hardware have also been connected to an estimated 1,500 fires between 2014 and 2017. The company's equipment allegedly sparked the

Camp Fire in 2018, the state's deadliest wildfire, which killed eighty-five people and destroyed close to fourteen thousand homes and five hundred businesses. The fire was the world's costliest natural disaster in 2018 with overall damages topping $16.5 billion.

It's become clear that declaring bankruptcy has become a tactic for PG&E to skirt responsibility for its poor safety practices and management. Chapter 11 involves a reorganization of the company's affairs, debts, and assets, but they tend to emerge from this process even more disorganized. Geisha Williams, the first female CEO of PG&E, who was appointed in 2017, stepped down in this most recent bankruptcy, taking with her a $2.5 million severance package. Perhaps her hire was an attempt at a fresh start to help distance the company from the San Bruno mess, but even with her more than thirty years in the utility industry, she was unable to make changes to the corporate culture. John Simon, the company's general counsel, has been (fittingly) named interim CEO. All eyes will be on the company's board to see if they will make the necessary changes to do the right thing in the coming years.

Meanwhile, BlueMountain Capital Management LLC, an asset manager owning more than 4 million PG&E shares, has said that the company is solvent and that a bankruptcy would be "damaging, avoidable, and unnecessary." In a letter to PG&E's board of directors, BlueMountain wrote, "There is overwhelming evidence that PG&E is solvent. We simply cannot recall a situation where such a valuable company filed for bankruptcy with such blatant questions about the necessity to do so."

The way I see it, PG&E has never accepted responsibility for any of their actions—going all the way back to Hinkley and dozens of other cases I've dealt with up and down the state for more than twenty years. They don't follow through on their obligations or reinvest the money they make in better safety practices and new equipment. As we continue to deal with climate change and changing weather conditions in California, it's more important than ever that this company have new infrastructure that can stand up to strong winds and storms.

"Rather than spend the money it obtains from customers for infrastructure maintenance and safety, PG&E funnels this funding to boost its own corporate profits and compensation" are the words used in one lawsuit filed against the company for the Camp Fire.

This is what happens when corporations are left to police themselves. They put profits before safety. This company's destructive and negligent past should not be overlooked in its bankruptcy proceedings. I believe the courts will hold PG&E

accountable, as it will essentially elect a judge as the new CEO. Plus, a newly elected governor in California is looking at the company with fresh eyes.

"PG&E, with respect, has not been a trusted player in the past," said California governor Gavin Newsom, just days after the utility made its bankruptcy announcement. "They have admitted knowingly misleading regulators in the past—very recent past. That is simply unacceptable."

In addition, he said, "Every survivor deserves to have their claims heard in a fair process that recognizes their pain and financial losses. I remain steadfastly committed to working with all stake-holders to find a solution that ensures consumers have access to safe, affordable and reliable service; treats wildfire survivors fairly; and enables California to continue making progress toward our climate goals."

Sadly, for residents of Kettleman City, where almost 30 percent live below the poverty line, their troubles have continued long past the PG&E lawsuit. This tiny community of about 1,600 people is dealing with many other contaminants besides chromium-6. More than half of the workforce are Latino farmworkers, who get exposed to chemicals sprayed in the tomato fields and almond groves. The town is also just three miles down the road from Waste Management, Inc., one of the nation's largest toxic waste dumps. For years, residents have suspected that these multiple toxic exposures are connected to their health problems, including a large cluster of birth defects—babies being born with enlarged heads and cleft palates. But the biggest problem for this town, and many others like it, is that scientists still have little data about how individual chemicals impact our health, and know even less about the effects of multiple chemicals on the body. It's difficult to trace the exact pathway these chemicals take to people's bodies, especially as they result in different kinds of diseases and health issues. We need more research and biomarker tracking to continue to improve our understanding of how these chemicals work and how they create havoc in the body, which I continue to advocate for. However, commonsense instincts tell us that they are related. From my years of work, I believe it's only a matter of time until the science catches up and helps us understand the cause and effects of exposure to an array of toxic chemicals.

I continue to get emails from people throughout California and work to raise awareness about Kettleman City and towns like it. If you've driven on California's Interstate 5, you've probably seen signs in gas stations and hotels that say, "Tainted Water, Use at Your Own Risk." In 2016, I posted an article on Facebook about two wells in Kettleman that tested positive for high levels of arsenic, three years after the EPA put California on notice for noncompliance with the Safe Drinking Water Act. Back in 2008, EPA tests found unsafe levels of arsenic, a known carcinogen, in the drinking water of Kettleman City. Five years later, the state started delivering thirty gallons of water each month to residents. It turns out that arsenic is commonly found in tap water throughout the Central Valley. In fact, fifty-five thousand people in ninety-five different public water systems throughout the state are drinking tap water contaminated with arsenic, according to research from the Environmental Integrity Project.

Public water systems are required to notify customers when the water does not meet federal regulations. The notices mailed to consumers about the arsenic read, "You do not need to use an alternative water supply (e.g., bottled water)." Yet the state sent a different warning to the owners of private wells (which are not covered by federal regulations) that read, "If you suspect that your well may have arsenic, you should not use the water until it is tested, and take appropriate measures to protect yourself and your family from potential chronic health effects if arsenic is present." We need more federal mandates to set strong, health-protective standards for contaminants in drinking water. Without them, states will continue to use inconsistent and potentially unsafe guidelines, leaving citizens confused about the safety of their drinking water.

Imagine living somewhere your whole life and never filling up a glass of water from the faucet. That's exactly what Kettleman City resident and environmental activist Maricela Mares-Alatorre's daughter has experienced. Maricela fights for her community, whose claim to fame is poor water quality and high levels of pollution, by organizing rallies, joining task forces, and talking on radio and TV to bring more awareness to these issues.

She relayed the story about her daughter to a local news station saying, "My daughter last year we were watching a movie, and she saw somebody in the movie went to the sink and poured themselves a glass of water, and she said, 'oh he's drinking from the sink!' Because she has never lived in a place where you can actually drink from the sink." She described how her daughter never leaves home without bottled water, but many other local kids drink from the water fountains at school, which only recently installed water filters. The California state government has promised to help build a $9.6 million water treatment plant to help treat water from the California Aqueduct, which runs close to the town.

Now imagine being so afraid of the water coming out of your tap that you don't want to wash your dishes, so you switch to paper plates, permanently. It sounds like some futuristic dystopia, but it's just a small picture of what was happening in

Midland, Texas, a midsized town wedged between two larger ones. Midland gets its name from the fact that it was once the midway point between Dallas–Fort Worth and El Paso on the Texas and Pacific Railroad in 1881, but the state already had another town named Midway, and so they named it Midland instead. It's the hometown of former first lady Laura Bush and the childhood home of former president George W. Bush. It's also located near the Permian Basin oil fields, so petroleum and gas have run the local economy for years.

After Hinkley and Kettleman, I continued to get thousands of emails and to respond as quickly as I could to each of them. One of those emails came in 2009 from Sissy Sathre, a community activist in Midland, who wrote pleading with me to help her neighborhood, where most of the families were afraid to use their water—they were making green ice cubes. Sissy had written more than a thousand letters to her local government, congressman, and legislators, to no avail. I wrote Sissy back in thirty minutes, after her email came through on my phone while Bob was driving us through a snowstorm at 1 a.m. We had just finished a town hall meeting in Michigan for another case and we were on our way to the Chicago airport. She sent me photos of her green swimming pool and told me her daughter was waking up with open sores and skin rashes. She said her neighbor Sheldon and his wife had both been diagnosed with kidney problems. Other folks in her community were dealing with rashes, earaches, headaches, hair loss, and rare forms of cancer. The animals were having health problems too, with residents reporting dogs with multiple tumors. The images were too familiar, and I had a strong hunch that the water was contaminated with chromium-6. Bob hopped on a flight the next day to test the water. Sure enough, it had some of the highest hexavalent chromium readings we had ever encountered in well water, and higher than anything I'd seen in Hinkley.

This case once again opened my eyes to the issue of domestic wells in our country. So many of the cases I work with even today are part of this omission from the Safe Drinking Water Act. The EPA only regulates public water systems. Many states and towns do not require sampling of private wells once they're installed, so the responsibility of maintaining clean drinking water falls to the homeowner. The problem arises when industrial neighbors dump toxic chemicals that seep into the groundwater without alerting the locals about it. About 15 percent of Americans (about 43 million people) get their drinking water from private wells, which should be protected from this kind of contamination.

The good news for the forty families in the Cotton Flats community in Midland was that within two weeks of Bob and me showing up for a town hall meeting, state health officials began installing home water treatment systems for the residents. We saw the power of people coming together to get results. It wasn't about a lawsuit this time; the work shifted to helping community members get organized and united. Sissy and many others went door-to-door, charted the contamination on maps, and put together health questionnaires. It was grassroots organizing at its best, and I know they did a great job raising awareness. But the filters were only a temporary fix as many people reported frequent issues with them. Affected residents got into the habit of filling up white buckets of water to test the color before they would drink it. If that green color came out, then they knew the filters weren't working. The next step was to figure out where the pollution was coming from, and Bob worked with local activists to identify the largest user of chromium-6, an industrial neighbor just north of and adjacent to the polluted groundwater wells: Schlumberger, an oil field services company.

In a statement Schlumberger said, "Chromium has not been used in any of the processes performed at the Schlumberger facilities in Midland, Texas, and independent water samplings indicate that the source is likely an adjacent site unrelated to our facilities."

If I had a dollar for every corporation that denied responsibility for the use of toxic chemicals, boy, would I be living it up! Back in 2005, Congress passed an exemption, now commonly referred to as the Halliburton loophole, for hydraulic fracking from the Safe Drinking Water Act. At the time, Halliburton was raking in about $1.5 billion annually from fracking and this exemption allowed them and others, like Schlumberger, to keep profits up and keep the chemicals they were using secret. Despite the hush-hush ruling, independent research has shown that hexavalent chromium is commonly used in fracking compounds.

The Texas Commission on Environmental Quality essentially told residents that its priority was to identify the contaminated sites and provide clean water for people with chromium-6 contamination. They did not pursue further action against Schlumberger or any other potential polluters. The TCEQ maintains these contaminated wells with filters at a cost of more than $1 million annually. The site was also added to the EPA's National Priorities List of Superfund sites. Much like Hinkley, this site could be contaminated for generations to come.

The Midland case speaks to how so many of us have become complacent. We think some agency is overseeing our health and well-being, but case after case has shown me that they are not. Part of the problem with water is that we don't see it. We have these incredible water systems underneath our feet, but we don't think to check on them until the water coming out of our tap is green or smells foul. Sissy, who had become a friend during this case, died in 2015 from cancer. Unsafe levels of chromium-6 have been detected in tap water in all fifty states, affecting more than 200 million Americans. How many more people will we have to lose before we all get motivated to do more? We still don't have national regulations for hexavalent chromium, nearly twenty years since I first exposed these issues.

ARE WE ASLEEP IN THE POPPY FIELD?

In both the book and the movie versions of **The Wizard of Oz,** there's a scene where Dorothy and her friends are following the Yellow Brick Road and come across a poppy field that makes them fall asleep. It's a trap set by the Wicked Witch to derail them from their cause—getting to the Emerald City.

> Now it is well known that when there are many of these flowers together their odor is so powerful that anyone who breathes it falls asleep, and if the sleeper is not carried away from the scent

of the flowers, he sleeps on and on forever. But Dorothy did not know this, nor could she get away from the bright red flowers that were everywhere about; so presently her eyes grew heavy and she felt she must sit down to rest and to sleep. . . . "If we leave her here, she will die," said the Lion. "The smell of the flowers is killing us all."

—The Wonderful Wizard of Oz, 1900

In the story, the poppies represent the dangers of apathy and complacency. I think that as a society, we've been lulled to sleep. We believe that someone else is taking care of things—whether it's government agencies or large corporate entities. But I'm here to tell you that no one is out there working to save us; we have to start saving ourselves and creating better systems that work for all of us.

Think about the poppies in your life. Are you busy watching the latest reality show on Bravo? Are you constantly checking your smart devices and social media? I'm not here to judge, but take a moment and realize how you might be avoiding the real issues that we face. I'm not saying don't ever watch TV, but don't let it take over your life. Stay awake and keep learning. Imagine what would happen if you read one article a day about water issues or talked to one friend about your concerns. Find out when your next city council meeting is happening and bring a neighbor with you. Any little action forward can get you going in the right direction. Now is the time to get out of the poppy field and get into action.

WHAT'S YOUR WHY?

It's so important to remember your why. For me, it's my grandchildren. I think of their sweet, innocent faces and my love for them. Then, I think of all the children who need our voices and need us to fight for their future. I think of their happiness and for a healthy, clean world for them to live in and enjoy. It keeps me motivated, especially when the work seems daunting. Think about your why and let that fuel your fighting spirit.

7

SAYING NO TO "UNINTENDED CONSEQUENCES"

On the western edge of Dutchess County, New York, sits Poughkeepsie—a town of thirty-two thousand people who rely on the Hudson River as their drinking water source. The 315-mile Hudson runs from the Adirondack Mountains in upstate New York down through the Hudson Valley farmlands and into the Atlantic Ocean near New York City. General Electric (GE) dumped more than 1 million pounds of polychlorinated biphenyls (PCBs) into the river from the late 1940s until the '70s, when environmental regulations started kicking in. Exposure to these odorless man-made chemicals has been linked to a range of health effects in humans and animals, including suppressing the immune system, elevating blood pressure, low birth weights, changes in thyroid hormone levels, and cancer.

Musician and activist Pete Seeger spent years raising awareness about the contamination, and two hundred miles of the river was declared a

Superfund site in 1984, one of the largest in the country. Years of grassroots organizing and political pressure drove GE to start working to remove the toxic sediment in the river. PCBs are just one of the chemicals, along with sewage and industrial waste, that have also been dumped into the river, causing problems for both the wildlife and the people who drink from it. In one of the largest and most complex environmental cleanups in U.S. history, efforts have included dredging—a process that removes sediment and debris from the bottom of the river. The EPA and GE have worked together on this project, and extensive monitoring and remediation efforts continue today.

Poughkeepsie is one of many small towns located alongside the Hudson that depend on its water. The city is known for its prestigious private colleges like Vassar and Marist, its often gray skies, and its high property taxes. For years, an unpleasant smell wafted from the wastewater treatment plant, described by residents as a mix of sulfur and sludge, and it likely contributed to the town's spot on **Forbes**'s list of "Most Miserable Cities." Upgrades at the plant, which included improving the processing system, addressing maintenance issues, and installing a new odor scrubber, helped reduce odor complaints. In addition, the town has become a model for honest drinking water treatment, despite long-term pollution to their source water.

Randy Alstadt, water plant administrator at the Poughkeepsie Water Treatment Facility, has been working diligently since 1997 to provide clean water to Poughkeepsie's residents. One of the biggest challenges he has faced is controlling disinfection byproducts in the water—a problem now rampant throughout our country. The plant started using chloramines, a mixture of ammonia and chlorine, in 2000 to help control the amount of DBPs (disinfection byproducts) in the water to meet EPA regulations. It was a cheap fix that only required a chemical feed pump, a chemical storage tank, and the cost of the ammonia. At the time, Randy said he was satisfied with the low-cost solution, and if he encountered any future problems, he would explore alternatives.

As soon as the water plant turned on the chloramine, they started to see increased corrosion activity in the distribution system, along with gaskets failing—both at the plant and in customers' homes. Randy's customers reported brown water coming out of their taps, no matter how many times he flushed the distribution system. Health problems, such as skin and respiratory issues, showed up too.

"Right when we made the switch, we had people calling and complaining about skin rashes and breathing problems, and they said their houseplants were dying," he told me.

He was not aware of the health effects at that time, and to be fair, we did not have as much information then as we have today. These issues are consistent with what I've seen in so many of the communities that use chloramine today. The difference is that not all water companies seem to be as self-aware and honest as Randy. The water board approached him repeatedly, frustrated with the continuing rust and corrosion in the system as well as the customer complaints, so he hired an outside engineer to study the system and find a better solution. In 2010, he stopped using ammonia altogether.

"As soon as we turned off the chloramine, the brown water went away," he told me. So did the health complaints. The problem with chloramine, Randy said, is that it masks the problem of organics in the water. It doesn't get rid of them and it forms even more byproducts, which are currently unregulated. We certainly don't need more unknowns when it comes to treating our water. Since then, the Poughkeepsie plant has approved funding and finished building a new $18 million system using ozone and biologically activated filters to help remove organic material from the water. The new system not only eliminates the need for chloramines but also reduces the amount of chlorine needed to clean the water.

Bob and I have spent countless hours traveling

from community to community expressing our concerns about the use of chloramines. I was also curious about how Randy raised the funds to make the switch. Chloramines cost the city about $25,000 a year, so a new multi-million-dollar system was a big ask.

"It's a lot of money, but if there's one customer out there suffering because of my water, that's not right. I don't agree with that," Randy said. "Nobody likes to hear that it will cost more than a million dollars to make upgrades. But I think that the health effects of chloramine don't justify using it. Once the cost of the upgrade is divided amongst all the customers, the monthly increase is typically not that great. It turns out to be about the price of a meal per month. I let customers know it's for better quality water, and people can agree to that."

Randy says he's a salesman as much as a water treatment operator. It's all about doing what's right to get the best quality drinking water to his customers. Think about paying $2 for a bottle of water when Randy can make clean water at a cost of $1 per thousand gallons. Which would you choose?

The new ozone system has been up and running in Poughkeepsie since October 2016. Randy says the disinfection byproducts have gone down to about a third to a half of what they were, depending on the time of year. That's effective in reducing DBPs and exactly the kind of numbers any operator would hope for. In addition, using ozone has also helped him reduce the amount of chlorine needed to clean the water. While PCBs remain a concern in his area, he says he's never detected them at the plant.

Randy makes it look easy. He has integrity and used his common sense to provide the safest drinking water possible to his customers. I applaud his efforts and I hope that Poughkeepsie can stand as a model for more cities and towns that are still weighing their options.

Unfortunately, the use of chloramines has soared in the last decade at many water municipalities simply to meet compliance with the EPA's Stage 1 and Stage 2 Disinfectants and Disinfection Byproducts Rules. It's worth mentioning that a few cities have used chloramines relatively safely to treat their water—Denver since 1918 and Boston since the 1930s—but these are exceptions, not the rule. No two water systems are the same, and it has worked in these cities because chloramine takes up long-lasting residence in the water, which is helpful to treat water that journeys through miles of pipes. If you don't have extensive pipelines, you end up with more complications than solutions, as we saw in Poughkeepsie and in many other cities across the country. Drinking water treatment facilities need to look at the compatibility of chloramines with their distribution system and work to predict the challenges and safety concerns of adding ammonia to their treatment plan.

In a paper for the Water Research Foundation, Djanette Khiari essentially summarizes thirty years' worth of research on chloramines, writing: "Chloramination can be a complex process and improper management can lead to unintended consequences."

In almost every community meeting where Bob and I have discussed the issue of chloramines, we've been met with confusion and resistance— usually in the form of a "plant," or someone who tries to deny the science and complications we've seen in many communities. Randy's story in Poughkeepsie shows exactly the kind of problems we are trying to help communities avoid. Brown water coming out of taps. Health complaints. Corrosion in the system. Breakdowns in already deteriorating infrastructure. The June 2017 issue of the **American Water Works Journal** focused on chloramines and confirmed these same problems. The guest editor, Stuart W. Krasner, discussed how drinking water utilities have "cost-effectively optimized their treatment and disinfection processes to control a variety of micro-pollutants to meet state and federal regulations, operational requirements, and aesthetic issues." He also discusses another downside: using chloramines has led to the discovery of new pollutants, presenting even more challenges to the drinking water industry. One of those health and regulatory challenges is an emerging class of DBPs called nitrosamines (e.g., N-nitroso-dimethylamine or NDMA), a suspected carcinogen and an unregulated DBP. When exposed at high levels, NDMA can cause liver damage to both humans and animals.

"NDMA is preferentially formed by chloramines, where chloramines have been increasingly used to control the formation of the regulated DBPs trihalomethanes and haloacetic acids," Krasner wrote.

On top of that problem, switching to chloramines can cause lead to leach from pipes, fixtures, and other components in the water distribution system, which means that even if the water is meeting regulations at the treatment plant, by the time it reaches customers it may be unsafe to drink. A 2007 study looked at drinking water sources, blood lead data, and census data for 7,270 children in Wayne County, North Carolina, to determine lead exposure. The county has two main public water systems: Wayne Water Systems, which uses chlorine for disinfection, and Goldsboro Water System, which tried chloramines for disinfection for about seven years. The Goldsboro Water System's change to chloramines was associated with an increase in children's blood lead levels, suggesting that the switch could have created an increase in lead exposure.

Even the U.S. EPA considered changing regulations related to chloramines in 2016 amid cities reporting issues with it. A 2009 EPA report says that the appropriateness of using chloramines varies with water types and water utilities and that gaps in research on chloramines exist, including the fact that there are few studies on its impact on human health and few studies on the DBPs that form when chloramines react with natural organic matter in the water, and that chloraminated water may contain higher concentrations of unregulated byproducts. A study published by the Water Research Foundation, a nonprofit that receives funding from the utility industry, looked at data from eleven cities and concluded that utilities should look at other options and avoid chloramines when it comes to reducing disinfection byproducts.

"We're questioning the wisdom of using chloramines as much as we do in this country," said the lead author of the study, David Reckhow, a national expert on the treatment of drinking water and the head of the UMass–Amherst Water Innovation Network for Sustainable Small Systems.

As of the writing of this book, the EPA has not changed its stance and still lists chloramine as safe for disinfecting drinking water when used at regulated levels.

TULSANS AGAINST CHLORAMINES

While Poughkeepsie stopped using chloramines in 2010, other parts of the country were just starting to consider it. In 2011 officials in Tulsa, Oklahoma, announced plans to start using chloramines as a secondary disinfectant to "meet more stringent EPA requirements," according to Robert Brownwood, the city's water supply manager at that time. The switch was reported to cost the city less than $1 million, and Brownwood said that most residents wouldn't notice the change. In contrast to Poughkeepsie's title of "Most Miserable Cities" from **Forbes**, Tulsa made their list of "Most Livable Cities." The downtown has one of the country's largest concentrations of art deco buildings thanks to a construction boom in the early twentieth century. The Tulsa metropolitan area is often called "green country," because of its rolling, forested hills and mountains that stand in stark contrast to other parts of Oklahoma, which look more like the rest of the dry, dusty Great Plains.

Even though Tulsa is the second-largest city in Oklahoma, Jeanine Kinney, who was born and raised there, says Tulsa is a tight-knit community that feels much more like a small town. In fact, she found out about the plan to start using chloramines when one of her neighbors approached her on a walk and handed her a water bill. In tiny print, it addressed the conversion from chlorine to chloramines, assuring customers that they would not notice the change. At the time, Jeanine didn't know much about her water or anything about chloramines, but said she would look into it, as her neighbor seemed concerned. When she started doing research later that day, she learned about the chloramine water crisis in D.C. and found groups like Citizens Concerned About Chloramine (CCAC), a nonprofit organization based in California. The information scared her, and she said she couldn't understand why Tulsa was suddenly looking to add ammonia to their water. She wrote me an email saying, "Erin, my name is Jeanine Kinney, I live in Tulsa, Oklahoma. I've been doing some homework and research, they are doing a chloramine conversion here. What do I do?" I wrote her back, explaining that yes, this change is happening rapidly throughout the country. It's the cheapest way you can go. I told her to start reaching out to her city council members.

So she did. She called her city councilman at the time, who told her he wouldn't touch the subject with a ten-foot pole. It was not on his agenda. Next, she reached out to some locals who knew more about water issues and they put her in touch with Jim Mautino, a council member who was concerned about chloramines because he had a son who could be sensitive to it. As soon as they met, Jeanine was impressed. He had done his homework on the topic and was willing to put chloramines on the agenda whenever he could. Jeanine didn't stop there. She contacted Denise Johnson-Kula, president of CCAC, who guided her to more information and helped her write a statement she could read at the council meeting to clearly state her concerns.

Here's the statement she read on October 4, 2011, at the Tulsa City Council committee meeting:

> The health department, the water department, and the EPA are claiming that chloramine is safe for all everyday uses, drinking, bathing, and cooking. Yet, the EPA itself admits that it has no respiratory, digestive, skin, and epidemiological studies on the human health effects of chloraminated water. The limited cancer studies on chloraminated water are so few that they are considered inadequate for assessment. Even though these studies show some evidence that chloramine itself is a carcinogen. No determination can be made from those handful of studies. There is not enough scientific data to know if chloraminated water is safe for any uses for human beings.
>
> Thousands of people all over the country, and even in other countries, have reported

severe and life-threatening respiratory, digestive, and skin symptoms whenever they are exposed to chloraminated water. These people have proven by avoidance and re-exposure that the chloraminated water is the culprit for their symptoms. They do not have these symptoms when they are not exposed to chloramine and as soon as they are re-exposed their symptoms return. These symptoms fall into exactly the "gaps" in the scientific data about chloramine's safety and the respiratory, digestive, and skin studies that do not exist.

In addition to the immediate health effects that people are reporting from chloraminated water is the grave concern about the emerging science in the very little-known disinfection byproducts (DBPs) of chloramine. These DBPs are not yet regulated but are turning out to be many magnitudes more toxic than those of chlorine (THMs & HAAs).

Finally, chloramine is much more corrosive to plumbing, lead pipes, and copper pipes with lead solder and brass plumbing fixtures, which contain lead. Lead is being leached into drinking water because of the corrosive effects of chloramine on combinations of these metals. Sometimes the level of lead leached into the drinking water is extremely high. Children from chloraminated water districts are showing high levels of lead in their blood. And for those of us concerned about our environment, chloramine is much more toxic to fish, frogs, amphibians, and to other aquatic life. Water main breaks with water disinfected with chlorine rarely do any damage unless the level of chlorine is extremely high. But with chloramine even small traces from breaks and leaks, as well as from people washing their cars or watering their lawns, can wipe out fish, frogs, and amphibians in nearby ponds, streams, and lakes. Why risk our fragile environment if there are better alternatives?

In closing today, I really want to believe in my heart that each of you nine city councilors took your position on the city council in order to help, protect, and look out for the best interest of the people of Tulsa. I plead with you to help protect the health of Tulsa's water consumers. Please oppose the use of chloramine as it has not been studied for the very health effects that people all over the country and all over the world are reporting.

Not bad for a newbie water warrior! Jeanine told me that after the meeting the council members looked like their heads were going to spin off their necks. It validated all the points that she and Jim Mautino had been trying to convey. When she attended many meetings similar to this one, council members would approach her afterward and some would say, "You are never going to get anywhere," while others would say, "Good for you. Thank you for doing what you are doing."

She just kept thinking that if they won or lost, at least she could sleep at night knowing that as a mother and as a Tulsan she had tried to use her voice to speak up for so many people in the city. She would rather try and fail than not try at all. Jeanine soon discovered the Tulsa Metropolitan Utility Authority (TMUA), a public trust organization created by city charter, made up of seven members—the mayor and six other nonelected officials who were appointed to four-year terms. They were the ones responsible for managing and maintaining Tulsa's water and sewer systems. They held the decision-making power and the final say for the entire Tulsa metroplex area (more than half a million people). Jeanine was worried about how much they knew about chloramines and wondered if they were taking into consideration people on dialysis, people with COPD or respiratory, skin, or digestive issues, cancer patients, and others with compromised immune systems. What about women filling up their babies' bottles with tap water? How could just few a people make such an important decision for so many? She started showing up to the TMUA open meetings to get more answers and put pressure on them to make the right choice for everyone.

She also created a Facebook group called Tulsans Against Chloramine (which still has more than eight hundred members) with Meghan Lampkin and Victoria Clarke, who were also very concerned about the water. The women worked together and met with Mayor Dewey Bartlett Jr., the TMUA, and state legislators, who eventually agreed to do testing to see if they could switch to carbon filtering instead of chloramine. Once the tests were complete, the city came back saying it was too expensive to go that route. They also discovered that one of the appointed TMUA members owned a company that manufactured chloramine-resistant parts that could replace rubber gaskets and other parts damaged by chloramines—a huge conflict of interest.

Jeanine, Meghan, and Victoria pushed forward with their fight, continuing to collect more supporters and helping to educate more people in Tulsa. They reserved free rooms at the library for group meetings and worked to create informational pamphlets that delivered facts about the switch so that people could learn about the risks associated with chloramines. Bob and I saw how serious the group was getting, and he flew out to Tulsa several times to meet with both the activists and the city officials to try to educate, spread awareness, and create a bridge between them. He gave a presentation at the very first open public council meeting on the topic and they voted 7–2 to hold off on implementation. They were confused by the discrepancy between his information and what the water department was saying so they arranged for Bob to present directly to the members of the TMUA. But before Bob could come back to town, Jeanine got word that the TMUA was trying to push the decision through before his presentation. Bob came to town early and showed up to the meeting, and the TMUA members just about dropped their jaws. Bob called out their behavior, telling them, "I see what's going on here. You are trying to pass it through before I came to town to give my presentation."

In addition, Jeanine had helped organize more than one hundred Tulsans to come to the meeting to give public comments, but the TMUA crammed so many city officials in there that the fire marshal told everyone the room was at capacity and wouldn't let them in. This meeting was not meant for city officials; it was meant for the residents of Tulsa to voice their opinion. The hallway was flooded with people. Bob did give his presentation and showed other reliable, affordable ways to clean the water, but despite his information and the people who showed up, the TMUA voted to approve chloramines anyway. By the summer of 2012 both the Mohawk Water Treatment Plant and A. B. Jewell Water Treatment Plant had started using chloramines, and they continue to use them today. The city could have set an example for the U.S. and proved that they could stay compliant with EPA standards without the addition of ammonia. They may have found a cheap fix but in the long run they have unraveled other problems with water main breaks, needing to replace pipes and fixtures, and customer complaints about the water.

When I recently talked to Jeanine, who now lives in San Diego, she said that even though they didn't win, she felt like they turned the lights on in her town. She was thankful for the tools she gathered along the way and the validation and support that we provided.

While researching chloramines Jeanine found a list of communities that rejected the use of chloramines:

- Seminole County, Florida: investigated and rejected chloramines.
- Tennessee: discourages its use because they recognize the potential problems but does not forbid it.

- Ohio: requires that the water company prove that they cannot meet EPA regulations without chloramines.
- Leesburg, Virginia: considered and rejected chloramines.
- West View, Pennsylvania: tried chloramines, but had lead issues and now uses it only three months of the year.
- West Columbia, South Carolina: reverted back to chlorine in 2007.
- Charlottesville-Albemarle, Virginia: considered and rejected chloramines.
- Scottsdale and Glendale, Arizona: did not entertain the option of chloramines and went with GAC (granular activated carbon).

She also talked with Randy in Poughkeepsie. She asked him, "Why did you do the conscious thing and decide not to go with chloramines?" He told her, "Because it was the right thing to do and we could do it. I wanted what was best."

It's funny how one of the country's "most livable" cities with all its art, culture, and green space couldn't do what one of the "most miserable" cities did successfully: give their residents clean, safe water and not make them guinea pigs for a questionable water treatment process.

BOILING WATER IN CORPUS CHRISTI

In the humid coastal city of Corpus Christi, Texas, aging infrastructure combined with chloramine use was just one of the issues causing three boil-water orders in the 320,000-person city in less than a year. In May 2016 a two-week citywide order was announced to residents, sparking both public outrage and the resignation of the city manager. The city detected low levels of chlorine in the system, making it risky to drink. My inbox was once again flooded by concerned residents.

Public utilities issue "boil-water orders" as a preventive public health advisory, usually when heightened levels of bacteria are detected in the water. Boiling water helps kill both harmful bacteria and parasites. Residents are usually advised to bring water to a full rolling boil for at least one minute to kill any unwanted organisms. Many people opt to drink and cook with bottled water during an advisory. Either way, telling residents to boil water before they drink it helps make it safe for consumption, but certainly causes a lot of headaches for consumers and city officials alike. An estimated 1,550 boil-water advisories were issued in Texas in 2015, up from about 1,100 in 2012 and 650 in 2008, according to data from the Texas Commission on Environmental Quality.

In the case of this "Texas Riviera" town, the

troubles began in September 2015, when the city switched from chlorine to chloramine, which was billed as a "new disinfectant." But larger problems also existed with deferred maintenance and lack of money to update the system. Another perfect storm! Corpus Christi has 225 miles of cast-iron water pipes, more than half of which need replacement and are vulnerable to decay.

"We historically have not replaced anywhere near what we need to keep up with [the system's] life expectancy and failure rates," Dan Biles, a former Corpus Christi assistant city manager, told the local paper. "You're running on a system strung together and one mistake or problem can be the downfall of the system. Replacing the pipes doesn't make it invulnerable to boil notices, but it does make the system more resilient to mistakes or isolated issues. And it's not just a Corpus Christi issue. We, as a society, need to invest more in our infrastructure."

When my water expert, Bob, visited Corpus Christi, he spoke with city council members, investigated the facilities, and made recommendations. A special city council meeting was called to talk specifically about the water crisis, and at the meeting he told them, "When you see three boil-water notices in nine months, it tells me you're chasing your tail. You are not unique. This is a problem that is happening across the country."

The city formed a water task force in the summer of 2016 in response to the boil advisory and other water issues. Bob recommended not only equipment and system upgrades but also more training on how to use the systems in place. In 1996, the city attempted to use granular activated carbon to filter water, but according to documents from that time, it was a failure because employees didn't understand how to use the product, which caused bacteria levels to skyrocket. In Bob's words, "They couldn't have used it in a worse way." But used properly the same system can replace their current system, which uses an ammonia mixture that can further damage an already ragged system.

The city had more troubles in December 2016 when officials abruptly ordered residents to stop using their tap water altogether due to possible water contamination from an asphalt chemical leak. Unlike the boil-water notices or advisories, residents didn't have the option of boiling their tap water; they had to cease use of all taps. Local government described it as a "back-flow incident in the industrial district," and later confirmed that one of the chemicals was Indulin AA86, a toxic asphalt emulsifying agent known to cause severe burns on skin contact. The announcement caused schools and businesses to close and long lines to snake around grocery stores as residents scrambled to buy bottled water. In total, the ban lasted four days but was lifted when test results showed no contamination from the leak in the water supply. This water crisis, combined with the string of boil-water advisories, left many residents on edge, and public officials on notice that they needed to rebuild trust with their constituents.

Despite all their troubles, as of the writing of this book, the city has been listening to recommendations, allocating more funds to the issue, and making progress. Bob believes that if the city continues down this new path, they could have one of the best water treatment plants in the nation, but ultimately their fate hinges on whether they can keep making choices that will create safe drinking water for all and not cut corners with chloramines.

VOTING CHLORAMINES OUT OF HANNIBAL

Hannibal, Missouri, the childhood home of Mark Twain, is a town of almost eighteen thousand people whose drinking water comes from the Mississippi River. "Whiskey's for drinking; water is for fighting" is a maxim that exemplifies the water issues in this town. In April 2016 two women, fed up with water problems in their hometown, rallied their community, making them the first citizens in the nation to file an ordinance aimed at prohibiting the use of ammonia in their public drinking water system. The city had begun using chloramines to disinfect the water in September 2015. Bob Stevenson, general manager of the Hannibal Board of Public Works, told **The Wall Street Journal** that the ammonia mixture helped the city comply with federal and state regulations for byproducts in drinking water.

"In our view, chloramines are like a miracle cure," he said. "They got us out of a tough problem pretty cheap."

Many citizens were not convinced that chloramines were the answer to the town's water issues, as many factors can contribute to water issues, including not maintaining or upgrading the water system, which can lead to a buildup of naturally occurring organic matter in the water, even when chlorine is the primary disinfectant. Local water tests in Hannibal revealed that two disinfection byproducts—total trihalomethanes (TTHMs) and haloacetic acids (HAAs)—had exceeded federal regulated limits from September 2011 to August 2015. Long-term exposure to water with high levels of THMs is known to cause liver, kidney, or central nervous system problems, along with an increased risk of cancer.

Just like those in other communities who have considered chloramines to help regulate these dangerous byproducts, the people of Hannibal had concerns about both their health and their water quality. They believed their community should be able to vote on whether they wanted ammonia in their water, and they wanted to explore alternative treatments, such as a granular-activated-carbon filtration system, to fix their water woes. At the heart of this community effort were Kellie Cookson and Melissa Cogdal.

Kellie, a forty-seven-year-old lifelong resident of Hannibal, raised her kids and grandkids there and still owns a popular hair salon in town. She admittedly didn't know anything about water for most of her life but told me that her house used to stink like a sewer at times and her kids would complain about the smell. The water would also stain her family's white clothes in the washer. She remembers getting letters in the mail from the Hannibal Board of Public Works (BPW) about issues with the water, but she didn't pay much attention to them.

"I was of the mindset that they do water, and I do hair," she told me. "I thought they were doing the best they could."

She began to take interest in the water in June 2015 when her husband Jay got very sick and was diagnosed with Legionnaire's disease, a waterborne bacterial infection that kills one in ten people who contract it. Legionnaire's feels like a bad pneumonia and is still relatively rare—close to ten thousand cases were documented by the CDC in 2017. But incidence of Legionnaire's is on the rise, almost doubling from 2016 to 2017. A **Legionella** outbreak with ninety-one confirmed cases contributed to twelve deaths reported by Michigan health officials during the Flint water crisis, with more suspected deaths still in question. Another outbreak at California's Disneyland in December 2017 made headlines when nine people who visited the theme park got sick, and the number of cases has been rising in communities in Connecticut, New York, Ohio, North Carolina, and Florida.

Legionnaire's is not contagious; people contract it by breathing in droplets of water contaminated with **Legionella pneumophilia** bacteria. Some of these cases can be traced to water systems where conditions are favorable for bacterial growth, such as cooling towers, hot tubs, humidifiers, and large air-conditioning systems, but CDC research has shown that people can easily be exposed to **Legionella** from hot water that comes out of faucets and showerheads. Kellie still does not know how her husband contracted it. In fact, the only reason Jay was diagnosed was because the doctor treating him at the hospital had recently read an article about Legionnaire's in **Reader's Digest**. Jay had been admitted for pneumonia, but his high fever and hallucinations prompted the doctor to run the test. After Jay was released from the hospital, his health problems persisted. He got pneumonia every month for the next seven months. When he got sick in July, only a month after being in the hospital, Kellie decided she needed to learn more.

"Every time he would get pneumonia, I was fearful that it was **Legionella,** because that's how it started the first time," she said. "None of the doctors around here could tell me anything about it. They really didn't know a lot."

She contacted her local health department to see if they would be willing to test the water and conduct a thorough investigation of her home and her shop. She wanted more information so she could protect the rest of her family, but they refused to help. The woman at the health department told her, "Since he did not die and no one else is sick, there's absolutely nothing we will do."

Those words just rang in her head. "I feel like they were saying he didn't matter," Kellie said.

She wrote the sentence "Since he did not die and no one else is sick, there's absolutely nothing we will do" on a piece of paper and let it fuel her, over and over. On staying motivated, she said, "If I ever got tired or wanted to quit, I would just read that statement."

Jay's life did matter to his family. They had accumulated thousands of dollars in hospital bills and were no closer to understanding where his illness came from or if he was ever going to get sick like that again. Kellie was required to call the CDC to report Jay's case of Legionnaire's, and they too declined to perform any investigation. She decided to take matters into her own hands. Kellie started studying water issues to the point where she was up all hours of the night. She converted her daughter's old bedroom into what she called her "water room." While researching, she would come across so many unfamiliar words that she had to look them up one by one.

"I would literally put a word on the wall and then dissect it and break it down to the point where the room had words all over it. Every time I would read something new, I would have to go back and look up what that word meant," she said. "This didn't come easy to me. I had to dissect six words out of one sentence because it was like a foreign language to me."

She did most of her research online, reading as many articles as she could find. At first, she didn't know what to believe. For every article that sounded like chloramines were bad, she would read another describing about how they have been used for years without problems. Then she heard that water expert Bob Bowcock was coming to town, so she decided to attend the public forum and get more information. Bob was invited to speak by another group of people in town who were also upset about the state of their water. About halfway through his presentation, he started hitting on **Legionella** and Legionnaire's disease, which turned on a light for Kellie.

"He had never met me or talked to me, so he didn't know that my husband had been sick with it," she said. "A lot of people in town didn't know either. I stuck around after and talked to him. I knew from the moment I walked out of the American Legion that I was going to do something about it."

Kellie had seen an old friend from school at the meeting: Melissa Cogdal. When she ran into her a few days later at a festival downtown, she asked, "Hey, how interested are you in the water and this whole chloramine thing?"

Melissa, a forty-six-year-old mother of two, describes her family as typical middle-class Americans. She and her husband have been married for twenty-seven years, and they have always been active in their community, though not necessarily political. She had custody of her nephew Christian, who was living with her family, and she was worried about how chloramines would affect his health. His mother had died of kidney disease and he had tested positive for the precursors to the disease. When she researched chloramines, she discovered they could be especially dangerous for people with kidney issues.

Melissa says her water has had a strong smell

for as long as she can remember. She recalls getting out-of-compliance notices as well but didn't think the chemicals involved could hurt her family or her home appliances. She said the notices were written to be very reassuring to the customer and didn't make the problems seem alarming. The sentiment was "Everything is fine. You can continue to drink your water." She was very trusting of her utility system at that point. Melissa was also one of the many Hannibal residents who voted on a bond referendum in 2013 to raise money for upgrades to the water and sewage treatment system. They approved a $13 million water bond and a $9 million sewer bond to help finance improvements through low-interest revenue bonds.

"I knew that the issues were being addressed and that these things take time," Melissa said. But once she got the notice about the city using chloramines to disinfect the water, she was confused. They had voted to spend millions of dollars on upgrades and yet they were proposing the cheapest option. Where had all the money gone?

The women decided to team up and work together on the issue. Kellie called a friend who had a way with words and told her she needed a name for a new water group. Two hours later, they had it: Hannibal to Oppose Chloramines or H20-C. Now with a name, Melissa and Kellie started a Facebook group and began centralizing their information, raising awareness, and gathering supporters. Kellie described to me a lot of late-night phone calls between the two of them, since they both had kids and jobs to tend to during the day. They started attending board of public works meetings and city council meetings. They felt it was important to work with the system and beside their local officials.

"We wanted to work with them and try to get them involved, not go after them," Kellie said.

Unfortunately, they were not met with open arms. They described their experience at meetings as uncomfortable, with BPW members talking down to them and asking if they had degrees. The board dismissed them as moms, not experts. But the chilly response only fueled their fire and helped them to work harder and find more solid research to present. I can certainly relate to their struggle! For every door that has been slammed in my face, another one gets opened somewhere else. At this point, Bob and I encouraged them not to back down and to keep going to meetings.

Looking for ways to move forward, Melissa, upset, called her councilman, looking for more options. He tipped her off to a new direction that could initiate change when he said, "If you don't like the answer that council is giving, you can always start a petition and put it on the ballot and let the voters decide."

Within two days, Melissa had learned everything about how to write and submit a petition. The women could write one to oppose adding ammonia to treat the water. If they could get 10 percent of voters in Hannibal to sign it, then the city council could vote on it. If the council opted not to vote, the issue would automatically go to the ballot as a referendum, which is when the general population can vote on a single issue and get it written into law. Not all states allow it, but Missouri is one that does. Melissa, Kellie, and Jay (and a few others) hit the streets going door-to-door to get the 1,100 signatures needed. They attended big events in town and spent time at the park to connect with as many people as possible. Within four months, they had written the proposal and collected all the signatures they needed. No citizen-driven petition had ever gone in front of the city council before, and they could have voted it in to become a city ordinance. Not wanting to ruffle any feathers with the board of public works, council members let the petition sit for sixty days with no action. They didn't read it or act on it in any way. By law, the issue then went to the ballot.

Meanwhile, Melissa's councilman in the Third Ward, Kevin Lionberger, resigned in September 2016. Immediately, many people in town, knowing her involvement with the water question, encouraged her to run for that seat. She thought it was a crazy idea, and that she didn't know enough to run, but she was angry. She had lived in Hannibal all her life and felt like none of the elected officials cared about her concerns about the water and the health of her nephew.

"I decided to do it," she told me. "I never dreamed in a million years that I would get it and here's why: because a seat had been vacated, it was up to the current council members to appoint another member until the election."

Melissa had spent the previous few months showing up at their meetings and putting them on the hot seat and now she was asking to sit next to them. But the only other people who signed up for the position were even less qualified—one person had just recently moved to Hannibal and didn't know about the water issues.

At this point it was September 2016, and the election wasn't until April 2017. Much to her surprise, Melissa got appointed to the seat. When she found out, she was stunned. Her first council meeting was in October and when she ran in the April election she won with about 87 percent of the vote.

Before the election, the **Hannibal Courier-Post** interviewed her, and this was her response to the question: Why are you running for city council?

Having spent much time at city hall the last year, I decided to step up and serve my community. Having lived in Hannibal all my life I recognize its strengths and weakness. I have felt the same hardships and struggles as my neighbors with decaying neighborhoods, streets, and infrastructure. I have been affected by job loss, drug addiction, and abandoned buildings left in the middle of neighborhoods. I also appreciate the history and beauty of our river town. I would like to help bridge the gap between citizens and administration. Making ideas, concerns, and programs work to improve our community and neighborhoods. Giving the citizens a voice then working together for improved living conditions for our residents.

When we talked more about joining the council, she said she thought people were excited to see somebody who wasn't afraid to say and do things differently. Melissa said getting appointed gave her slightly more sway with the board of public works too. When she asked for a piece of information, they had to give it to her. But she did have to give up her work with Kellie and H20-C, and she couldn't campaign specifically for the ammonia issue. The two stayed in touch as friends while Melissa maintained ethical standards for her new position.

Hosting a town meeting with Bob Bowcock in 2017
at the clubroom of the American Legion in Hannibal,
Missouri, to help citizens understand the risks associated
with putting ammonia in their drinking water

By January 2017, Kellie had started to campaign
in a big way for Proposition 1, which was essentially a chemical reduction act. Voters would be
asked to say yes or no to ammonia in their water.
Like other towns, Kellie and others created bright
red signs for people to display on their lawns and
at businesses that said, "Vote Yes on Prop 1" to
help get the word out.

"Every neighborhood had our signs in it," Kellie
said. "We were just seeing them everywhere."

Creating a Facebook group was an effective
tool for helping spread the word and getting

more people to put up signs. While most group members were supportive, Kellie did have to deal with naysayers and those who were not in favor of Prop 1 on the social network too. In every community, you have people who are not willing to look at the gaps in the research and who think that those who oppose chloramine use are troublemakers. She endured personal attacks on her character and her family, but Kellie said she stuck to the facts and did not engage with smear campaigns. Bob and I came to Hannibal for another town meeting to help educate the community about the proposition and offer more facts so voters could make an informed decision. That same week the city sponsored their own forum with an engineering firm they had hired to research the issue. Hannibal officials commissioned a study from Jacobs Engineering, an independent firm, to look at the cost and feasibility of a granular-activated-carbon system to clean the water and help meet EPA standards. The engineers also told residents that getting rid of ammonia would create cleaner, safer water and help extend the lifespan of home plumbing and appliances.

On April 4, 2017, voters showed up to the polls in Hannibal and the ordinance passed by a vote of 1,259 to 894, giving the BPW ninety days to stop using ammonia to treat the city's drinking water. This shows exactly the kind of impact everyday citizens can have simply by standing up, just like the Margaret Mead quote: "Never doubt that a small group of thoughtful, committed citizens can change the world; indeed, it's the only thing that ever has."

"We have worked very hard and have had many doors slammed in our face, but each time, we got back up and proceeded forward," Kellie said about the election. She and other organizers celebrated at a local restaurant that night, and I posted on Facebook to celebrate with them.

April 5, 2017

You say you want a REVOLUTION . . . weeeeeellllllllll you know . . . In the United States of America, we do it at the ballot box. It's hard, it's mean, it gets ugly . . . but in Hannibal, Missouri, last night it worked.

The Drinking Water Revolution has begun. No longer will consumers just be served unsafe Drinking Water and be told—tough, it meets the regulations. No longer will we be lied to. This is about information. This is about TRUTH. This is about action. Who wants to be next?

Unfortunately, the story does not end here. Justice comes with many nuances. In May of that same year, the BPW board of directors held a meeting to discuss an alternative treatment plan, one that would exclude chloramines, which had been submitted by yet another group of engineers. The proposal estimated that initial testing would not be complete until December and that the whole process of switching away from chloramines would take at least two years. When the board notified the Department of Natural Resources (DNR) about its intent to stop using ammonia as a disinfectant, DNR officials refused to approve it. They needed a water system plan with a proposed alternative treatment process. Even with public support, the city had a lot of red tape to work through to make the switch.

On July 17, 2017, the Hannibal Board of Public Works filed a lawsuit against the City of Hannibal to stop the enforcement of Prop 1, alleging that the ordinance was unenforceable because of its conflict with state law. Not exactly the route I would have chosen for them, but here's local politics in action. Hannibal BPW board president Randy Park released this statement:

> If the Board removes the ammonia from the disinfection process as required by Proposition 1, Board members could be subject to prosecution and fines and penalties for violation of state environmental statutes and regulations. Also, certified

operators that directly manage the treatment system will be subject to suspension or revocation of their certifications from DNR. On the other hand, if the Board complies with state statutes and refuses to remove the ammonia from the treatment process, Board members and employees operating the water treatment and distribution system will be subject to municipal fines or penalties. The Board and its employees are subject to fines or penalties whether they enforce the ordinance or not and the ordinance is unjust.

Melissa said this lawsuit was a pivotal moment in her journey. She had now been elected by the people and was tasked with protecting her constituents. They were depending on her to make a sound decision. It was an excruciating time for her. As a council member, she knew that the lawsuit could drag on for years, and she didn't want to cost the taxpayers hundreds of thousands of dollars in attorney fees. On a personal level, she wanted the chloramines out of the water as soon as possible.

"I knew that they were going to try to get a judge that knew nothing about Hannibal and cared nothing about Hannibal to make this decision on everything that Kellie and I and others had done to get the ammonia removed," Melissa told me.

She knew there was a good chance that the judge could rule that the ordinance or its timeline was unconstitutional. The city now had to hire an attorney because they had the same attorney as the BPW. Once they hired a new attorney to represent the citizens and the city, the council met with him to discuss every possible outcome that could come from the lawsuit. One way forward became clear: if the council rewrote the ordinance and passed it into law, the courts wouldn't be able to fight it. Melissa felt like that was the only way to keep the fight for clean water alive.

The council kept the Prop 1 wording intact, except that the ninety-day clause was pushed to twenty-four months, along with some leeway for pilot testing, which Melissa tried to fight. They also added a provision that Bob Stevenson had to update the council and the community every ninety days until the new system was in place.

"If we let that lawsuit go on, we'd be nowhere," Melissa said. "We would all be sitting around waiting for our next court date."

While Melissa took heat from many in her community, she learned a valuable lesson. Once you get involved in these issues, you realize all the complications in dealing with politics, legal matters, and more. Sometimes you end up fighting for the best possible scenario, and a lot of times it might feel like a no-win scenario. You might have to compromise, but at least you keep going. From the outside, it may look like you are dragging your feet but in truth you are keeping the issues at play. Melissa was able to bring a lot of awareness to the council and to city officials, helping them see another point of view instead of just the one from the utility company.

"Listen, the ammonia is going to be removed," Melissa told me. "They have until January of 2020

Bob Bowcock meeting the moms who became
water warriors in Hannibal, Missouri, in 2016,
and the first citizens in the nation to file an
ordinance aimed at prohibiting the use of ammonia
in their public drinking water system

to do it. I truly believe when this is over, we will have the cleanest water in the U.S."

Her advice to others looking to get involved in their community? Be willing to sacrifice time with your family, knowing that you are working to create a better life for them. Be sure to remind yourself why you started in the first place and keep that thought front and center.

"When I started working on this issue, I had always voted and educated myself on the issues, but I couldn't tell you the difference between an ordinance and a charter," she said. "Now, I've learned so much. Don't be afraid to put yourself out there and run for those offices because you might just win."

On February 20, 2018, the directors of the Hannibal Board of Public Works unanimously decided to move forward with a granulated-activated-carbon system for the city. The new water treatment facility is expected to be up and running by March 2020.

COLUMBIA'S SAFE WATER COALITION

Every Monday morning at 9 a.m., Julie Walsh Ryan and Marie-Josee Brown meet at their local coffeehouse in Columbia, Missouri, just a two-hour drive away from the activists in Hannibal. They are the founders of COMO Safe Water Coalition (CSWC), a group created to discuss and improve their city's water quality. Since 2009, Columbia Water and Light has used chloramines to disinfect its drinking water and to control high levels of trihalomethanes. The city uses free chlorine in the summer months when the weather is warm, and then switches to chloramines the rest of the year. But both women took interest in their water to get to the bottom of health problems they and their children were having.

Julie and her family moved to Columbia in 2010 from North Carolina. In 2013, she was diagnosed with breast cancer. Though her cancer is now in remission, she couldn't help but wonder what might have caused her illness. Less than 10 percent of breast cancer cases can be traced to genetic factors, and she did not test positive for any mutations. But she did take notice when I posted on Facebook in 2015 about Columbia's water being treated with chloramines to combat high levels of trihalomethanes, which show carcinogenic activity in lab animals. Many factors could have contributed to her diagnosis, but she wasn't the only one with health issues. She started talking to other women in her neighborhood who were also dealing with breast cancer. Her kids had itchy, burning skin after showers and started having allergies—symptoms they had not exhibited in North Carolina.

When she received a boil-water advisory that lasted for two weeks straight in the summer of 2016, she knew it was a red flag and she committed to calling the city, doing more research, and speaking to the media to get answers about the water. The city said the advisory was related to irrigation, but Julie wanted more information. Meanwhile, Marie had known Julie from around town and was also concerned about the water. Her daughter was dealing with dry skin, severe migraines, and asthma. She suspected the water was not helping with any of it. They decided to team up, start meeting regularly, and make a Facebook group for the COMO Safe Water Coalition, which now has more than 350 members.

Like the women in Hannibal, they made it a priority to work with their local officials to start more conversations about the water quality to enact change. They have attended meetings with the mayor, the city manager, the city council, and the water advisory board. But they also met with resistance. Since Columbia falls into the category of compliance with EPA standards, it's harder for some officials to understand why chloramines may not work for all of the city's 120,000 residents.

In a 2016 letter to the mayor, the city's public drinking water branch chief, David Lamb, wrote:

Currently, 2.5 million citizens, or roughly half of the Missourians who are customers of a community water system, use water that is disinfected through chloramination. Chloramination is a common disinfectant technology used throughout the country and the world. It is the most common solution implemented by public water systems working to prevent the formation of disinfection byproducts.

As previously mentioned, each community has discretion to decide what treatment process it would like to utilize, as long as the technology is safe and will effectively provide treatment in all conditions. It is our opinion that, as long as the city properly operates and maintains its system, chloramination will prove to be an acceptable method for addressing the city's problems with disinfection byproducts.

Another issue the women hope to change is how the water is classified. Currently, Columbia's drinking water comes from wells that tap into an aquifer beneath land bordering the Missouri River and is classified as groundwater. But groundwater that sits close to surface water, such as a river, is at a higher risk of contamination and requires more stringent EPA treatment requirements. Julie and

Marie believe their water source should be reclassi-
fied as "groundwater under the direct influence of
surface water." This switch would help the city as
it moves forward with new treatment methods to
disinfect the water. Right now, the drinking water
has high turbidity, which makes the water look
cloudy and is a potential indication of pollution.
Turbidity is caused by tiny particles in the water
that can come from algae, dirt, minerals, proteins,
oils, or bacteria. EPA standards don't require turbidity treatments for groundwater, but they do for
groundwater under the direct influence of surface
water.

"We feel it's very short-sighted to plan for this
treatment plant to expand and be upgraded without ensuring that it is built to process water that is
classified as under the influence of surface water,"
Julie told her local paper.

Setting a regular meeting time has helped the
women connect with others in their community
who were interested in getting involved or learning more. They have had journalism students,
engineers, and other moms join them. It also
helped them to connect with Dr. Enos Inniss, a
civil and environmental engineering professor at
the University of Missouri, who is also a member of the university's Water Resources Research
Center and an expert in water treatment process
design and control. He invited them to sit in on his

classes so they could better understand issues like how chlorine and ammonia act in water, the difference between groundwater and surface water, and other water quality issues. He also sends relevant articles their way and helps answer questions when they reach roadblocks in their own understanding of these complicated topics. Marie says that many nights she takes her research to bed, starting at 8 p.m. and reading until 1 a.m.

The CSWC women have focused on little wins since their inception. They have researched the wastewater and stormwater initiatives in Columbia and looked into infrastructure improvements and financial requirements. Marie was asked to represent the group on a panel for a presentation by Missouri River Relief. It was a great opportunity to highlight the work of CSWC and show the respect the group has gained in the community. Julie was appointed to a Drinking Water Planning Work Group for the city, whose work helped pass a $42.8 million water bond issue in the 2018 primary, funding improvements to the city's water treatment plant.

They both continue to make their voices heard in the community by attending various city meetings. They still hold weekly coffee gatherings, where they focus on research and talking with concerned citizens. COMO Safe Water Coalition celebrated its three-year anniversary at the end of

2019. Though they still have work ahead, these partners are energized knowing the work they do is making a difference.

ACTION STEPS
Attend Meetings

As you can see from these stories, one of the best steps to getting involved in local politics is simply to show up to your public meetings. It could be a city council, a board of supervisors, a public works commission, or whatever it is called in your town or city. Decisions about local policies, whether it's raising taxes, funding new parks, or approving new water treatment techniques, are made at these meetings. We need to show up. Have you ever been to one? They are in there just talking to themselves. Most of the time it's a small group deciding on issues for the whole town. You need to tell them what's going on. Tell them what you care about. What would it look like to start showing up en masse to these meetings? I think we would see more democracy in action.

City council meetings are set up to be a public affair, so anyone and everyone is welcome. You can access the agenda at your city hall, on the city's official website, or often at your local library. You can add agenda items, usually by submitting written or verbal comments to the city clerk. You can also request a speaker card at the meeting and speak about any agenda item already listed (usually you only get a few minutes, so be sure to do your homework before you attend). Remember that every member on your council has been voted in by your community to represent the people, so they are there to listen to your opinions. Most of these meetings are happening throughout the country with too many open seats, but I'd like to see that change. I recommend just going to a meeting to see how it works. You might be surprised how much you will learn about what's really happening in your town.

You can also create your own meetings. If the thought of researching these issues on your own is daunting, start your own study group with a friend or friends in your community. Each person can take on one aspect of the local water issues, such as understanding the chemicals found in your water quality report or understanding your water source, and then you can report back to your group. Imagine if you were to meet regularly like the women in Columbia and then take informed questions and ideas for action with you to the next city council meeting.

Cut the Noise

The first thing anyone needs to become a water warrior (or activist of any kind) is to assess what you believe and care about, which can't happen unless you learn to "cut out the noise." The noise is all around us these days, from what's happening in the news or on social media to the meeting you had with your boss or the issues your kids might be having at school. We all have a lot going on. As someone who has been at this work for a long time, I want to tell you that you need to engage in self-renewal first. For me, it's taking the time to look at the sunset or watching my granddaughters play in the yard. What could it look like for you? A short meditation practice? An adult coloring book? Do what you can to hear your own voice, whether it's playing a round of golf or getting a spa treatment. Take the time to reboot as often as you can so that you can carry on with your cause.

Managing Pushback

You might notice a common thread in the stories of these water warriors. Despite what people said to them or even their own fears and doubts, they kept fighting for what they believed in. It's so important to listen to your own instincts and not to get bogged down by other people's opinions. The most important rule when it comes to other people is not to take their opinions personally. Remember, everyone has an agenda.

Usually, the people who are the most critical of my work are the ones who have the most to hide. Think about it. A city like Poughkeepsie welcomes tours of their plant and speaks about how they have learned from their mistakes. But the cities and companies that are misappropriating funds or intentionally covering up pollution or other problems are the ones who will try to take you down. They will use harsh language or personal attacks in an attempt to discredit you. They benefit when no one holds them accountable. I've learned over the years that the more pushback I get, the more I know there's a story to uncover. The truth always comes out, and it starts with your voice. Don't be afraid to speak out and keep asking the hard questions.

Know Your Why

Knowing what you stand for is one of the most liberating feelings in the world. I would not have made it this far in my career without knowing why I fly all over the country or stay up late in strange cities talking to the local people about how they can enact change in their town. Take a moment now to get crystal-clear by asking yourself a few simple questions and write down your answers.

- Why do I want to join this cause to fight for clean, safe water?
- Who will it impact?
- What vision do I have for myself and my family for the future?

Once you know your why, consider sharing it with three people you are close to in the next few weeks. When you say something out loud, it gives the statement even more power. Maybe they will share their "why" with you too.

Here's mine for some inspiration:

I am an advocate for awareness, the truth, and a person's right to know. I believe that in the absence of the truth, all of us stand helpless to defend ourselves, our families, and our health, which is the greatest gift we have.

8

LOCAL POLITICS RUN AMOK

It was the summer of 2014 when LeeAnne Walters, a thirty-seven-year-old mother of four, realized something was terribly wrong with her water. Every time her kids took a bath or swam in their pool, they broke out in tiny red bumps. Like any concerned mom, she went to the pediatrician. At first, she got the diagnosis of dermatitis. The doctor thought her children's skin was reacting to some kind of allergen. When it didn't clear up, she went back to the doctor's office and came home with a second diagnosis: eczema. This time she had a cortisone cream to rub right on the rashes. When that didn't work, she was told it must be scabies. After three diagnoses and the kids' skin still erupting in red bumps, she realized it might be something their skin came in contact with every day. When the water started flowing out brown from her taps, even with a water filter, she started stocking up on bottled water, about forty gallons a week for drinking, cooking, and bathing. The red bumps went away, but a bigger problem was brewing. LeeAnne's home became what is now considered ground zero in the Flint, Michigan, water crisis. To understand what turned her water toxic, you have to look at what was happening in the state of Michigan at that time.

Governor Rick Snyder, elected in 2010, started assigning emergency managers to take the place of elected officials in cash-strapped cities throughout the state. Snyder and the Republican-led legislature passed a bill in 2011 officially called the "Local Government and School District Fiscal Accountability Act," but known to many as the "Emergency Manager Bill," essentially replacing government officials elected by the people with Snyder's political appointees. The new law gave these high-paid managers unprecedented powers, such as taking over pension systems, setting school schedules, and removing elected officials from office. In the law's own words, the managers were allowed to "exercise any power or authority of any officer, employee, department, board, commission, or other similar entity of the local government whether elected or appointed."

Michael Brown, who was born and raised in Flint and served as temporary mayor in 2009, became the city's emergency manager (EM) in November 2011. In his first few days, he eliminated pay for the mayor and city council, laid off key city officials, and even shut down some city offices. He was the first in a series of four emergency managers appointed to help mend Flint's economic challenges. At the time, the city's unemployment rate of nearly 20 percent was one of the highest in the state, the population was declining, and the city was operating with a consistent deficit in its general fund.

An elected official dealing with issues in their district has to answer to the people, while an emergency manager is accountable only to the governor. EMs are charged with saving money at all costs, while being paid six figures to do it. Brown's salary in Flint was approximately $170,000 a year. And he was not alone. These managers were appointed to many cities, and residents throughout the state were not happy about it. By 2012, Michigan voters had repealed the emergency manager law, ousting Brown in Flint for a time, but just six weeks later the legislature passed a new bill that was nearly identical to the original one. Flint put a new manager in his place, Ed Kurtz, who originally kicked off the exploration of how the city could save money on its water bill. The plan was to stop buying water from the Detroit Water and Sewerage Department, which had been steadily increasing its rates.

Darnell Earley, the emergency manager from October 2013 through January 2015, took the reins in Flint and promised bold steps to address the city's continuing problems. He made the final decision to switch the water source away from Detroit's water system, which drew its source water from Lake Huron, the third-largest body of freshwater in the world. Flint would join the Karegnondi Water Authority (KWA), requiring the city to build its own pipeline to transport water from Lake Huron into the city.

As a temporary drinking water solution, the city resurrected the Flint Water Service Center (FWSC). The center was maintained for years as a backup facility, but that's not the same as being equipped to supply water to 100,000 residents. In addition, the Flint River would become the city's main water source while the pipeline was built. The river flows through the center of town and served as the main drinking water source for residents from the 1880s until the 1960s, when the city began buying water from the Detroit system.

For years, Flint's river was inundated with unregulated industrial waste, starting with lumber mills in the 1800s, then paper mills at the turn of the twentieth century, and finally, General Motors automotive factories before World War II. As the population swelled in Flint and the river accumulated more toxins, it made sense to find a cleaner, more reliable water source. The Flint River also has two important differences from Lake Huron:

it's warmer and its flow is less constant. Both factors make it friendly to bacterial growth and rising levels of organic matter. With high concentrations of bacteria and organics, the river water would require extra chlorine to properly clean it. Chlorine can react with organics in the water, causing the amount of disinfection byproduct trihalomethanes (THMs) to skyrocket. Flint also has an antiquated lead pipe system, which is reactive to treatment chemicals like chlorine and can cause major corrosion.

Some local experts did express concerns about switching to the river as the city's water source. Brian Larkin, then associate director of the Governor's Office of Urban and Metropolitan Initiatives, sent an email message to others in the governor's office, writing, "The expedited timeframe is less than ideal and could lead to some big potential disasters down the road."

The water quality supervisor at FWSC, Mike Glasgow, also said in an April 2014 email sent to the State of Michigan Department of Environmental Quality (MDEQ), "I do not anticipate giving the okay to begin sending water out anytime soon. If water is distributed from this plant in the next couple weeks, it will be against my direction."

That is exactly what happened.

Flint River water started flowing through the city's pipes in April 2014. The switch was estimated to save the city millions of dollars. Flint mayor Dayne Walling called it "regular, good, pure drinking water, and it's right in our backyard. This is the first step in the right direction for Flint, and we take this monumental step forward in controlling the future of our community's most precious resource."

By May, almost immediately after the switch, residents started complaining about both the smell and the color of the water. In August and September, the city issued three boil-water advisories after high levels of bacteria were detected. In October, General Motors announced its plans to stop using the water because it was corroding auto parts. The company negotiated a private deal to buy Lake Huron water for its Flint plant. GM was one of the largest water consumers in town, so the city was now looking at the loss of close to half a million dollars a year.

In January 2015, residents were issued another notice, alerting them to high levels of THMs detected in the water. When LeeAnne received this notification in the mail, she decided to attend her first city council meeting. Many of the city's residents were showing up to these meetings, reporting the same problems with their water—strange odors and colors. They described health problems ranging from rashes to hair loss to neurological conditions. While the city continued to assure residents that the water was safe to drink, common sense told them otherwise.

Through persistent calls, LeeAnne got through to water utility manager Mike Glasgow, who agreed to test her water. At this point, the water coming out of her sink had an orange hue. Service center employees went out that week to flush the hydrants, as per procedure. But a week later the water color was unchanged, so he tested the water at her faucet. The results came back at about 104 ppb for lead, when the legal limit is 15 ppb. He instructed her not to drink, cook, or brush her teeth with the water at those levels. If she was going to shower or wash dishes, he told her to run the water for up to fifteen minutes first, as flushing the water would help to lower lead levels. At a follow-up test a week later, the numbers had more than tripled.

By March 2015, the Flint City Council voted 7–1 to stop using the river water and reconnect with Detroit's system, but Jerry Ambrose, the emergency manager in place at that time, overruled the vote and issued the following statement:

> Flint water today is safe by all (U.S. Environmental Protection Agency) and (Michigan Department of Environmental Quality) standards, and the city is working daily to improve its quality. Users also pay some of

the highest rates in the state because of the decreased numbers of users and the age of the system.

It is incomprehensible to me that (seven) members of the Flint City Council would want to send more than $12 million a year to the system serving Southeast Michigan, even if Flint rate payers could afford it. (Lake Huron) water from Detroit is no safer than water from Flint.

I started receiving emails from Flint around this time. One day, more than thirty emails stacked up in my inbox from people living in Flint. Hundreds more poured in. What stood out most to me were the pictures of the water coming out of the faucet. It was yellow, brown, orange, and mucky. If we saw this kind of water running from taps in a developing country, we would send aid. People were reporting health issues to me, such as rashes and diarrhea, and they were scared for their children's health.

Melissa Mays, a mom to three boys, was one of the first people to email me. The water at her house was coming out of the faucet yellow. She said depending on the day, it would smell like rotten eggs, dirt, or bleach. Her family started developing rashes and having clumps of hair fall out. Her young boys were complaining about muscle and bone aches. Even their cat was throwing up and losing fur in large clumps. Melissa started talking to her neighbors, who said they were having the same issues. These symptoms started shortly after the city switched the drinking water source, which is an important observation.

I sent my water quality expert, Bob Bowcock, to test the water. He was on a plane one day after I forwarded him a few of these emails. Bob found high levels of chlorine in the water supply, much more than levels found in a swimming pool! Levels that high are certainly known to create rashes, but not such drastic changes in water color or odor. One of the biggest missteps in Flint was to not add corrosion-controlling chemicals at the water treatment plant. Officials at the MDEQ have since admitted that it was "a disastrous mistake when they failed to require the city to add corrosion-control chemicals as part of the treatment process."

The corrosive water caused lead to leach from pipes, joints, and fixtures. Flint eventually reconnected to the Detroit water system in October 2015, after nearly a year and a half of denial, and once major damage was already done to the antiquated water infrastructure system, not to mention all the people drinking the water. Fire departments became bottled water distribution centers; police officers went door-to-door handing out bottled water and water filters. Yet, all of it was preventable. For almost eighteen months, people were told to relax and that nothing was wrong, but it all proved to be lies and cover-up.

I called out the water problems in Flint a year before it became a media frenzy. Flint Water Treatment Plant employees were responsible for operating the water supply and purification system, plain and simple. Responsibility for the crisis and cover-up was in the hands of those operating the water municipality, the local officials, and all the way up to Governor Rick Snyder.

In a Facebook post, I wrote:

January 20, 2015
Dangerous Undrinkable Drinking Water
Flint, Michigan, adds its name to the list of hundreds of cities, towns and community water systems that are failing. Bottom line, they have made many bad choices . . . and yet there are real solutions.
EXCUSES . . . EXCUSES . . . EXCUSES
Until the Safe Drinking Water Act is really enforced . . . Drinking Water in the United States will be equal to a third world country.
Today, Mayor Dayne Walling says access to clean, safe, affordable water is a basic human right, and Governor Rick Snyder has

the responsibility for helping to deliver it. Now is not the time for the blame game . . . Detroit has failed, and Flint jumped ship. So much for local control . . . Everyone is responsible from the top down: USEPA, Michigan Department of Environmental Quality, the State of Michigan and the local officials.

Within a year Susan Hedman, the EPA's regional administrator; Dan Wyant, the director of Michigan's Department of Environmental Quality (DEQ); and Brad Wurfel, MDEQ spokesperson, had resigned from their posts. The governor had issued a public apology vowing to fix the situation, but the people were left with the mess. The response to my post from the public was huge! Thousands of people from all over the country commented, especially people from Flint.

One woman wrote: "I live in Flint and over the past 3 months just showering has caused my skin to break out in rashes all over. Can't drink the water and boiling it does not help, it actually makes it taste worse. We have to buy any water we drink or risk getting sick. Both my grandkids have had repeated bouts of diarrhea when they drink the water because we have run out of bottled. Flint charges insane rates for water we can't even use. Help us please!"

Another woman wrote: "My father lives in Flint, he's 85 years old and the city sent him a letter telling him that elderly people are advised not to drink the water. We have been buying him water from the store for a couple of years now, thank God he can afford to do that. But what happens to the elderly and the mothers of infant children that are advised not to drink the water that can't afford to pay for store bought water? And by the way, my father lives alone, and his water bill is $100 a month for something he cannot drink."

Another wrote: "It is sad that in a state surrounded by freshwater lakes, the 'great lakes,' we don't have any clean healthy water to drink."

In February 2015, Bob toured the city's water treatment plant and did more investigation into documents related to the water source switch. After his assessments, he sent a letter to the mayor, the water municipality, and the Flint City Council, outlining his recommendations.

They included the following:

- Update and implement the Source Water Protection Plan.
- Define and identify groundwater quality and quantity inflow variables to the Flint River, specifically from the contaminated sources identified adjacent to the river.
- Define and identify reservoir release

surface water quality and quantity variables to the Flint River, specifically from the Holloway Reservoir.

- Thoroughly evaluate the Detroit Water Supply quality characteristics.
- Conduct a detailed "cost of treatment assessment" of the Flint River Water Treatment Plant and compare it directly to the cost per unit of water purchased from Detroit. Publish said results and allow for public input as to the choice of water supplied based upon actual costs versus quality.
- Optimize the ozone disinfection system.
  - Discontinue the use of sodium bisulfate to reduce pH in the ozone contact chamber.
  - Trust the Plant Operator to use the optimum amount of ferric chloride required for coagulation.
  - Investigate the use (jar tests) of ferric chloride and various water treatment polymers to reduce the use of corrosive ferric chloride.
  - Discontinue the practice of lime softening. Continue the flow through the softener facility and consider adding a low dose of filter aid (additional polymer) as necessary during seasonal high turbidity.

- Discontinue the practice of fluoridation.
- Discontinue the practice of re-carbonation.
- Discontinue the use of pre-filtration chlorine.
- Remove the anthracite coal media from the filter beds and replace it with a granular activated carbon (GAC) material. There are specifically engineered products for use in dual media filters. The use of GAC for organic Trihalomethanes (THM) precursor removal will immediately reduce THM formation in the drinking water supply.
- Post chlorinate disinfect based on residual demand requirements. Post chlorination will not be as intensive as the organic material will be dramatically reduced. The GAC will also serve as a barrier to other types of contamination events (petroleum, chemical, and algae blooms).
- Distribution System Operations
  - Complete development of the water distribution hydraulic flow model.
  - Immediately increase distribution system velocities.

– Re-engineer the distribution system
   to encourage directional sediment
   transport for evacuation of system
   contaminates (sludge, biofilm,
   sediment, and other debris). This
   will further aid in chlorine demand
   management.

- Take at least one of the water system
  storage reservoirs out of service.
  Thoroughly clean the storage reservoir,
  perhaps a program of alternative years of
  service. With the 2 MG elevated tank,
  perhaps both reservoirs could be removed
  from service this year.

- Prepare a budget that accounts for
  all fixed/variable debts: loans, capital
  depreciation of infrastructure, retirement
  system obligations, etc. This will allow
  the community to understand exactly
  where it stands in relation to its debt
  obligations . . . before one drop of water
  is produced. The total of the compilation
  can then be divided among the consumers
  based on number and class size of services.
  It is simple, straightforward, and easily
  understood.

- Prepare a budget that accounts for all
  commodity/variable costs: salaries,
  chemicals, energy, contract services,

etc. This will allow the community to
understand exactly where it stands as
it relates to the cost of water. Using
historic production and sales numbers,
project a water sales figure and divide the
commodity costs among the units; this is
the true cost of water.

His recommendations were ignored, and we
were basically told by the municipality and local
officials to "go to hell." To this day, Bob is still
willing to help Flint and yet they have rejected his
help and many other expert opinions. It was a full
year until the national media picked up the Flint
story and major officials finally started to come
clean.

Disasters like Flint don't happen overnight.
While I can understand that the city was trying to
gain some autonomy and cut costs, they did not
have the measures in place to do it safely. As soon
as the water treatment operators, the city, and the
state became aware of the problem, they should
have taken action. But they didn't. They covered
it up. They told residents everything was fine,
exposing 100,000 people, including thousands of
children, to dangerous levels of lead and cancer-
causing disinfection byproducts, which is why so
many officials have stepped down, been fired, or
are facing felony charges.

So far, fifteen officials have been charged with everything from misconduct in office and willful neglect of duty to involuntary manslaughter. The highest-ranking official to stand trial (so far) is Nick Lyon, the director of the Michigan Department of Health and Human Services, who has been charged with involuntary manslaughter in two deaths related to the outbreak of Legionnaire's disease. Lyon denies wrongdoing, but the district judge on his case said that withholding health information from the public was "corrupt." Flint brought to light exactly how the very agencies that are set up to protect us can put us in very real danger.

By the way, people in Flint pay some of the highest rates in the country for their undrinkable water. On average, Flint residents pay eight times more than the national average. Bills for many residents have continued to soar throughout the crisis. When Bob assessed these rates in 2015, he said they were the highest he had seen anywhere in the country. He found that Flint residents were paying $15.80 per thousand gallons of water for service and use fees, compared to the national average of about $2 per thousand gallons. Budget documents from the city don't provide enough information for residents to understand how their money is being spent. In 2018, Melissa Mays was paying about $350 a month for her water and was still unable to drink, bathe, or cook with it.

But within this story of local corruption, more water warriors were born, including citizens and scientists working together to get the truth out.

At a February 2016 meeting of the House Oversight and Governmental Reform Committee, LeeAnne offered her testimony of what happened to her family. "My home was being tested because of the discoloration of my water and the health issues my family was experiencing. We fought the city and the state, saying there was something wrong, and we were dismissed. I decided we needed to get to the science if anyone was ever going to believe us."

She had three tests conducted by the city of Flint, which used extra steps to minimize the amount of lead detected—a common practice. The numbers were still 104 ppb, 397 ppb, and 707 ppb, which prompted LeeAnne to contact the EPA and start working with water expert Miguel Del Toral. Through her own research, LeeAnne discovered that the city was not using corrosion control in its water treatment, and Miguel was able to confirm it. He also introduced her to Dr. Marc Edwards, a scientist at Virginia Tech with thirty years' expertise in lead pollution, who helped LeeAnne to independently test her water. Of the tests she performed, she found an average of 2,500 ppb of lead in the water coming out of her tap. Her highest reading was 13,500 ppb. The EPA classifies lead measuring at 5,000 ppb as hazardous waste.

"At that point, you do not just have smoke, you have a 3-alarm fire and should respond immediately," Marc told the **Detroit News**.

But despite this information and the fact that one of her sons tested positive for lead poisoning, the city and the MDEQ still contended that the water was safe.

"With the help of Virginia Tech, we conducted citizen-based sampling," LeeAnne said in her congressional testimony. "We educated and distributed 300 samples equally throughout the city. We collected back 277 samples. All of this was done in a 3-week turnaround."

Just a few months after Bob and I became aware of what was happening in Flint, these Virginia Tech scientists confirmed that more than 40 percent of the homes in Flint had dangerously high levels of lead. The people learned how to conduct field tests from these scientists, and that science backed up their common sense. Now, that's what we call boots on the ground action!

The researchers also posed the question: How is it possible that Flint "passed" the official EPA Lead and Copper Rule sampling overseen by the Michigan DEQ?

In their report, the Virginia Tech scientists wrote, "In our experience, following the EPA site selection criteria targeting homes with the highest risk for lead, the MDEQ sampling should have found much worse results than our sampling. Instead, MDEQ is asserting that the lead levels in Flint are much lower. Hence, we call on the U.S. EPA and others, to conduct a detailed audit of the 2014 and 2015 LCR sampling round overseen by MDEQ in Flint, to determine if it was conducted consistent with requirements of the law."

This citizen work caught the attention of two other women in Flint who played a pivotal role in helping the city's children: Elin Betanzo, a certified water operator and engineer, and her friend Dr. Mona Hanna-Attisha, director of the pediatric residency program for Hurley Medical Center, a public hospital in Flint. They were talking in Dr. Mona's kitchen one night, shortly after learning about the elevated lead levels in Flint's water. Elin said she had concerns about the water switch back in 2014, when she attended a training session sponsored by the Michigan American Water Works Association. It's where she first heard the news that Flint was planning to switch their water source, which as a water professional she thought was an unusual move. Cities don't typically switch from a clean water source to a more polluted one unless there's a serious reason such as a drought or a toxic spill.

"That's not something that happens every day," Elin said in an interview. "It surprised me. . . . They were saying that they were moving off of Detroit water to save money, but usually you don't save money by going independent. There's economies of scale, and by having a larger water system, it seems theoretically, if all the economics are working properly, Flint would be saving money to be staying on Detroit. So, from an expense point of view, it seemed unusual that they were changing off of the Detroit water."

As the women were talking, they realized that Dr. Mona had access to children's medical records in the city, and that she could use this information to show whether or not the children's health had been impacted by the water. As I've mentioned, lead is a known neurotoxin that can cause irreversible damage and is most toxic to the developing brain. About ten thousand children under the age of six lived in Flint at the time.

"If you do the study and if you document the increase in childhood blood lead levels, this is what would need to happen to make people pay attention to this and actually listen to the residents in Flint," Elin said to her friend.

Dr. Mona pulled hospital records as data for her study, looking at children's lead levels before and after the switch to the Flint River. The medical center routinely screened children for lead poisoning, especially at ages one and two, so she knew they had the data. Sure enough, once the data was collected from nearly two thousand children, she found that their blood lead levels had nearly doubled throughout the city and tripled in certain high-risk areas. Her study was eventually published in the **American Journal of Public Health**. Her research also called out important facts about children drinking water with elevated lead levels:

"Lead in drinking water is different from lead from other sources, as it disproportionately affects developmentally vulnerable children and pregnant mothers," she wrote in the study. "Children can absorb 40 percent to 50 percent of an oral dose of water-soluble lead compared with 3 percent to 10 percent for adults. In a dose–response relationship for children aged 1 to 5 years, for every 1-ppb increase in water lead, blood lead increases 35 percent. The greatest risk of lead in water may be to infants on reconstituted formula."

She held a press conference in September 2015, recommending that the city stop using the Flint River as its drinking water source as soon as possible, but she was quickly vilified by city officials, who called her an "unfortunate researcher, causing near hysteria." She was accused of splicing and dicing numbers that were not consistent with state data. But numbers don't lie, and soon those same officials were forced to retract their statements about her work and come clean about what was really happening in Flint. Dr. Mona calls the water disaster one of the greatest environmental crimes of this century and says that the people of Flint were betrayed by every agency that was supposed to protect them.

"Our data is just a snapshot of a small group of children at one point in time," she said in 2016 testimony to the House Democratic Steering and Policy Committee on "The Flint Water Crisis: Lessons for Protecting America's Children." "Due to the extended time period of potential exposure, the likelihood that most living in the area ingested the water directly or cooked with it, and the short time period in which we are able to detect blood lead levels in children, it is highly likely that there are a large number of children whose elevated blood lead levels have gone undetected."

Dr. Mona now leads the Pediatric Public Health Initiative, a joint program of Michigan State University and Hurley Children's Hospital to address Flint's population-wide lead exposure. The initiative brings together experts in pediatrics, child development, psychology, epidemiology, nutrition, toxicology, geography, education, and community and workforce development. The initiative aims to continue to assess what happened, monitor the effects from the lead exposure, and intervene to help these children. Lead exposure in children has been associated with decreased IQ and an increased likelihood of ADHD, delinquent behaviors, total arrests, and increased rates of arrests involving violent offenses. Her team is using evidence-based interventions to mitigate the effects of the exposure on these children, and she intends to share best practices with medical professionals throughout the country.

The water situation is still a mess in Flint, and the fallout is ongoing. People still won't drink unfiltered water, and though money has been allocated to replace and update pipes, it will take years to complete this task. The state has poured more than $350 million into Flint to help fix the water problems, on top of a $100 million grant the EPA awarded to the Michigan Department of Environmental Quality to fund drinking water infrastructure improvements throughout the city.

In January 2016, Governor Rick Snyder and current Flint mayor Karen Weaver appointed Virginia Tech scientist Marc Edwards to oversee all water testing for the state and federal government. The City of Flint reported in April 2018 that Flint's water met federal standards and the water tested at 6 ppb for lead, below the federal action levels in the Lead and Copper Rule of 15 ppb. The city closed the remaining free bottled water distribution centers that same month. While the city has worked to replace lead service lines that connect homes to the municipal water source, lines inside homes can still be contaminated and many residents don't have the funds to replace them. Edwards has clashed with Flint activists, his former colleagues, and other Flint researchers based in Flint by filing lawsuits against them. Virginia Tech has been awarded almost $2 million by the EPA to create one of the largest citizen science engineering projects in U.S. history to better understand lead in drinking water. Marc Edwards is the principal investigator of the project.

But great tragedies do foster new possibilities, and in Flint many residents decided they wanted to help save their city. In February 2017, the city clerk's office had given out fifty-two petitions for city council seats. In order to run for a council seat, candidates have to pick up a petition, file it by the designated deadline, get at least a hundred signatures of registered voters from their ward, and be registered to vote in the ward that they hope to represent. After the primaries, seventeen candidates remained, giving voters the choice of two candidates in eight of the nine wards. Newcomers claimed five of the nine seats in the November 2017 election, taking out incumbents and offering fresh energy to the council. Santino Guerra won the Third Ward seat at just nineteen years old. This University of Michigan–Flint sophomore studying criminal justice and sociology proved that you are never too young to run for office and make a positive difference in your community. His top three policy priorities are safe and affordable drinking water, blight, and public safety.

Local officials are slowly gaining back control of the city. The financial emergency, which began in 2011 and led to emergency managers running the city, resolved in April 2015 with a Receiver Transition Advisory Board (RTAB) overseeing a switch back to local government control. As of January 2018, both the mayor and the city council have gained back most day-to-day decision-making powers, while the RTAB still reviews budgets and debt obligations. With local powers back in place, they have repealed a law enacted by former emergency manager Jerry Ambrose that required the state to approve all resolutions made by the mayor and city council before they could take effect.

It's not a perfect fix, and Flint still has a long road ahead. The real question in Flint, and in so many other places like it, is how do we begin to fix these broken systems? A lead crisis worse than Flint's happened in Washington, D.C., in the early 2000s, where thousands of children were exposed to lead-contaminated water and the city didn't disclose the increased levels until **The Washington Post** reported about them in 2004. It wasn't a cost-saving move as in Flint, but rather a switch from chlorine to chloramines to disinfect the water that caused lead to leach from the city's pipes. The EPA distributed thirty thousand water filters and offered blood testing for residents who were concerned about their exposure. Yet the Lead and Copper Rule from 1991 remains unchanged. How many more cases of amnesia will we get before something changes?

I think more self-reporting and technology advances can help. What if we could post water test results publicly and in real time? What if more people were informed about how those results would impact them? We have access to more technology than ever before and perhaps we can use it to create more transparent and accessible agencies. Imagine how we could enact change if everyone was more informed and felt ready to take part in creating solutions.

Here's one example. When eleven-year-old Gitanjai Rao from Lone Tree, Colorado, read about the water quality problems in Flint and throughout the country, she wanted to find an easier way to test the water and receive results. This solutions-oriented sixth grader used the skill of observation to get started. "I noticed articles about how there was no solution to detect lead in water that is fast, easy, and inexpensive," she told **Fast Company**. "I knew I wanted to solve this."

She developed a kit, which she named Tethys after the Greek goddess for fresh water, that uses carbon nanotube sensors to detect lead in the water. A Bluetooth attachment sends results straight to your smartphone so you can immediately see if your water's levels are elevated. Typically, a lead test strip has to be sent to a lab and results come back in a week or two. It can cost about $50 or more for both the test strip and the processing, while Gitanjai's kit is estimated to cost about $20. Her project won the 2017 Discovery Education 3M Young Scientist Challenge; the $25,000 prize will help her develop the prototype for production. Her kit could be expanded in the future to test for other toxic chemicals in the water as well. Wow! She is an amazing example of how one person can make a huge impact. She envisioned a world where no children drink lead-contaminated water and then did the research to develop an idea that could really help.

"You are not alone" is what I say to every community I speak with. These problems are everywhere. If you're thinking water problems are happening in a few cities around the country, but certainly not in your town, I've got news for you. Flint is not the only place that's dealt with lead contamination, not even close. I've heard personally from more than two hundred communities that have lead problems as bad as or worse than Flint's. More than 18 million Americans throughout the country rely on drinking water systems that have violated federal lead regulations, according to a 2016 report from the Natural

Resources Defense Council. Looking at data from EPA records, the report showed that more than five thousand systems failed to protect people on many levels—from not working to reduce high lead levels to not properly monitoring the water for lead, or simply not reporting results to the public or the government. The Philadelphia Water Department is facing a class action lawsuit due to questionable lead and copper testing practices, but cities throughout the country use similar techniques to minimize lead in their testing results by flushing water lines before they test.

Hinkley taught us how corporations conceal huge toxic scandals and how hexavalent chromium got into the public water supply and harmed the health and welfare of consumers. Flint taught us about the cover-ups happening in state and local agencies to protect themselves rather than the people they serve. Now, I want to show you how state and local officials have turned against their constituents in favor of fracking, and how people are fighting back.

FRACK-QUAKES

Let's look at Oklahoma. The oil industry is Oklahoma's bread and butter. People there live and die by it. The state capitol in Oklahoma City is the only one in the U.S. with active oil rigs outside it. World oil prices are set in Cushing, Oklahoma, a tiny town with fewer than eight thousand people, which is also home to the world's largest oil-storage tank farm with capacity for about 90 million barrels of crude oil. Cushing is also considered the "pipeline crossroads of the world," thanks to its vast infrastructure that supplies up to 6 million barrels of oil daily through thirteen major pipelines.

On November 7, 2016, a magnitude 5.0 earthquake rattled Cushing, damaging homes and large buildings and causing schools to close the next day. I can only imagine how a larger earthquake could disturb those pipelines and storage tanks. It was one of just nineteen earthquakes recorded that week throughout the state. Oklahoma is not known for natural seismic activity, but in 2015 it became the earthquake capital of the world. Before 2009, Oklahoma had about two earthquakes of magnitude 3.0 or greater each year. But activity began to increase in 2010, and from 2013 to 2018, the state had hundreds of earthquakes per year.

We are in the midst of a massive drilling boom across the U.S., in part due to new technologies like hydraulic fracturing, a process that pumps millions of gallons of water mixed with toxic chemicals and sand into the ground to retrieve oil and gas deposits. Fracking is happening near neighborhoods and Main Streets across the country. In many of these areas, drilling competes with farming for access to freshwater. From 2005 to 2015, Oklahoma used more than 19 billion gallons of freshwater in fracking operations.

I have a special connection to the tall grasses of Oklahoma, as I spent most of my summers as a kid visiting my grandparents in Ponca City, where my mom was born and raised. My older siblings were born in Oklahoma City. The Sooner State is known for tornadoes and thunderstorms, not earthquakes. It's not only bizarre, it's affecting people's lives.

The drilling isn't the problem in Oklahoma as much as the wastewater. Scientists have confirmed that the injection of mass quantities of fracking wastewater into disposal wells throughout the state is what's triggering the tremors. Water plays a crucial role in hydraulic fracturing. The water cycle has five parts to it, according to the EPA, and it's the last part that's causing havoc.

Five Stages

Stage 1: Water Acquisition

The withdrawal of groundwater or surface water to make hydraulic fracturing fluids.

Stage 2: Chemical Mixing

The mixing of a base fluid and additives at the well site to create hydraulic fracturing fluids.

Stage 3: Well Injection

The injection and movement of hydraulic fracturing fluids through the oil and gas production well and into the targeted rock formation.

Stage 4: Produced Water Handling

The on-site collection and handling of water that returns to the surface after hydraulic fracturing and the transportation of that water for disposal or reuse.

Stage 5: Wastewater Disposal and Reuse

The disposal and reuse of hydraulic fracturing wastewater.

The Oklahoma Oil and Gas Association has disputed scientific claims linking their activity to earthquakes. The association's president, Chad Warmington, said in a 2015 statement, "There may be a link between earthquakes and disposal wells, but we—industry, regulators, researchers, lawmakers, or state residents—still don't know enough about how wastewater injection impacts Oklahoma's underground faults."

Initially, state lawmakers kept their heads in the sand. Former EPA administrator Scott Pruitt, the former attorney general for Oklahoma, contended that the problem didn't exist. Oklahoma governor Mary Fallin took the side of industry, saying that the relationship between oil and gas activity and earthquakes was speculation and that more science was needed to understand it.

Man-made earthquakes, or "induced earthquakes" as scientists call them, are not a new concept. In an aptly titled 2015 lecture, "Yes, Humans Really Are Causing Earthquakes," a U.S. Geological Survey (USGS) research geophysicist explained that one of the first known human-made earthquakes shook Johannesburg, South Africa, in 1894, and it was caused by an increase in gold production in the area. In Europe scientists in the early 1900s found that mining activities could create seismic activity, and by 1908 Germans had built the first monitoring lab for further study. In the U.S., earthquakes related to oil production first happened in 1925 in Goose Creek, Texas, near Houston. Scientists concluded that the extraction of oil and gas changed the forces on the fault lines, making earthquakes more likely. When Nevada's Lake Mead was filled in 1935, scientists realized that the pressure of the water on faults below caused them to shift.

Earthquakes relating specifically to fluid injection into the ground were tracked in 1967 at the Rocky Mountain Arsenal, a chemical-weapons manufacturer located outside Denver, Colorado. The plant disposed of its waste fluids by injecting them into a well that was twelve thousand feet deep. Shortly after, more than a thousand earthquakes rattled the area, some measuring up to 5.0 on the Richter scale.

Seismologists start by asking a few questions to study and identify man-made earthquakes.

1. Is there a recent change in activity?
2. Are the earthquakes close to the source of stress?
3. Are they happening close to the time of the stress?
4. Are they close to the surface? (Many times, induced earthquakes show up closer to the earth's surface than natural ones.)

Of course, not all induced earthquakes can be traced to this set of questions, but they offer simple guidelines for tracking the activity. The first question—is there a recent change?—is one I use often to determine the source of water issues in an area. It's all about observing changes and then investigating how those changes can impact the environment.

When it comes to Oklahoma, the waste and cleanup from hydraulic fracturing activities is the source of trouble. During the natural-gas-extraction process, fracking fluids rise to the surface, along with ancient seawater, known in the industry as produced water. The water is so salty that it can't be dumped at the surface, as it can kill plant life and harm soil health. When it spills into waterways, it can kill fish. In fact, spills of this saltwater from fracking in North Dakota have caused outrage among landowners and farmers alike; they say that saltwater is far more devastating to our environment than oil. Companies dispose of this water by pumping it down another opening deep in the shale— a process called deep wastewater injection. As these wells fill up with the wastewater, it builds pressure on geological faults, causing man-made earthquakes to occur. Oklahoma's geology is particularly prone to quakes. The rock is highly absorbent of the wastewater and the buildup over time allows deep faults to slip, leading to dozens of earthquakes occurring in the same area for days. Since 2011, well operators have injected more than 2 billion barrels of fluids each year into the ground in Oklahoma. These disposal wells have also been linked to earthquakes in Texas, Arkansas, and Ohio. In fact, Arkansas lawmakers banned the use of deep injection wells in 2011.

The impact of these quakes on the people there includes structural damage to their homes, along with concerns for their water supply. One family I spoke with lives in a house that is essentially rubble on the first floor. It's dusty and is more like a cabin than a house. Another household is looking at $75,000 worth of repairs on a home valued at $65,000. Earthquakes also impact drinking water, as they are known to cause wells to dry up and to lower the quality of surface water.

The state did begin to take some precautionary measures after seeing the increase in earthquake activity. In 2015 the Oklahoma Corporation Commission began implementing restrictions on the number of wastewater wells. After nearly 4,000 earthquakes in 2015, the number dropped in 2016 to 2,500 thanks to those regulations. But when it comes to earthquakes, size matters more than frequency.

Oklahoma's Pawnee Nation has sustained some of the biggest earthquakes in the state, including the largest earthquake ever recorded in Oklahoma's history—a 5.8 magnitude that struck the 2,200-person town of Pawnee on September 3, 2016. The earthquake occurred on a previously undiscovered fault zone, according to researchers.

"That was the one earthquake that started out with a bang but then rumbled and rolled," Andrew Knife Chief, executive director of the Pawnee Nation, told **National Geographic**. "It was the one earthquake where I go, 'Oh, this is a big deal. This is a big one.' You could feel it. It kept going and going. It shook the ground for about a minute."

The Pawnee Nation's long history in this

country spans more than seven hundred years; the tribe has been based in Oklahoma since 1875. Several of their buildings are listed on the National Register of Historic Places. They have been dealing with physical damage to their structures, such as sagging beams and cracked walls. And buildings in Oklahoma were not designed to withstand earthquakes like those in California. The Pawnees are worried about their drinking water too.

"We are not anti-using our land's resources," Andrew said. "What we are trying to push back against is the irresponsible production of oil and gas and the irresponsible disposal of wastewater. If an earthquake comes through here and destroys the buildings, we can rebuild, but if you pollute our water, we're done. And we have warning sides [sic] and indications that our waterways are becoming more polluted."

In 2016, the EPA released results from a multi-year study that looked at the relationship between fracking activities and drinking water and confirmed that the practice does impact drinking water. This study provides valid research as more communities work to protect themselves from fracking. Some of its main points show that fracking activities can cause stress on surface water and groundwater supplies because of the withdrawal of large volumes of water; because spills and faulty well construction can contaminate underground sources of drinking water; and because the disposal of wastewater into underground injection wells can impact surface waters.

I came to speak at a Pawnee town hall meeting in early 2017 and came back with Bob for another talk at Oklahoma State University to discuss the earthquakes and their impact. Community meetings provide information to help everyone to understand the issue and help people who have been impacted through no fault of their own. "We should never be bullied for coming forward with concerns," I said to the audience. "You have a right to ask for the truth and to ask for solutions."

As I've mentioned, my father was a mechanical engineer who worked for Texaco running the pipelines. He worked for industry, but he also said, "When we cross the lines and jeopardize the environment and our public health and welfare, we've gone too far." He came from a place of respect and understanding the difference between right and wrong. The oil and gas industry—not communities or families—needs to pay for the damage caused by fracking. These companies knew they were causing the quakes, and they also knew that the state was friendly to industry.

In March 2017, the Pawnee Nation filed a lawsuit against more than twenty-five oil and gas companies operating wastewater injection sites near their home. It was the first earthquake-related litigation filed in a tribal court, and it accuses the companies of knowingly causing the tremors with "reckless disregard for public or private safety."

"It was important to the tribe because it's an assertion of sovereignty," said attorney Curt Marshall, co-lead counsel on the case. "There's hundreds of thousands of dollars of damage through no fault of the tribe and we are working to get them money so that repairs don't come out of tribal funds."

He added that they are not looking to shut down the industry, as the oil and gas activity is vital to the local economy.

When the case goes to trial, the jury will be made up of Pawnee Nation members. While the lawsuit focuses on property damage to historic buildings, it's also an opportunity to use the court system to fight against this practice. Other personal and class action lawsuits have been filed in the state, but so far they have either been dismissed or are still pending.

A TOWN THAT BANNED FRACKING

It doesn't get more idyllic than the fourteen-thousand-person town of Dryden, New York.

Frank Capra, director of **It's a Wonderful Life**, was inspired to make his movie after visiting this quaint place, known for its picturesque farmlands and historic homes. The town sits upon the Marcellus Shale, a rock formation that stretches from upstate New York into Pennsylvania, West Virginia, and parts of Ohio, one of the largest shale formations in the U.S. and one that contains about 84 trillion cubic feet of natural gas. This small farming town in upstate New York fought to preserve its way of life and won.

Mary McRae, a farmer in Dryden for more than thirty years, was first approached in 2007 by a young man who said he wanted to lease her land to drill for gas. She turned him down swiftly, but he was persistent. He called her on the phone, wrote letters, and even showed up at her door several times. She eventually signed the lease after he told her that her neighbors had already signed the deal and the company was moving forward with their plans. She had no idea what she had agreed to and eventually started reaching out to her neighbors for help. That's how she met Deborah and Joanne Cipolla-Dennis, recent transplants to Dryden, who didn't want to see the town's rural way of life ruined. The group started researching the issue and discovered that their town was slated to become a hotbed of fracking activity. They created the Dryden Resource Awareness Coalition as a means to explore the impact hydraulic fracturing could have—not only on their neighborhood but also on the state and region. They met up as often as three times per week for discussions that centered around what actions they could take to protect their land and water.

They connected with David and Helen Slottje, former corporate lawyers from Boston who now lived in Ithaca, just a twenty-minute drive from Dryden. The couple had been offering pro bono legal help to many nearby towns that were concerned about fracking. David and Helen knew there wasn't much legal recourse when it came to regulating the industry, but they discovered a potential loophole: a local land-use prohibition that could stop the drilling. Local zoning laws might be able to ban fracking, just as towns regulate noise activities or enact other ordinances to protect neighborhoods.

The first step toward making it happen was to start a petition drive. The group began collecting signatures from fellow residents and were able to present almost 1,600 signatures to the Dryden Town Board, an impressive accomplishment for a small town. They showed just how many locals were concerned about fracking, reaching out across party lines and to all parts of town, organizing information sessions, collaborating with neighboring communities, and pursuing other strategies.

They presented their signatures at a packed

town hall meeting with more than a hundred locals. One dissenting voice came from Henry Kramer, who spoke amidst the many who were in favor of the ban.

"You do not have the jurisdiction," Kramer told the town board. "Has the state given us any legal authority to overwrite or impede state policy?" He worried that the town would be exposing itself to lawsuits by enacting the ban: "If we are among the first to do so you can expect a major assault from the gas companies."

Still, after much support, the Dryden Town Board approved a change in its zoning ordinance, clarifying that oil and gas development activities, including fracking, were "prohibited uses" of land within the town.

Their fight did not stop there. Just six weeks after the town board passed the measure in a unanimous bipartisan vote, the privately held Anschutz Exploration Corporation sued the Town of Dryden to force the town to accept drilling within city limits. The case went all the way to the state supreme court, which sided with Dryden. In June 2014, the New York Court of Appeals ruled that Dryden could use local zoning laws to ban oil and gas operations in their town. By December 2015, after seven years of study by the New York State Department of Environmental Conservation and the Department of Health, the state announced that fracking was prohibited due to human health concerns.

This precedent-setting case serves as a model to more communities throughout the country. As of the writing of this book, about 165 local fracking bans have been enacted, according to research from Food & Water Watch. Three states have banned fracking entirely: Vermont's legislature enacted a permanent moratorium on fracking in 2012; New York governor Andrew Cuomo banned fracking in 2014 due to concerns about health risks; and Maryland governor Larry Hogan signed a bill banning fracking in 2017. In March 2019, Oregon passed a ten-year ban on fracking. Two other states, Florida and New Mexico, are also considering bans or restrictions.

Everyone wants energy, but we need to look at how we're extracting it and the price we're paying in the process. How are we handling the chemicals involved in fracking, including the wastewater? We can't get so greedy and careless that we stop observing what's happening to the environment around us. You can watch Josh Fox's films, **Gasland** and **Gasland Part II**, for even more stories and examples of how fracking is impacting communities across the country. If we want to continue this practice, we need to find ways to do it in a sustainable way so that it doesn't hurt the communities involved.

ACTION STEPS
Connecting Science, Schools & Communities

More partnerships between schools and communities can be a way to address water issues at the local level. If you have kids in school (any grade level), ask if the science teacher is willing to add water quality testing to the curriculum. Students can collect water samples from local sources, including school drinking fountains, a local pond, a home tap or well, a nearby stream, or a large lake. Using water test kits, they can measure the chemical components of their water samples and learn about the various factors that affect water quality. Find out if they can also tour the local water treatment operation to learn more about your source water and how the drinking water is treated in your community. Children are our future and we can teach them from an early age to value the water around them and learn more about water testing and treatment.

Water Testing & Sampling 101

Do you know who can test your water? Many times, a county health department will help you test for bacteria or you can have your water tested by a state-certified laboratory to get more details about the quality of your drinking water. You can find one in your area by calling the Safe Drinking

Water Hotline at 800-426-4791 or visiting www .epa.gov/safewater/labs.

Once you've connected with a lab, either you will have a technician come out and test the water, or they will send you a kit to do it yourself. Whether it's part of a school project or you would like to independently collect water samples, the EPA offers guidelines for collecting a water sample.

- Collect the sample before any water has been used. Water should not be used for 8–18 hours before sampling.
- Make sure you have clean hands.
- Complete the sample recording form.
- Only use containers (250-milliliter) supplied by your certified lab. (Containers should not be opened until you are ready to collect the sample and keep food and drink away from the sample and its container.)
- Make sure no water has been withdrawn from the tap or water fountain before you collect the sample.
- Place the container under the faucet or drinking water fountain that is being tested and collect 250 milliliters of water. If a faucet is being tested make sure you turn on the cold water tap.
- Turn on the water and fill the container without allowing any water to run down the drain.
- Close the container according to the instructions from your certified lab.

- Make sure the container is labeled with the same information from your sample recording form.
- Prepare the container for shipping according to the certified lab's instructions.
- Ship containers according to the certified lab's instructions.
- Samples must be delivered to the lab within fourteen days of collection for proper testing.

Petition Writing 101

There's an art and science to writing a petition. The first step is to make a clear main point at the top of your petition, which is your headline. You want to keep it to fewer than ten words: We oppose fracking in Our Town, USA (six words). We oppose using ammonia to treat our drinking water (nine words). Making a clear point at the top will make it easy to get signatures and build support.

Next comes the body of the petition. You'll want to write a few sentences or paragraphs that briefly explain the topic. Imagine that you have thirty seconds or less to convince someone of your cause. What would you say? Be sure to include research to back up your point and make sure you are offering a solution. Every petition has two audiences: the citizens who will sign it and the lawmakers who will decide on it. Keep the argument brief so that both the people signing it and the officials reading it can quickly understand your point of view.

Here's an example from Dryden's petition:

To: Town Board of the Town of Dryden, Tompkins County, NY:

We, the undersigned residents of the Town of Dryden, believe that high volume, slickwater hydrofracking for gas extraction threatens our water and our air.

Allowing this practice in our community will significantly endanger our health and well-being.

Hydrofracking is a heavily industrialized process that in surrounding states has snarled traffic and caused significant air, water and noise pollution, and severe damage to roads and other infrastructure. In many places, it has had deleterious effects on tourism, hunting, fishing, agriculture, and the local economy in general.

We urge the Town Board to ban slickwater hydrofracking in the Town of Dryden.

One of the easiest (and free) online platforms to begin a petition can be found at Change.org, which has lots of great tips for petition writing. Anyone can start a petition to help raise awareness and gain support for a cause you care about.

9

HEROES FIGHTING POLLUTION
AT MILITARY BASES

Joining the military is both an enormous commitment and a high honor. Our servicemen and -women work to protect our freedoms, maintain peace, and support U.S. policy throughout the world, often in dangerous, intense, and challenging situations. These individuals are held to a high level of self-discipline and maintain a dedication to excellence. Sadly, the agency that oversees these service members has not upheld those same standards. Every day military families write to me about contamination on military bases, and too many of them are suffering from related health issues.

The United States spends more than any other country on its military, and the U.S. Department of Defense (DoD) is one of the worst polluters in the world. Its footprint is bigger than any corporation—with toxins spread across 40 million acres of American soil. The EPA has identified at least 149 current and former military bases with groundwater contamination. More than two-thirds of all Superfund sites are closely connected to the military. The drinking water and soil at these bases has been polluted by a range of dangerous chemicals left over from military activities, including jet fuel, cleaning products, degreasing solvents, firefighting foams, and explosives.

Retired Michigan congressman and veteran John D. Dingell, who died in 2019 at age ninety-two as the longest-serving member of Congress in U.S. history, told **Newsweek** in 2014, "Almost every military site in this country is seriously contaminated."

Contamination from these bases, which are scattered throughout the American landscape, ranges from radioactive waste found in McClellan Air Force Base near Sacramento, California, to PFAS found at Wright Patterson Air Force Base near Dayton, Ohio, to PCBs, chemical warfare agents, and radioactive waste found at the former army installation of Fort McClellan near Anniston, Alabama. Just outside Salt Lake City, Utah, sits Hill Air Force Base, which is both a Superfund site and one of the state's largest employers. The EPA has found more than sixty chemicals in the soil and groundwater, describing the situation as having an "unsafe level of contamination" and saying that there's "a reasonable expectation that people could be exposed." These are just a few examples of the extensive contamination that threatens the health of the people who have lived and worked on these bases as well as the nearby communities that people call home.

For our heroes to return from war to discover they themselves, their families, and their children have been exposed to dangerous levels of toxins on their own soil is asking too much. The Department of Veterans Affairs (VA) mission statement is "to fulfill President Lincoln's promise 'To care for him who shall have borne the battle, and for his widow, and his orphan' by serving and honoring the men and women who are America's Veterans." I'm a military mom who holds all of them near and dear to my heart. Two of my children served in the U.S. Army, and my son served a tour in Afghanistan. These Americans sacrificed to protect and defend our country, and we need to take care of them. They shouldn't have to sacrifice their health in the years after their service is complete.

I started getting involved and doing more research into contamination at these sites as more people started contacting me. The DoD and the VA are not required to tell service members or veterans about potential exposure to contaminated water or toxins, with the exception of Camp Lejeune in North Carolina, which I will discuss in depth in the next section. In addition, the Feres Doctrine, an obscure and highly criticized policy stemming from a 1950 Supreme Court ruling states, "The United States is not liable under the Federal Tort Claims Act (FTCA) for injuries to members of the armed forces sustained while on active duty." The FTCA allows people intentionally or negligently wronged by a government employee to sue the government for their injuries, but the **Feres** ruling bars active service members from collecting damages when they are injured during their tour of duty, transferring the burden of investigating tort claims against the government from Congress to the court system. Instead, those injuries should be covered by VA benefits. The original **Feres** case was a collection of three cases, one involving a soldier who had died when his barracks caught on fire due to a defective heating system and two other instances of service members who experienced shoddy surgical procedures. One of the most fiery critics of the Feres Doctrine was staunch conservative Supreme Court justice Antonin Scalia, who died in 2016. In **United States v. Johnson**, Justice Scalia wrote, "**Feres** was wrongly decided and heartily deserves the 'widespread, almost universal criticism' it has received." Still, this national policy persists despite dozens of challenges to the ruling throughout the years.

State laws have also been used to protect polluters. A 2014 Supreme Court ruling upheld a North Carolina statute of repose, making it more difficult for plaintiffs to sue companies that pollute communities. Lawsuits must be brought within ten years of the contaminating act, even if residents don't discover the pollution until after that time, according to the archaic statute. Residents of Asheville, North Carolina, sued CTS Corp., a multinational manufacturer of electronic components, attempting to get the company to clean up pollution from their defunct factory (in business from 1959 to 1983), which had left the groundwater contaminated with dangerously high levels of TCE. The pollution wasn't discovered until thirteen years after the company closed its doors. The **CTS Corp. v. Waldburger** case argued that the federal statute of limitations—giving plaintiffs the ability to file suit two years from first discovery—superseded the state law. But the Supreme Court ruled 7–2 in favor of the corporation, upholding the state law rather than the federal one. Such rulings hurt the people who have been most affected by toxins, especially when you consider the latency period from exposure to experiencing symptoms. It played a part in the contamination at Camp Lejeune. In fact, the Department of Justice wrote an amicus brief for the **Waldburger** case in favor of the polluter, stating, "The United States has a particular interest in the interaction of CERCLA with the North Carolina statute because of ongoing litigation against the

United States under the FTCA [Federal Tort Claims Act] involving allegations of contaminated drinking water at the Camp Lejeune Marine Corps Base in North Carolina." In other words, the U.S. government wanted a favorable outcome in the case so they could use it as a precedent to block the mounting number of lawsuits coming from Camp Lejeune. Under the court's ruling, people affected by this toxic tap water would have had to file a lawsuit by 1994, despite the fact that most people did not know about the problem until at least 1997.

Science has shown that the latency period for many health problems caused by exposure to these contaminants can take up to thirty years or more. How can someone file a claim against a polluter who has given him or her cancer when they don't get diagnosed until twenty or thirty years after the exposure? Despite the Supreme Court ruling, Camp Lejeune lawsuits have continued. The text of the law says, "No cause of action shall accrue more than 10 years from the last act or omission of the defendant giving rise to the cause of action." That omission is where there's room for legal action, as many have argued that the Marine Corps omitted facts and documents in this case.

In 2017, I spoke at an event on the National Mall for Operation Stand Together, an organization of military veterans and their families who are working to raise awareness about chronic, lifelong illnesses and conditions resulting from contact with toxic exposures during active-duty service. While many people are familiar with the millions of Americans affected by the spraying of Agent Orange, a dangerous herbicide mixture that contained carcinogenic dioxin, during the Vietnam War, most people are unaware of the toxins found on our home soil and in our water. These issues have been swept under the rug for too many years, and the science continues to catch up, showing the real health impacts of exposure to these contaminants. It's a huge heartbreak.

The DoD has spent more than $11 billion reviewing and cleaning up closed bases, and an estimated $3.5 billion is still needed to continue such efforts, according to a 2017 report from the Government Accountability Office (GAO). Base Realignment and Closure (BRAC) is a process that's been happening since 1988 to help reduce excess infrastructure; it's overseen by an independent commission assigned by the president. The commission has closed 120 installations, including ammunitions plants, air force bases, army airfields, naval reserves, and research laboratories. But when these sites close, the contamination remains. Who is responsible for cleaning up this mess? Why has the VA continued to deny the fact that veterans were exposed to toxic chemicals? The current administration has said they want to take care of our veterans and military families. Here is your chance to read more about the people who have been deeply affected by all of this pollution.

CAMP LEJEUNE CONTAMINATION

Born on the Fourth of July, Jerry Ensminger is the picture of a patriot. He grew up on a small, rural farm outside of Hershey, Pennsylvania, and joined the U.S. Marine Corps in 1970, as soon as he finished high school. Jerry spent more than twenty-four years serving his country, retiring in 1994 as a master sergeant. On the drill field, he trained more than two thousand new recruits. He still believes in the Marine Corps motto "Semper fidelis," a Latin phrase meaning "always faithful."

Jerry had four children, all born during his military career, but his daughter Janey would change the trajectory of his life. Janey was the only child who was conceived, carried, and born while his family lived at the U.S. Marine Corps Base Camp Lejeune. Located in Jacksonville, North Carolina, it is the largest marine base on the East Coast, supporting a population of more than 100,000 marines, their families, and civilian employees. On a hot Sunday afternoon in July 1983, Janey, who had been dealing with a persistent case of strep throat, developed a high fever. Jerry took her to the hospital. He was not expecting her to come home with a diagnosis of acute lymphocytic leukemia, or ALL, which is the most common type of childhood cancer. Each year in the U.S. about three thousand children are diagnosed with ALL.

Jerry's life changed dramatically from that day forward as he watched his daughter go through hell. She received treatments from both Penn State and Duke University medical facilities, getting many procedures including chemotherapy treatments, bone marrow extractions, and spinal taps to try to bring her body back to health. She took steroids, which made her gain weight, and she also lost her hair. Kids at school called her "Cabbage Patch Kid," which made her feel even worse. Jerry said he spent many nights praying to God to take the illness away from his daughter, but those prayers went unanswered. Janey died on September 24, 1985, at the age of nine. Like any parent, Jerry was grief-stricken, but he couldn't shake the nagging question "Why?" He researched both sides of his and Janey's mother's family for a history of childhood leukemia and not one case existed. He didn't understand how this unspeakable tragedy had hit his family. The American Cancer Society states on its website that most childhood leukemias are not linked to any known genetic causes.

He found an answer in 1997, more than ten years after he lost his daughter. Jerry, who was now retired and living in North Carolina, was making himself dinner while watching the local news when the television reporter said, "The contaminants found in the water at Camp Lejeune have been linked in scientific literature to birth defects and childhood cancers." Jerry dropped his plate of food and said it felt like someone had just hit him on the head with a two-by-four. The Agency for Toxic Substances and Disease Registry (ATSDR), a federal public health agency, completed a public health assessment (PHA) of drinking water at the base and concluded that the people living and working at the base were exposed to "contaminants of concern" in their drinking water from 1953 through 1987. These chemicals included trichloroethylene (TCE), tetrachloroethylene (PCE), dichloroethylene (DCE), vinyl chloride, and benzene.

He jumped into research mode, searching for more answers and deciding to do everything he could to help other families who might have been affected by the contaminated drinking water. Marines have a tradition of taking care of their own, and he wanted to honor that custom. He couldn't help but think about the hundreds of thousands of people who had also lived on that base and had drunk that water. They were back home in all parts of the country and didn't hear the local news report. He bet many of them had the same nagging questions about their health problems as he had about Janey's. With help from others along the way, including Tom Townsend, a retired marine major, he combed through government databases and web pages and filed Freedom of Information Act (FOIA) requests for military files to find information about the contamination.

Jerry discovered the drinking water well that supplied his water at Camp Lejeune was contaminated with PCE, an industrial solvent used in dry cleaning. Located just steps from the base, a dry-cleaning facility where many marines would drop off their uniforms had been dumping their liquid waste into the ground, eventually polluting the water. The levels of PCE found in the water system near his home during that time were 215 ppb. The levels considered safe today by EPA standards are 5 ppb. But other pollution was happening on the base as well. TCE, a degreaser used to clean machine parts, was regularly dumped into the ground. The toxic sludge permeated through the soil and into wells that supplied water to residents. One of the wells tested as high as 1,000 ppb for TCE, while the current EPA levels are set at 5 ppb. Additionally, during that same time up until spring 1988 underground gasoline tanks leaked about 1,500 gallons of fuel each month, totaling more than a million gallons, which also found its way into the water supply.

As Jerry started contacting representatives at Camp Lejeune and the Navy Environmental Health Center in Norfolk, Virginia, he was surprised by their reaction. He said in a 2012 interview with C-SPAN that many of the people he spoke with acted as if the contamination was not a big deal, saying, "Oh, ATSDR doesn't know what they're talking about, these were very minute, trace amounts of these chemicals. You shouldn't have any reason to believe that this is what caused your daughter's illness."

His response was "Well, then why is ATSDR talking about doing a childhood leukemia study?"

He tried to maintain faith and confidence that the Marine Corps he had served for nearly a quarter of a century of his life would do what was right.

"As time went on, I started to realize that not only were they not doing what was right by their people, they were doing everything they could to do what was wrong," he said. "They were omitting facts. They told many, many half-truths and total lies. I'm polite to a point but whenever I feel that someone is giving me lip service, well then the gloves come off."

The Marine Corps said that the contamination happened before the days of stringent environmental regulations, notification requirements did not exist back then, and the water quality on the base was comparable to that of municipal water systems during that time. Regardless of their stance, it's worth noting that the very corporations responsible for creating these chemical compounds knew about the health implications years before the EPA was ever involved in regulating them.

Just as internal scientists at DuPont and Dow Chemical knew about the dangers of PFOA, so did those working with TCE. A letter written by Dr. Carey McCord, a medical advisor for Chrysler Corporation, said, "Promotional activities, seeking the extension of industrial uses of trichloroethylene, frequently fail to disclose the toxic nature of this chemical and the practical dangers that may attend its use. Any manufacturer contemplating the use of trichloroethylene may find in it many desirable qualities. Too, in the absence of closed systems of operations, he may find in this solvent the source of disaster for exposed workmen." This letter was published in a 1932 issue of the **Journal of the American Medical Association**.

The list of health issues associated with exposure to TCE and PCE includes everything from infertility to cancer—including a huge cluster of breast cancer in men—to neurobehavioral effects. A cluster of children with leukemia in Woburn, Massachusetts, made famous by the book and movie **A Civil Action**, has been studied as well. Jerry couldn't help but draw parallels between this story and his own, as it shows the toll that

TCE takes on the human body, especially young people's bodies.

In 1965 Anne and Charles Anderson moved to Woburn. Their son Jimmy was diagnosed with ALL in January 1972 at 3.5 years old. It was through conversations with neighbors that Anne discovered that two other children down the block had also been diagnosed with leukemia. Jimmy's doctor had told her that the cause of ALL was unknown, but she suspected otherwise. Woburn had a long history as a center for industrial and chemical production. It was home to leather-tanning factories in the 1850s and chemical factories throughout the twentieth century. For years, she had noticed that the tap water tasted bad and came out in strange colors, and she wondered if any of the chemicals from the town's past had found their way into the water supply.

At first, her observations and questions about the water were met with skepticism by doctors, local officials, and even her neighbors. No one believed that a connection could be made between the water and the children's health. In 1979, the local newspaper reported that buried chemical containers had been discovered near the city's wells, prompting them to be tested. Officials found dangerous levels of TCE and other chemical solvents. The case led to a major lawsuit and garnered a fair amount of media attention. In 1986, researchers from the Harvard School of Public Health published an analysis of the contaminated Woburn wells and their health effects, concluding that there was a link between the drinking water and the children's leukemia. A 1994 analysis of about seventy-five towns also suggested a connection between TCE/PCE and leukemia, and many studies since then have found similar results.

Even with all this information available, the EPA did not classify TCE as a human carcinogen until September 28, 2011. The agency estimates that 250 million pounds of TCE are either produced or imported into the U.S. each year. The EPA has proposed prohibiting its use in both degreasing applications and as a spot cleaner in dry-cleaning facilities—the first attempt to ban the use of any substance under the TSCA in more than twenty-seven years. We need the right science and policies in place, but they take time. Our agencies are overburdened and underfunded. Why do we allow these chemicals on the market when we don't know how safe they are? As I've explained, our laws give companies free rein to employ these compounds for profit, and years later we discover that they cause health problems.

So many babies born at Camp Lejeune in the '60s and '70s died that a nearby cemetery had a section that parents called "Baby Heaven." Children were born without craniums and with

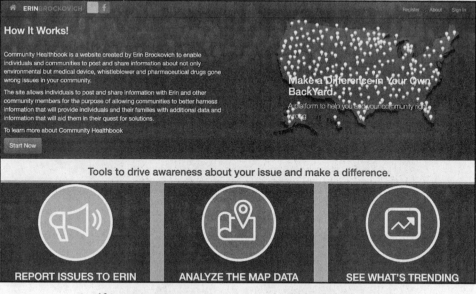

A self-reporting map, www.communityhealthbook.com is where
people can report illness and diseases in their communities.

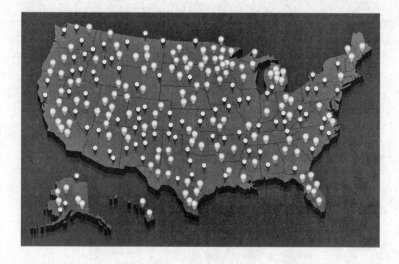

Tyler, Texas   Los Angeles, California

St. Joseph,   St. Bernard Parish,
Louisiana   Louisiana

Bridge City, California

Washington Heights,   Redding,
New York   California

I receive hundreds of emails every day from people throughout the country, many of which contain photos of discolored water. Here is a sampling from 2016, and the emails continue to this day with photos of brown water, orange water, and more, from all over the United States and the world.

Melissa Mays (left, with megaphone), a mother from Flint, Michigan, and founder of Water You Fighting For?, at one of the many rallies held during the Flint water crisis, a crisis that continues today.

Action begins at the local level, where everyday people get involved to fight for a better future and help their communities. Above are some photographs of the tainted water from just a few of those communities, including Hoosick Falls, New York; Tyler, Texas; and Sebring, Ohio.

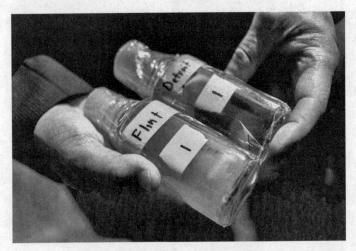

Lead-contaminated water during the Flint water crisis

A fish with tumors being pulled from the water in southwest Florida in the summer of 2018, during the red tide and blue-green algae crisis. It caused thousands of marine animals to die, and hundreds of tons of dead fish washed ashore.

Being presented with a tribal blanket by Casey Camp-Horinek,
a councilwoman of the Ponca Tribe of Oklahoma, in 2016,
while bringing attention to the escalating number of earthquakes
in Oklahoma as a result of fracking throughout the state

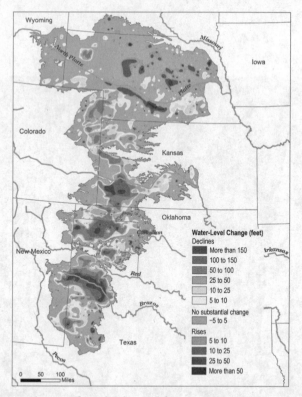

Climate change affects the demand for water, as well as the supply.
The Ogallala Aquifer lies beneath parts of South Dakota, Nebraska,
Wyoming, Colorado, Kansas, Oklahoma, Texas, and New Mexico.
Farmers are extracting water faster than it is being replenished.

Miami, Florida, faces chronic flooding challenges, even on
days when the sun is out. As sea levels rise, saltwater will seep
into the groundwater that residents rely on for drinking.

In 2017, DuPont paid hundreds of millions of dollars to settle two environmental lawsuits just before its nearly $150 billion merger with the Dow Chemical Co. In one of those lawsuits, DuPont paid more than $50 million to resolve claims of mercury leaking from its former facility in Waynesboro, Virginia. In the other, DuPont and Chemours agreed to pay more than $670 million to settle 3,500 lawsuits related to the release of PFOA, a toxic chemical used to make Teflon.

Camp Lejeune, in Jacksonville, North Carolina, the largest Marine Corps base on the East Coast and considered the site of the worst water contamination case in United States history

Clean water is not a Democratic or Republican issue. Make sure that the next time an election comes around, the candidates know that you, their constituents, care about water issues.

neural tube defects, such as spina bifida and anencephaly (a condition where part of the brain or skull is missing). Many died of leukemia and lymphoma. Any walk around a cemetery is somber but when you see stones that list names with only one year beneath them, the realization hits home of how many young children died there within their first year of life. As I mentioned earlier, my friend Trevor Schaefer, who survived brain cancer at the age of thirteen, believes we need more funding to study how children's bodies are affected by these toxic chemicals. If a young man can see these correlations, why is it so difficult for our elected leaders?

Camp Lejeune closed most of the contaminated water wells in 1985—that's five years after they first discovered the pollution. Documents uncovered by Jerry and others suggest that leadership was slow to respond when water tests showed evidence of contamination. The base was declared a Superfund site in 1989, and estimates state that at least 1 million people were exposed to this contaminated water. It took another twenty-four years with help from Congress to inform veterans and their families about the contamination and its health risks.

Jerry has been the face of this case in Washington, D.C., for more than twenty years, pushing for legislation that could help affected military personnel, veterans, their families, and civilians. In fact, his retirement has been overtaken by it. He has made countless trips to D.C., trading his overalls and mud boots for a suit and tie to meet with legislators and testify before Congress.

"I've got a very forceful voice and a very forceful personality, so it served me well," he said. "In many ways the Marine Corps trained me to be doing what I'm doing now."

Jerry never pursued legal action, even though lawyers approached him years ago, wanting to file a lawsuit for Janey. He said no. "I knew if I got involved in suing the government the people I was working with, who make the laws, would drop me like a damn hot potato. No amount of money can help Janey. But people out there are still suffering the consequences of this shit. These people are losing their homes. They have to make a choice between keeping everything they've worked for their entire life or dying. I've got to give these people some help."

Jerry has redefined what it means to be a veteran and an activist. He has found success working directly with legislators and their staff, saying, "It's one thing to deal with a senator's staff back in their home state and it's another thing to sit with an elected member and their immediate staff in Washington, D.C., and look them in the eye."

On each trip he would try to fit in several visits

to congressional offices, so he didn't waste the entire ride on a five-minute meeting.

"My butt knows every bump on I-95 between exit 49 and Capitol Hill," he said. "I've made that trip that many times. When I started going to Capitol Hill, I didn't have the money for hotels. I didn't have the money to stay up there and eat out at restaurants. I would leave my farm at 3:30 a.m. and drive straight through so I would miss rush hour in D.C. I would make my appointments for late in the morning or early afternoon, so I could leave before the end-of-day rush hour would start. Eventually, I got to know people up there that were nice enough to put me up."

That's dedication to a cause. That's knowing your why.

"If you're going to hold somebody accountable, you better get on your pony and start riding," he told me about his work.

Jerry has also dealt with his share of naysayers, including retired marines, who thought the water issue was not real.

"I've discovered throughout the years that a lot of those naysayers changed their tune when it came and landed on their doorstep," he said.

Camp Lejeune is considered by scientists and federal investigators to be the worst and largest water contamination our country has ever seen.

Janey's story is just one of many tragedies that
came out of Camp Lejeune.

I could write hundreds of these stories, but here
are two more—one from a civilian whose mother
worked on the base and one from a family member
of another marine stationed there.

Rosanne Warren's mother, Patricia, worked
at Camp Lejeune during her pregnancy, according to court documents. Rosanne was born in
1971 and as a child frequently stayed with family
friends who lived on the base while her mom was
working. At twelve years old, she began having
kidney problems, eventually receiving multiple
stent implants. By her mid-twenties she was diagnosed with cervical cancer and went through the
standard treatments of chemotherapy, radiation,
and surgical removal of her uterus. Despite these
medical interventions, the cancer returned to her
hip and kidney. Rosanne died in 2000 at the age
of twenty-eight. Patricia did not find out about
the exposure she and her daughter experienced at
Camp Lejeune until 2008, when a friend told her
about a community meeting to discuss it.

Mike Partain, born and raised at Camp Lejeune,
lived in the same housing complex as Jerry and
his family. Both his father and grandfather were
marines. Mike joined the navy but was later
discharged due to a debilitating and unexplained
full-body rash. He eventually moved to Florida,

got married, and had four children of his own. He was diagnosed with male breast cancer at the age of thirty-nine, despite lacking any genetic markers for the disease. Breast cancer in men is rare, making up less than 1 percent of all cases of the disease. Yet, more than a hundred men who lived or worked at the base during the time of the contamination have been diagnosed with it.

Mike became aware of the toxic water where he grew up when he saw Jerry on the news, testifying at a congressional hearing in 2007. It's a testament

In D.C. with retired marine Jerry Ensminger and cancer survivor Mike Partain, both instrumental in increasing awareness of water pollution issues at Camp Lejeune. Both men were present when President Obama signed the Honoring America's Veterans and Caring for Camp Lejeune Families Act of 2012 in Washington, D.C.

to how one person really can make a difference for so many others. Mike soon joined forces with Jerry, reaching out to him after he saw him on television. He wanted to learn more about the contamination and how he could help, which led to many late nights working determinedly to find other men who had been diagnosed with breast cancer by posting on breast cancer websites and working with local and national media. He also created a timeline of events linked to public records and navy and Marine Corps documents. The timeline became one of the most important weapons in uncovering the truth of what happened at Camp Lejeune.

A CONDENSED TIMELINE OF CAMP LEJEUNE EVENTS FROM 1980 TO 2009 (ORIGINALLY CREATED BY THE ASSOCIATED PRESS)

October 1980: Tests through March 1981 show water at the Hadnot Point treatment plant is "highly contaminated" with chlorinated hydrocarbons. A lab chemist urges further analysis. Officials do not test individual wells to find the contamination source.

May and July 1982: Tests identify TCE and PCE as contaminants in water systems for Hadnot Point and Tarawa Terrace, which served housing, schools, other buildings, and swimming pools at Camp Lejeune.

July 1984: The base begins testing individual wells and by February 1985 shuts down ten contaminated wells. One drinking water sample measured 1,400 parts per billion of TCE. The U.S. government eventually set 5 parts per billion as the maximum safe level for TCE at the tap.

January 1985: A fuel spill closes a clean water system. Homes and a school are connected on an emergency basis to the Hadnot Point system for twelve days. They receive contaminated water.

March through April 1985: A contaminated well that had been shut down is turned on to pump water to residents on four nights to ease a temporary water shortage.

April 1985: The base commander, Maj. Gen. L. H. Buehl, urges families in Tarawa Terrace to conserve water. He says wells were closed as a precaution over "minute" amounts of organic chemicals. He does not mention that contamination exceeded maximum recommended exposure limits several times over.

March 1987: The water treatment system for Tarawa Terrace is shut down and homes are connected to a new water treatment plant.

October 1989: Camp Lejeune is added to the Superfund list of the nation's highly contaminated hazardous waste sites.

August 1997: The U.S. Agency for Toxic Substances and Disease Registry concludes that adults had little or no increased cancer risk from the past contaminated water but raised concern about effects on developing fetuses. It recommended studies on the fetal effects.

August 1998: The health agency finds a link between toxic water and low-birth-weight babies born to some women at Camp Lejeune during the years of contamination. The study undercounts mothers who were exposed because it assumes a clean treatment plant provided water for four years before it was constructed.

1999: The health agency begins searching for leukemia cases and birth defects among babies who were in utero at the base from 1968, when birth records first were computerized, until 1985, when contaminated wells were believed to have been shut down.

2003: The health agency begins to study whether Camp Lejeune's contaminated water is linked to birth defects and elevated leukemia rates in its survey of 12,600 children.

October 2004: An outside panel convened by the Marines determines that Camp Lejeune did not understand the significance of its water contamination early on and that Navy environmental advisers were "not aggressive" in assisting them. However, the panel concludes that Marine leadership acted responsibly and provided water quality consistent with general practices at the time.

April 2005: Criminal investigators from the Environmental Protection Agency find no illegal actions or cover-up in Camp Lejeune's handling of its water contamination. The Justice Department declines to prosecute.

June 2007: House Energy and Commerce Committee hears testimony from what it calls "poisoned patriots," families who blame their cancers on Camp Lejeune water.

October 2007: The Senate directs the military to find former Camp Lejeune residents and workers and notify them they may have been exposed to contaminated drinking water.

June 2008: The federal health agency concludes it is feasible to do cancer and mortality studies of adults who were exposed to the tainted water. The agency is laying groundwork for the studies while completing its study of fetal health effects.

April 28, 2009: The health agency withdraws its 1997 public health assessment, stating it contains omissions and inaccuracies.

(A new PHA with updated research was released in January 2017.)

Jerry first testified in front of the U.S. House Committee on Energy and Commerce in April of 2004 after **The Washington Post** wrote an article about Camp Lejeune and the contaminated water. He was invited by Congressman Dingell, the ranking member at that time of the Energy and Commerce Committee, who saw the **Post** article. The DoD was considering how to get immunity from increased environmental regulations.

In July 2004, North Carolina Republican senator Elizabeth Dole filed an amendment requiring the Marine Corps to notify all former and retired marines and their families, along with all civilian employees, about their possible exposure to the contaminants. By August, she and four other senators introduced a bill requiring the EPA to establish a health advisory for TCE and a National Primary Drinking Water Regulation that would set limits for TCE in public drinking water sources. While these proposed actions didn't make it past the Senate floor, that didn't stop Jerry.

But by August 2012, President Barack Obama signed a bipartisan-supported bill called Honoring America's Veterans and Caring for Camp Lejeune Families Act of 2012 [HR 1627], also called the Janey Ensminger Act. The bill provided hospital care and medical services through the VA for veterans and family members who resided at the base for longer than thirty days between January 1, 1957, and December 31, 1987, for up to fifteen health conditions that scientists have linked to the contamination, including the following:

- Lung cancer
- Breast cancer
- Bladder cancer
- Kidney cancer
- Leukemia

- Esophagus cancer
- Multiple myeloma
- Renal toxicity
- Miscarriage
- Myelodysplastic syndrome
- Female infertility
- Scleroderma
- Hepatic steatosis
- Non-Hodgkin's lymphoma
- Neurobehavioral effects

The president signed the bill during a ceremony in the Oval Office with Mike and Jerry standing next to him, saying that the bill ended "a decades long struggle for those who served at Camp Lejeune" and that the country had a "moral and sacred duty" to care for those sickened by the toxic drinking water. It was a great first victory, but like many good laws on the books, it was slow to lead to action. Veterans were not automatically provided services, prompting lawsuits by veterans organizations. Some died while waiting for their benefits to be approved.

In 2017, the VA passed a rule granting disability compensation to Camp Lejeune veterans. Veterans who were at Camp Lejeune for at least thirty days during the contamination and who later developed adult leukemia, aplastic anemia, multiple myeloma, non-Hodgkin's lymphoma, Parkinson's

disease, and bladder, kidney, or liver cancer are
eligible. The compensation is estimated to cost the
government about $2.2 billion.

Jerry continues to advocate for issues related to
Camp Lejeune, including helping civilians who
worked on the base and their dependents, along
with people who lived near the base who were also
affected by the contamination. The Marine Corps
has still not admitted fault for what happened at
Camp Lejeune, and while thousands of claims have
been approved by the VA, many veterans
have been denied health care.

"You cannot put your faith in anyone but yourself, because no one is going to be as energized
as the people who are directly impacted by these
issues," Jerry told me in a recent conversation.

I've opened dozens of further investigations
at military bases in Pennsylvania, Alabama,
Michigan, Washington State, New York, Florida,
Vermont, New Hampshire, and West Virginia, and
continue to work with groups like Poisoned Veterans, Operation Stand Together, and the Veterans
& Civilians Clean Water Alliance to help raise
awareness and help veterans and service members
get the help and services they deserve.

"The American people need to wake up," Jerry
said to me. "We have a beautiful country and it's
still salvageable. We can save our environment. We
can save it for future generations and stop all this

With veterans—among them Jerry Ensminger—in
D.C. in 2017 bringing attention to toxic
drinking water at U.S. military bases

cancer. But we need to wake up and we need to
live lives in accordance with our environment or
we are all doomed."

I'm grateful for his service both in the Marine
Corps and all these years after.

PFAS CRISIS

The fear of drinking water contaminated with perfluorinated chemicals (often referred to as PFCs
or PFAS), particularly PFOA and PFOS, has been
building as more research has been amassed about

how these substances impact the body at toxic levels. The manufacturers of these chemicals, such as Arkema, DuPont, and 3M, knew about the dangers associated with them and failed to warn those who would come in contact with them. I've already discussed how DuPont knew about the risks with PFOA. Multiple studies dating back to the 1970s found health risks associated with PFOS, which was a chemical used from the '70s on, in firefighting foams used to help put out aircraft fires at military bases throughout the country. Despite a deal made with the EPA and the foam's main manufacturer to cease making it more than eighteen years ago, the air force and many other military installations continued using it.

As I was writing this book more news broke about the dangers of these chemicals. In May 2018, White House officials were caught suppressing the publication of a new ATSDR health study, calling it a "public relations nightmare." The study shows how PFOA- and PFOS-contaminated water at military bases and neighboring communities nationwide has reached unsafe levels, posing risks to human health at a lower level than what the EPA currently considers safe. The Union of Concerned Scientists reported that the research suggests that the health advisory should be set at 12 ppt for certain populations.

"The public, media, and Congressional reaction

to these numbers is going to be huge," one uniden-
tified White House aide said in an email published
in a **Politico** piece. "The impact to EPA and [the
Defense Department] is going to be extremely
painful. We [DoD and EPA] cannot seem to get
ATSDR to realize the potential public relations
nightmare this is going to be."

The EPA estimates that both these chemicals
resist most conventional water treatment and
require more robust systems, such as granular
activated carbon and ion exchange resins, so it's
particularly problematic when they make their
way into the drinking water supply.

"It is unacceptable and irresponsible that the
release of this study has been blocked for five
months out of fear that it would create a 'potential
public relations nightmare,'" U.S. Senator Maggie
Hassan from New Hampshire said in a statement.
"Families who have been exposed to emerging
contaminants deserve to know about any potential
health impacts that the contaminants may involve,
and it is completely unacceptable that your agencies are withholding science-based information
and failing to provide details to these families."

Congressman Dan Kildee also called on the
Trump administration to release the study, which
affects his district, including the groundwater
around Oscoda and the former Wurtsmith Air
Force Base in Iosco County, Michigan, and

communities across the country. Groundwater in western Michigan contains PFOA and PFOS concentrations up to 37,800 ppt or more than five hundred times the EPA's current health advisory of 70 ppt. PFOA and PFOS have also been found throughout Michigan's bodies of water including the Flint River, Kalamazoo River, and Saginaw River, and in parts of Lake Michigan, Lake Huron, and Lake Erie. He has continued to urge the administration to address PFOA and PFOS contamination, by working to include language authorizing a health study in the National Defense Authorization Act, which became law in December 2017. Federal lawmakers approved a budget in 2018 providing $10 million to fund this nationwide health study to further understand the impact of PFAS compounds on the human body and added more than $85 million to the air force and the navy budgets to specifically address this contamination.

In New Mexico, these chemicals have contaminated groundwater near Cannon Air Force Base and Holloman Air Force Base, including agricultural wells, at a cost to the local dairy industry. Senators from the state are also calling for the EPA to develop federal drinking water standards for PFOA and PFOS. In the absence of national standards, states have created their own drinking water regulations—and the lack of coordination among states has created a patchwork of conflicting guidelines and various MCLs. Communities continue to question if their regulations are sufficient.

In a bipartisan letter to acting EPA administrator Andrew Wheeler, New Mexico senators Tom Udall and Martin Heinrich wrote, "Without enforceable drinking water standards for PFOA and PFOS, it is doubtful that a national management strategy will sufficiently confront the challenges PFAS chemicals pose to states and affected communities. This decision would also fail to consider ongoing interagency efforts to determine the human health implications of contamination from PFAS, including the nationwide study being conducted by the Agency for Toxic Substances and Disease Registry (ATSDR)."

In Newburgh, New York, a small city perched next to the Hudson River, the drinking water tested positive for these same chemicals. Researchers from the New York Department of Environmental Conservation identified nearby Stewart Air National Guard Base as the source of the PFOS, suspecting that PFOS leaked into a stream leading to the city reservoir.

Newburgh has twenty-nine thousand residents and is just one of many places across the country affected by the EPA's update to its health advisory of PFOA and PFOS. In 2014, the chemicals were detected at 170 ppt there, but when the

EPA set a new health advisory of 70 ppt in 2016, the city declared an emergency. Because of the elevated levels of PFOS found in Washington Lake and Silver Stream, the city of Newburgh announced on May 2, 2016, it would stop using the drinking water and would connect to a different water source. I rarely get the opportunity to congratulate Safe Drinking Water Act administrators, but when they do it right, I enjoy saying it. The city has since been testing a new water filtration system designed to eliminate PFOS from the city's water source and has launched a free health screening program offering blood testing to residents. But Newburgh has a long road ahead when it comes to cleaning the reservoir and providing medical services to residents exposed to the contaminated water.

Meanwhile, the military has been investigating about 400 sites for water contamination of PFOS and PFOA. A March 2018 report from the House Armed Services Committee showed that 126 sites, either on-base or off-base, have drinking water or groundwater testing above the EPA's standard for PFOS and PFOA, including 25 army bases, 50 air force bases, 49 navy or Marine Corps bases and two Defense Logistics Agency sites. In addition, the DoD tested another 2,688 groundwater wells on and nearby base communities and found that about 61 percent of them tested above EPA recommended levels. These chemical compounds have been linked to cancer and other health issues such as ulcerative colitis and low birth weights. While the military is also working to develop a replacement substance, the damage from years of exposure to this chemical has already been done.

Residents of Portsmouth, New Hampshire, home to the former Pease Air Force Base, another abandoned military outpost, are dealing with this mess as well. You would need an old map of the city to recognize the base as it is now home to bright brick apartment buildings, trendy restaurants, offices, and daycare centers. When the base closed in 1991, the state of New Hampshire wrote a redevelopment plan to create a state-of-the-art business park, even though the area had been called "one of the most contaminated sites in New England" and declared a Superfund site in 1990. It was the first (former) military base in the country to discover PFAS in the local drinking water.

In 2014, Andrea Amico learned from a newspaper article about the drinking water in her community and how it was highly contaminated with these toxic substances. As has happened to so many other community members I've worked with, state officials did not respond to her calls or emails asking questions about how the water could affect the health of her family. So she started her own campaign to raise awareness and get blood tests provided to everyone exposed to the toxic

water. Along with residents Michelle Dalton and
Alayna Davis, they started Testing for Pease, a
community activist group whose mission is to be
a reliable resource for education and communication while advocating for a long-term health plan
on behalf of those impacted by the water contamination at the former Pease Air Force Base.

The women learned from communities like
Hoosick Falls, New York, less than two hundred
miles away, not to wait for those in charge to
take action. Officials there waited more than a
year to warn residents about the tainted drinking water and even longer to test blood levels
of locals. While the water in Hoosick Falls was
tainted by PFOA from industry rather than the
military, the contamination was not announced as
part of a federal testing program. One concerned
citizen—Michael Hickey, whose father worked at
the local plastics plant and died of kidney cancer
in 2013—paid out of his own pocket for water
tests, which detected PFOA at levels well above
the EPA's health advisory. Just like in Flint (and so
many other towns), local authorities downplayed
the threat, but Hickey and other community
members kept making noise.

In December 2015, the EPA finally issued a
warning to residents not to drink or cook with the
water. By June of 2016 residents of Hoosick Falls
stormed the state capitol, demanding answers,

bio-monitoring for their health problems, and cleanup. Children, moms, and grandparents marched with signs and their blood contamination levels scrawled on their bodies. With a PFOA blood level of 51.5, more than twenty-five times the national average, Hailey Bussey carried a handwritten letter asking Governor Andrew Cuomo why the administration "left us to die like sick kittens." Hailey was ten years old at the time.

Why does it take federal, state, and local governments such a long time to warn people about the dangerous toxic chemicals in their water? A nationwide EPA program samples water for unregulated contaminants and found PFOA in more than one hundred public water systems in twenty-seven states. In the case of Hoosick Falls, the town was skipped because their water supply serves fewer than ten thousand people. This town and many others are not big enough and likely don't have the resources to perform the tests. The fight for clean water continues there and in many other towns across the country.

In Portsmouth, three drinking water wells tested positive for PFCs. One in particular tested at levels more than twelve times above the EPA provisional health advisory, and that well was closed. After a community meeting in May 2014, Andrea felt as if local officials were not taking the problem seriously, so she turned to her local newspaper, the **Portsmouth Herald**, to cover the story.

"That article ran and that was the catalyst that brought all this to a head," Andrea said in a local article. "But to look back now and see how far we've come it truly amazes me and it gives me a big sense of pride in how far we've come."

Since then, two city officials, city councilor Stefany Shaheen and assistant mayor Jim Splaine, along with the state have agreed to test anyone exposed to the contaminants—after Andrea and others lobbied for almost two years for blood testing. Almost 1,500 people were initially tested, and results showed the blood levels of PFCs of people exposed to the city's tainted water were higher than national averages. The air force began a water quality sampling program to monitor the other wells and surrounding areas of Pease. The city began piloting activated carbon and resin treatment systems in October 2017 on those wells.

The air force also denied community requests to conduct a health study on the residents affected by the contamination at Pease in 2017, but by 2018 ATSDR announced it would include the town in their first-ever multi-site health study on PFAS exposure. New Hampshire senator Jeanne Shaheen worked with locals and helped to write the legislation that made the study possible.

The study will take years to complete and create a full picture of the impact to this city and its people, but it is a step in the right direction.

Portsmouth resident Lindsey Carmichael got involved with the local water issues after learning her son had been exposed to the contaminated water at his daycare. She became a member of Pease's Community Assistance Panel, a group of citizens who work with federal agencies to look at health effects on the community.

"All of us are guinea pigs and we bear the burden of proving a product or chemical's safety—or lack thereof—and the consequences are what we're seeing here," she said in an article.

Working with community members in Michigan in late 2017, raising awareness about PFOS. Note their T-shirts!

MILITARY CONTAMINANTS OF CONCERN

Below is a partial list and brief "official" statements about the conditions at these facilities from a Facebook post I wrote in 2015. Hundreds of other bases, forts, munitions stations, annexes, depots, centers, and unnamed facilities are also dealing with pollution issues.

U.S. ARMY

Aberdeen Proving Ground, MD

Essentially every land portion in the Edgewood, Maryland, area (on which a portion of the base is located) is contaminated or potentially contaminated. Monitoring in 1977–78 indicated contamination of surface and ground water. Four standby wells were shut down in 1983 due to detected organic compounds. The base's active drinking water supplies come from two off-post sources, Deer Creek and Winters Run, which are unaffected by the contamination on the base.

Fort A. P. Hill, VA

Three problems exist here: (1) An herbicide contaminated the soil near an old pesticide storage building and the soil has been placed in sealed drums. (2) Herbicide- and dioxin-contaminated soil and debris are stored at a base warehouse in 33-gallon drums inside sealed 55-gallon drums. A study will be done to recommend an environmentally sound method of permanent disposal. (3) The base plans to remove some 70 tons of soil contaminated by DDT. The base water comes from a deep aquifer and is not contaminated, the army says.

Fort Belvoir, VA

Several contaminants—benzene, trichloroethylene, chloroform, toluene, ethylbenzene, and 1,2-dichloroethane—have seeped from the Building 324 tank farm into an unnamed creek. None of these contaminants were detected in surface water at the installation boundary, and no health hazard is apparent, the army says. Post drinking water comes from the Fairfax County Water Authority.

Fort Devens, MA

A sanitary landfill that is a potential source of contamination is being closed. It was used as an open burning site, then for incineration of waste and burial of residues. Water quality meets state standards.

Fort Dix, NJ

Nine potentially contaminated sites are known. One, the sanitary landfill, was placed on the National Priority List (Superfund) due to the presence of organic solvents. However, the army says no significant health hazards have been identified. To avoid any risk, the landfill may be capped with clean soil and planted with grass. The other eight sites were identified only recently. Organic solvents and/or petroleum products were located at an old magazine area, a tank farm, a fire station, the golf course, a motor pool, a firing range, a pesticide storage building, and a National Guard facility. Investigation is under way to determine any problems. The sites do not endanger the base water supply, according to the army.

Fort Lewis, WA

There are two problems. One is Landfill No. 5. Plans call for a landfill liner and leachate collection to preclude groundwater contamination. There are also plans for a refuse-fired incinerator to reduce reliance on the landfill. Also, TCE has been found in the groundwater beneath the Logistics Center. Post drinking water comes from a spring unrelated to that aquifer.

Fort McClellan, AL

Ten old training areas and three former disposal sites have a slight chance of subsurface contamination from mustard agent and its breakdown products and possible byproducts of chemical agent decontamination. Only very small quantities of the agent were used, and all sites have been closed, decontaminated, and fenced. No evidence of any surface or surface water contamination has been found in the past, the army says. The post receives its water from the city of Anniston.

Redstone Arsenal, AL

A $30 million cleanup was recently completed by Olin Corporation, which made DDT in a leased factory that was closed in 1970 for environmental reasons. Manufacturing waste was contaminating soils and streams. DDT was found in the wildlife food chain but not in potable water supplies inside or outside the base. In addition, the presence of PCBs, heavy metals, and other organic compounds is known or suspected. An investigation is under way to determine if they contaminated the active sanitary landfill, a DDT waste landfill, open burning and detonation grounds, and twenty-two old disposal sites. Also, a $5 million program is in progress to remove all asbestos from post buildings.

U.S. NAVY

Brunswick NAS, ME

A study is under way to determine contaminants and their migration habits.

Lakehurst Naval Air Engineering Center, NJ

Soil and shallow groundwater at the tetraethyl lead disposal site are contaminated, perhaps from aviation fuel. The groundwater in some areas is covered with a six-inch layer of JP-8 jet fuel. Elsewhere, the carcinogen nitronomine may be present. Waste oils, battery acid, and solvents are suspected of having been discharged into some dry wells. The soil stabilization field test received 362 gallons of aniline and 161 of furfural (toxic by ingestion, inhalation, or skin absorption) and ferric choride solution; personnel and animals that come in contact with the soil may be endangered. A landfill received thousands of gallons of hydraulic fluids, five tons of asbestos, and also cutting oils, solvents, sludge, and heavy metals. A site for PCB testing and storage is near the environmentally sensitive Ridgeway Branch. The western portion of the base may be contaminated by ordnance: shells, gas-loaded projectiles, phosgene, phosphorus, mustard agent, explosives, flares, and depth bombs. The shallow aquifer in this area may also be contaminated.

Moffett Field NAS, CA

The major contaminants in the groundwater are volatile organic compounds.

Whidbey Island NAS, WA

The groundwater could be contaminated. Waste oil, solvents, fuel, and caustic rinse water containing heavy metals have been discharged through the storm sewer system and into Dugella Bay. Waterfowl and fish that feed or live in the drainage area may be affected. Subsurface migration at the seaplane base may have affected fish or shellfish in Oak and Crescent Harbors. A backup well at Ault Field is threatened by potential migration of contaminants.

Other Contaminated Navy Bases:

- China Lake, CA
- Indian Head NOS, MD
- Jacksonville NAS, FL
- Miramar NAS, CA
- Pabmont River NAS, MD
- Roosevelt Roads NS, Puerto Rico

U.S. AIR FORCE

Castle AFB, CA

On-base drinking water supply has been contaminated with TCE. Work is under way to install a new well drawing from a deeper, uncontaminated aquifer.

Dover AFB, DE

Ground on the base is contaminated with arsenic and other metals, and a stream on the base is contaminated with TCE. The base well, however, is free of these contaminants. Remedial action has been under way since 1985.

Griffiss AFB, NY

Phenols, ethyl benzene, and benzene have been detected in groundwater on the base, and toluene in surface water on the base.

Hill AFB, UT

Seepage water near two disposal areas contains toxic organic chemicals, such as trichloroethylene (TCE), 1,2-dichloroethane, and 1,1,1-trichloroethane. None of the affected water is used for human consumption. Remedial action to date includes construction of a slurry wall and landfill covers as well as pumping and treating contaminated groundwater.

Mather AFB, CA

Water in thirty-six homes was affected by TCE contamination of a well on-base. A new permanent water supply is to be provided to these homes.

McChord AFB, WA

Various chemicals—methylene chloride, chloroform, benzene, arsenic, chromium, and mercury—have been detected in test wells and in surface drainage leaving the base. One site is a liquid waste spill next to the wash rack and industrial waste treatment system. Contracted work for the American Lake Gardens Water Supply Project began in 1985; a contractor installed shallow wells and one deep well.

McClellan AFB, CA

An estimated 160 sites have been identified. Contaminants include organic compounds, such as TCE, methylene chloride, and 1,1-dichloroethylene. Wells both on and off the base that had contaminants exceeding government standards have been shut down. McClellan is considered a leader in cleanup efforts. Completed projects include alternate water supply for off-base residents and a groundwater containment system and treatment plant.

Norton AFB, CA

TCE was detected in concentrations exceeding state drinking water standards. All base wells were contaminated to various degrees with silver and PCE. Closure of a lagoon and sludge removal was begun several years ago.

Robins AFB, GA

Contaminants include halogenated solvents, heavy metals, pesticides (DDT, chordane, etc.), cyanide, and oil products. The toxic organic compounds TCE and PCE have been detected in groundwater on-base. Groundwater is not used as drinking water, but the contaminants could eventually appear in surface water.

Tinker AFB, OK

Some base wells were closed due to contamination from chlorinated solvents. Chlorinated solvents were also detected in the aquifer that is the primary water source in the region. Organic compounds have been detected at all sites, though migration is limited. Remedial action, begun in 1984, includes capping Landfill No. 6, and stopping leaks from underground storage tanks at the fuel farm.

Wright-Patterson AFB, Ohio

Fourteen organic compounds, including TCE and PCE in relatively high quantities, have been found in wells serving the base. Nearly half the seventeen wells have been shut down due to contamination or age. An air stripper, a technology in which volatile organic compounds are transferred from extracted water to air, has been put on two wells to remove the organics, and installation of two other strippers is planned.

Other Contaminated Air Force Bases:

- Beale AFB, CA
- Chanute AFB, IL
- Charleston AFB, SC
- Columbus AFB, MS
- Edwards AFB, CA
- England AFB, LA
- F. E. Warren AFB, WY
- George AFB, CA

- Hanscom AFB, MA
- Hickam AFB, HI
- Kelly AFB, TX
- Kirtland AFB, NM
- Langley AFB, VA
- Lowery AFB, CO
- Luke AFB, AZ
- MacDill AFB, FL
- McGuire AFB, NJ
- Moody AFB, GA
- Mountain Home AFB, ID
- Otis Air National Guard Base, MA
- Pease AFB, NH
- Plattsburgh AFB, NY
- Pope AFB, NC
- Reese AFB, TX
- Seymour Johnson AFB, NC
- Shemya AFB (now Eareckson Air sStation), AK
- Travis AFB, CA
- Vandenburg AFB, CA
- Wurtsmith AFB, MI

ACTION STEPS
Contacting Media 101

Working with the media can be an important step to help educate the public and have your message reach a larger audience. You can pitch stories about your cause to media outlets or offer to be a source for stories, meaning they will interview you about your experience. The best way to start is by contacting local media agencies such as local papers, blogs, or television stations. These local stories often get picked up by larger news outlets.

Ingredients for a Successful Media Pitch

Traditionally, one way to get more media attention for a cause is to write a press release. A press release is an official announcement regarding something new or noteworthy about you, your group, or an event. It should answer the who, what, why, where, when, and how of your story. These days, it usually takes the form of email, but the same principles apply. If you are working with a group of people in your community, find the person with the best writing skills to take on this task.

Start with a captivating headline or email subject. Reporters and editors get hundreds of emails a day, and you want to catch their attention. One way to do this is to think outside the box. Don't be afraid to put your most important point first or to make a powerful statement, as long as it is factual. Don't shy away from the personal: tell your story, as journalists appreciate a personal angle that can represent an issue, especially when it's a complex case such as water contamination. Be sure to include any national statistics that might be relevant as these facts will help those covering the story to understand the larger impact. Be sure to define and spell out key terms that might not be familiar, such as chemical names.

Keep these questions in mind as you write:

What's the story?
Why should we care?
Why is it relevant now?

Here's a template for a press release or pitch:

- Headline/Email subject line
- Opening sentence
- Body (What's the story, why does it matter?)
- Any other previous news coverage (with links)
- Contact information

Don't forget that it's a real person you are reaching out to so always be respectful of them and their time. It's also okay to send a follow-up email or two, if you don't hear back from them on the first outreach.

Additional Camp Lejeune Resources

If you are a veteran, and have concerns about your health, you can find out more information here:

Department of Veterans Affairs (VA): www.publichealth.va.gov/exposures/ camp-lejeune

ATSDR: www.atsdr.cdc.gov/sites/lejeune/ index.html

The Few, the Proud, the Forgotten: www .tftptf.com/5801.html

Semper Fi: Always Faithful (documentary film): semperfialwaysfaithful.com

A Trust Betrayed: The Untold Story of Camp Lejeune and the Poisoning of Generations of Marines and Their Families by Mike Magner (Da Capo Press, 2014)

Poisoned Nation: Pollution, Greed, and the Rise of Deadly Epidemics by Loretta Schwartz-Nobel (St. Martin's Press, 2007)

10

TAKING BACK THE EPA & FLORIDA'S SHORELINES

Gutted. It's the best word I can think of to describe the current state of affairs at the U.S. Environmental Protection Agency (EPA) in the second year of the Trump administration. Tasked with protecting the water we drink and the air we breathe, our No. 1 eco-agency is made up of many well-intentioned scientists, researchers, and administrators who have what many call an impossible job.

When Congress passes a law such as the Clean Water Act, the EPA must work to enforce and maintain it. That means finding solutions to some of our biggest problems, including water pollution and toxic waste. They use all available science and spearhead new research efforts, especially when it comes to studying emerging contaminants of concern. Each year, the list of potential toxic chemicals gets longer, right next to the backlog of thousands of unstudied and unregulated chemicals. We live in a triage situation where thousands of heavily polluted sites across the country sit untouched because they are too large, too expensive, and too complicated to tackle. These include many urban waterways.

What we need is a well-funded, robust agency full of our best and brightest. What we have is an underfunded, understaffed, overstretched federal department. This agency can't keep up with all the pollution and corruption happening across the country. Making laws and policies is already a slow, delicate dance between proposals, negotiations, implementation, and enforcement. These policies are based on the scientific research available and the funding to continue studying how pollution affects our daily lives.

These days, the EPA is more focused on cutting programs and killing regulations than on protecting us from toxic chemicals. Regulations without proper enforcement and oversight are moot. If we don't shift gears soon, we may never pull out of this mess.

"It's not wrong for Americans who care about the EPA to be concerned right now," climate change writer Robison Meyer wrote in **The Atlantic** in 2017. "Many Republicans want to see its powers diminished or removed altogether. But Congress will not attempt to curb the EPA's influence by closing it outright. Instead, it will wage war on the agency through a thousand little cuts—through bills, through joint resolutions, and through budget riders."

It might sound like I'm taking a political side here. I'm not. I hate politics being involved with our water, since we should all support this essential need. For years, I've watched as environmental tragedies have unfolded under both Republican and Democratic leadership. The EPA is not a perfect agency, but the situation has grown much worse since the election of Donald Trump in 2016, when he vowed to reduce the EPA's finances to "little tidbits," proposing a budget not seen since 1976. He called for a 25 percent reduction in staff and made plans to eliminate significant regional water quality programs such as the Great Lakes Restoration Initiative and the Chesapeake Bay program, which work to help keep our local waterways safe. He's also proposed to significantly cut the Superfund program, which works to clean up hazardous waste sites, and to slash funding for federal enforcement of environmental protection regulations. Cutting staff and budgets means fewer inspectors monitoring the laws we have on the books, fewer resources to study the impact of toxins, and more companies contravening environmental regulations.

When you take a closer look at the numbers, you will find that the EPA's budget and number of employees has been slowly shrinking for decades, according to a report from the Environmental Data & Governance Initiative (EDGI), an organization made up of academics and nonprofit employees that promotes open and accessible government data and information along with evidence-based policy making. In 1999 the EPA's staff size peaked with more than eighteen thousand employees. Staff numbers have dwindled since then for a variety of reasons including retirements, pushing out good people, and many employees feeling too fed up to stay and watch the agency crumble. The EPA now works with an estimated fifteen thousand employees on a budget of about $8 billion to ensure that Americans have clean air, land, and water. Consider the fact that studying one toxic chemical can cost an estimated $1 million and it becomes easy to see why the agency is operating at a snail's pace. The current administration has further snapped an already broken system.

"The Trump administration currently poses the greatest threat to the U.S. Environmental Protection Agency (EPA) in its entire 47-year history," reads the first sentence of an EDGI report titled "The EPA Under Siege."

The report also points to how the EPA, in its early days, had bipartisan support from Republican and Democratic presidents alike. All that changed during the first Reagan administration in the early '80s when he appointed EPA administrators with deep corporate ties, known for complaining about government overreach. Anne Gorsuch Burford, the first female EPA administrator serving from 1981 to 1983, resigned less than two years into the job amid a scandal concerning her mismanagement of the Superfund program. Many experts now refer to this conservative former state legislator as the original overthrower of the EPA. She proposed deep budget cuts to the agency and rolled back clean water and air protections while touting an industry-friendly agenda. In the first year of the Reagan administration, the number of enforcement cases filed from regional offices to the U.S. EPA dropped by 79 percent, while cases filed from the U.S. EPA to the Department of Justice dropped 69 percent. Most national environmental laws did survive that time and the agency did regain resources, but it never fully recovered. Even with good laws on the books, the agency has been hamstrung by enforcement issues and outdated science.

But we did gain one new law from Anne Burford's attempts to weaken the agency and that's the doctrine of Chevron deference. It's named for the 1984 Supreme Court case **Chevron U.S.A., Inc. v. Natural Resources Defense Council**, which worked to address a rule that the EPA created under Burford called "bubbling." It refers to a piece of the Clean Air Act (CAA) that puts stricter limits on new emission sources than older ones, since cleaning up old factories is harder than building new, cleaner facilities. The law essentially says new power plants, oil refineries, and other sources of toxic emissions need to meet the stricter standards. "Bubbling" was an interpretation of that law saying that as long as a new part of the facility did not cause any increases in emissions for the whole facility, the new section could pollute more than the CAA regulations allowed. The court disagreed with this logic, but ultimately decided that ambiguous language in any law should go back to the expert agency for interpretation. Despite the judges favoring a different interpretation of this law, **Chevron** established that federal agencies have the power to interpret and enforce the laws made by Congress. This doctrine becomes tricky in a politically divided world, as Democratic administrations tend to use Chevron deference to expand the EPA's authority, while Republican administrations generally use it as a weapon to weaken the agency.

In January 2017, the U.S. House of Representatives passed a bill aimed at changing Chevron deference. Called the "Regulatory Accountability Act," it appeared to create more transparency in how the government makes rules, requiring agencies to do more fact-finding, conduct scientific studies, and ensure that the benefits of regulations outweigh the costs. The problem is that agencies like the EPA are already stalled on so many levels and making them jump through more administrative hoops to do their jobs sounds dangerous. The bill introduces more than fifty new rule-making requirements before an agency can take action on new regulations and it also requires analysis of **any** alternative proposals—including ones from special-interest groups that are looking to delay regulations. It could impact how the EPA regulates everything from toxic chemicals to emissions at power plants, requiring the agency to adopt the cheapest regulations rather than what's best for public safety. Also, in an interesting twist of historical fate, one of the newest members of the Supreme Court, Neil Gorsuch, son of EPA-slayer Anne, says he opposes Chevron deference. So not only are we living under an anti-regulation administration, but we have a member of the Supreme Court who doesn't think expert agencies should have the power to interpret laws.

Not surprisingly, both pollution cases and charges to polluters from the EPA have dropped during the Trump administration, as documented by the Environmental Integrity Project (EIP). The organization's review of federal records found that during Trump's first year, penalties charged to companies for violating regulations dropped by 49 percent compared to former president Obama's first year. The Trump administration filed 48 civil cases against polluters and collected $30 million in penalties from inauguration day in January 2017 through January 20, 2018. In comparison, in Obama's first year 71 civil cases were filed and $71 million in penalties were collected. The Bush administration filed 112 settlements and collected $50 million in penalties; and the Clinton administration filed 73 consent decrees and collected $55 million.

"President Trump's dismantling of the EPA means violators are less likely to be caught, making illegal pollution cheaper," Eric Schaeffer, executive director of the Environmental Integrity Project and former director of EPA's Office of Civil Enforcement, said in a statement. "The president's 'law and order' agenda apparently wasn't intended for fossil fuel companies and other big polluters."

THREATS FROM THE TOP

The president's job is to appoint leaders to run the EPA who will uphold the office and work to protect both the environment and the people. Let me ask you a simple question: Do you think the person picked to run the EPA should care about the environment? I'm guessing your answer is yes. Should that same person have ties to big business and the very industries that the agency is meant to regulate? No. It's like asking a fox to guard the henhouse. Common sense tells us that those in charge of the EPA should operate independently without ties to private or corporate interests.

"You have all this stuff that goes on—political pressures, breakdowns in the system on all sides, a huge disparity in influence," Andrew Rosenberg, the director of the Center for Science and Democracy for the Union of Concerned Scientists, told me in a recent conversation. "Now Trump comes in. The people that he's putting in place are the people who not only developed these strategies for stopping environmental regulation but were the ones that were implementing them. They're running the EPA."

Andrew, who has worked as an academic and scientist in government and in regulatory positions for more than twenty-five years, is referring to a very well-known set of tactics that have been developed by industry to fight regulations. Many of these tactics were developed by the tobacco industry and then used by the oil industry, the food industry, the chemical industry, and many more. These practices are designed to confuse the science, helping delay or throw out regulations. While it's easy to set simple limits for pollutants or enact zero tolerance for certain toxins, we rarely do because of industry influence. Publicly, corporations love to criticize the complexity of regulations, but privately they are the ones working behind the scenes to complicate them. Impartial, objective studies don't always present corporate products and practices in a flattering way, so industry constructs controversy by casting doubt on scientific results that conflict with their interests. Other times, they simply bury the science. As I've discussed, these businesses also work to buy science that affirms their products or to influence the scientific process so they can keep polluting.

These tactics are at the heart of why the U.S. is one of the few industrialized nations that has not banned asbestos, even though independent scientific review has shown its harm to humans since the 1970s. In 1989, the EPA issued a rule, known as the Asbestos Ban and Phase-Out Rule (ABPR), which proposed a ban on manufacturing, importing, and selling products that contain asbestos. But the chemical industry fought back by suing the EPA, and they won. Asbestos is still used in many commercial products today while more than three thousand new cases of mesothelioma, a cancer directly related to exposure to asbestos, are diagnosed each year. That's just one example of one chemical.

Industry's biggest play to date may be taking over the EPA. It's a who's who of industry now sitting in top positions there. These are the same insiders who have for years been diligently pushing back on most, if not all, environmental and public health and safety protections. The government is supposed to protect public interest, not to uphold the bottom line for some of the world's biggest polluters.

President Trump's first pick to run the EPA, Scott Pruitt, is a former senator and attorney general of Oklahoma, an oil-producing state. Oil and gas industry executives were elated when he was selected to run the regulatory agency, as he promised to protect the fossil fuel industry. While attorney general of Oklahoma, he sued the EPA fourteen times in an effort to block clean air and water safeguards. He resigned as head of the EPA in July 2018, a little more than a year into the job, but his short tenure was riddled with ethical scandals around his personal spending habits and his secret schedule for private meetings with industry representatives, along with setting the wheels in motion for rollbacks to public health protections. He terminated half of the advisors on a key science advisory board, replacing them with industry-friendly representatives who he felt were better equipped to "understand the impact of regulations on the regulated community."

The acting administrator put in his place, Andrew Wheeler, began his career at the EPA, as a special assistant in the toxics office under President

George H. W. Bush's administration, but he went on to work as a top lobbyist for coal and chemical companies. Wheeler became the fifteenth administrator of the EPA in February 2019. Bill Wehrum serves as the assistant administrator for the Office of Air and Radiation at the EPA. He spent years as a corporate lawyer fighting the EPA to mitigate air pollution regulations on behalf of Big Oil, Big Coal, and the chemical industry. Now on the inside, he's helping the clients his law firm represented— coal-burning power plants—by relaxing national regulations for power plants and allowing states to set their own standards. His former client roster was also full of large trade associations like the American Petroleum Institute, the American Fuel and Petrochemical Manufacturers, and the Utility Air Regulatory Group. Federal ethics rules are more lenient for lawyers than for former lobbyists, so his transition hasn't raised many red flags.

Nancy Beck, Trump's pick for deputy assistant administrator of the Office of Chemical Safety and Pollution Prevention, may be the most egregious choice of all. She comes straight from the halls of the American Chemistry Council, a lobby group whose members include 3M, Dow Chemical, DuPont, Monsanto, Merck & Co., ExxonMobil Chemical, Chevron Phillips Chemical, Honeywell, and Bayer. By definition, lobbyists represent private interest groups in order to influence the decisions of government. Before working for the EPA, Beck advocated for these companies, helping write the industry's position on chemical legislation for Congress. She is now the EPA's key decision maker on chemical safety, and her actions will affect all Americans for years to come. It's an incredible breach of democracy.

But the president is ultimately the one who sets the tone for federal oversight. When Nixon created the EPA, he wasn't necessarily an environmentalist: he was responding to huge public outcry over environmental issues. More than 20 million Americans participated in the first Earth Day event in April 1970, which sent a strong message to government. By December of that same year, Congress created the EPA to tackle these issues.

"My primary objective in planning Earth Day was to show the political leadership of the Nation that there was broad and deep support for the environmental movement," wrote Wisconsin senator Gaylord Nelson in the **EPA Journal**. "While I was confident that a nationwide peaceful demonstration of concern would be impressive, I was not quite prepared for the overwhelming response that occurred on that day."

Since his inauguration, President Trump has imposed regulatory freezes and rollbacks across the government that will most likely continue throughout his term. His administration has already repealed rules meant to safeguard our drinking water by dismissing the "stream protection rule"—giving mining companies more leeway in dumping debris into our streams. His team has repealed the Clean Water Rule, also known as the "waters of the United States rule," which was adopted in May 2015, as a means to clear up confusion about which waters are protected by the Clean Water Act and helped further define the scope of federal protection, particularly for streams and wetlands, which millions of Americans rely on for drinking water. In August 2018, the agency announced plans to transfer regulation of coal-fueled power plants to the state level, which experts believe will help increase profits in the coal industry. The move will also increase carbon emissions throughout the country. The EPA has also proposed to freeze fuel-efficiency requirements for carmakers and even withdraw California's Clean Air Act preemption waiver. California and about a dozen other states follow this rule, which applies to about a third of all passenger vehicles sold. Former California governor Jerry Brown called the proposal "reckless."

"For Trump to now destroy a law first enacted at the request of Ronald Reagan five decades ago is a betrayal and an assault on the health of Americans everywhere," said Brown in a statement. "California will fight this stupidity in every conceivable way possible."

According to the EPA's own studies, the national clean car standards have preserved consumer choices when buying cars, helped reduce fuel costs, and lowered greenhouse gas pollution.

Now much of the slack will need to be picked up by the states, which literally have to clean up the messes of national and multinational corporations.

Why do companies want regulations managed at the state level?

"There's a lot of state agencies and legislatures that do a good job on certain issues, but the capacity of the states to do the scientific work, to do the regulatory work, and to follow through on the law enforcement and inspection work is much lower than the federal government," Andrew Rosenberg said to me.

Generally, states have neither the means nor the will to substitute for federal enforcement of environmental laws, according to a 2017 report from the Institute for Policy Integrity. Large corporate entities know that. Just look at the many examples I've already covered in Michigan, Texas, West Virginia, Kentucky, North Carolina, and other states.

The report discloses that while states are responsible for much of the enforcement, research from the EPA's own Office of the Inspector General concluded that state enforcement efforts were both inadequate and inconsistent and that states "frequently do not meet national enforcement goals." In just one example, only two states had complied with an EPA goal that all large-quantity generators of hazardous waste be inspected every five years. If a company knows that enforcement is a slap on the wrist or that inspections are lax to nonexistent, they will continue with business as usual. Federal violations tend to be much more severe with higher penalties attached than state violations, and companies know that too.

Fracking is an example of skirting federal oversight. Remember, the industry took care to ensure that the EPA and the Department of the Interior (DOI) were not regulating them, as it could cost them big-time. The Halliburton loophole, part of the Energy Policy Act of 2005, exempted fracking from key provisions of the Safe Drinking Water Act, putting its activities outside the jurisdiction of federal EPA enforcement and inspection. Fracking companies also have more influence at the state level. Just think about when one of these natural gas businesses come into a state offering ten thousand jobs—that's a big deal and the state is going to roll out the red carpet for those jobs. If that same company goes to the DOI offering ten thousand jobs, it doesn't have the same impact. Now add to that the issue that states will do fewer inspections and have less means to prosecute environmental violations and you can see why the industry pushed so hard for state or even local control.

We need both federal and state authority, but we also need to recognize the strengths and weaknesses at each level. When more of the burden is put on states to enforce environmental laws, less enforcement happens. In addition, reducing the U.S. EPA's budget means fewer grants go to state and regional offices to fund their enforcement programs. Most states already lack the resources and political clout to implement environmental laws. When politicians say that states know best how to handle their affairs or that states can become "laboratories of democracy," I urge you to look at exactly where this rhetoric comes from and who is funding their campaign. This experiment is risking public health throughout our country, while polluters continue to make their messes in our backyards. Just look at what's happening in Florida.

"DRAINING THE SWAMP" & CLEANING UP GREEN GOO IN FLORIDA

When most people think of Florida, they picture slender palm trees, sun-drenched sandy beaches stretching for miles, and an abundance of pelicans, manatees, and other wildlife. As I write these words, I'm watching one of the worst water crises unfold in the Sunshine State. Beaches and other waterways throughout southwest Florida, which are usually packed with locals and tourists alike, are empty thanks to what many describe as the smell of death near the water. The summer of 2018 was the lost summer across Florida. Hundreds of tons of dead fish and other marine wildlife washed ashore. One man became ill and went to the hospital after harvesting and eating clams from Fort Myers Beach. Respiratory issues were reported by those breathing in the toxic air near the water. In addition, more than eighty-six people sought treatment in hospitals after contact with water in Florida's St. Lucie River. When I visited the state in September of 2018, health officials had closed the beaches along Jupiter Beach because of the airborne toxins.

The devastation came from a one-two punch of microorganisms. Floridians are accustomed to red tide, known to scientists as **Karenia brevis**. It's a recurring harmful algal bloom (HAB) that's been reported along Florida's Gulf coast since as early as the 1500s and written about since the 1840s. Red tide blooms most frequently occur in saltwater but can make their way into estuaries and bays. The environmental impacts of red tide are widely documented and include massive fish kills, along with death to dolphins, sea turtles, and birds. Red

Fish with tumors pulled from the water in
southwest Florida in the summer of 2018 during
the red tide and blue-green algae crisis, which
caused thousands of marine animals to die and
hundreds of tons of dead fish to wash ashore

tide season usually lasts from October to February,
but the 2018 red tide season affected hundreds of
miles of coastline for more than ten months and
counting. Scientists believe that HABs are increasing in frequency, duration, and geography. They
are also increasingly investigating how humans
might be contributing to the problem.

Along with the red tide is cyanobacteria, more
commonly known as blue-green algae. The images
sent to me of thick bright green goo overtaking
canals look toxic and unnatural. When these
microscopic bacteria grow out of control, we call

it a bloom. These blooms cause a depletion of oxygen in the water and a flood of toxins including hepatotoxins, cytotoxins, and endotoxins, which cause destruction to any life in the water. Blue-green algae thrive in freshwater, inundating lakes, rivers, and streams. The combination of red tide in coastal waters and harmful blue-green algal blooms in freshwater has severe consequences for the local economy, human health, and the environment of Florida. Red tide blooms begin miles offshore, but the situation became severe in 2018 when the blooms came inshore right to the mouth of the Caloosahatchee River and surrounding bays, as these microorganisms use man-made nutrients to grow and spread.

Toxic algae blooms have increased thirtyfold since the 1960s with more than three hundred coastal systems impacted and nearly every state in the U.S. experiencing HABs, according to the National Centers for Coastal Ocean Science (NCCOS). The EPA says that nutrient pollution (too much nitrogen and phosphorus) makes the problem worse, leading to more severe and frequent blooms. Other contributors are warm water, water stagnation, and storm water runoff that contains pesticide residue from lawns and commercial farms.

"When nutrients from agricultural and urban areas are transported downstream, they can cause cyanoHABs in reservoirs, which can impair drinking water quality and result in closures of recreational areas," according to the U.S. Geological Survey.

How the HABs took over Florida's waterways is a more complicated tale. A water crisis doesn't develop overnight, and the state has been mismanaging its water for more than a hundred years. The heart of the issue comes down to draining a swamp. In this case, it's the Everglades, a large, interconnected marshland ecosystem in South Florida that once spanned some four thousand square miles, and now is less than half that area.

The region was one of the most biodiverse areas in our country, rich with exceptional flora and fauna, but the "swampland" was considered a nuisance to development. Michael Grunwald writes in **The Swamp:** "Americans believed it was their destiny to drain this 'God-forsaken' swamp, to 'reclaim' it from mosquitoes and rattlesnakes, to 'improve' it into a subtropical paradise of bountiful crops and blooming communities. Wetlands were considered wastelands and 'draining the swamp' was a metaphor for festering problems."

Starting in the nineteenth century, both politicians and business leaders schemed how to turn the wetlands into something productive. They discovered that if they drained the water, they could transform the land into the perfect spot for sugarcane fields. In fact, the region became one of the largest areas of rich, fertile soil in the country; it is now home to hundreds of thousands of acres of sugarcane crops. Other developments followed and population boomed. Today, we are dealing with the effects of rerouting nature's waterways and losing an ecosystem that acted as a natural water treatment system that helped to filter waste and purify the water.

The Everglades begin far north of Lake Okeechobee, one of the largest natural freshwater lakes in the country, in the Kissimmee River Basin. Water from this great watershed once traveled the Kissimmee River through creeks and tributaries to the lake, from which it then passed into the Florida Bay. Underlying the river of complex grasses is porous limestone that captures massive amounts of freshwater that supply scores of lakes, springs, and marsh systems. The Kissimmee River was an important component of the Florida Everglades until it was cut off by the Army Corps of Engineers in an attempt to manage Florida's freshwater for agricultural, industrial, and residential development. More than a hundred miles of winding river and tributaries that flowed gradually down the spine of the state to Lake Okeechobee got converted into a massive manually controlled canal, a fifty-six-mile channel direct to Lake Okeechobee, a massive sewer of wastewater discharge that would have otherwise been cleaned of most nutrients in the natural grasses of the meandering river.

Through the late 1920s, a series of hurricanes and resulting floods shifted the focus from draining agricultural fields to flood control, two vastly divergent tactics. In the 1930s, the Army Corps of Engineers was brought in to construct a continuous ridge of levees around Lake Okeechobee, together with four massive canals connecting Lake Okeechobee to the Atlantic Ocean. This is when agriculture took off, and with the ability to rebuild, agribusiness gained permanent control of the region and has refused to let go. Sugar was and still is the predominant crop in the Everglades, and production more than doubled within the first decade after the Army Corps demonstrated they could maintain control of the floodwaters, much to the pleasure of federal representatives who were obliged to their financial benefactors.

In the late 1940s, there were a series of hurricanes and record rainfall where hundreds of thousands of acres in both agricultural and urban areas were drenched in 108 inches of rainfall in just six months. Post–World War II construction began on a series of dikes, dams, and canals with the ability to control the flow of 1 billion gallons of water a day. South Florida experienced a postwar population explosion, which continues to this day. The impacts: the Kissimmee River and its important nutrient-cleaning grasses were devasted by drought, and the Florida Bay is no longer brackish, as was intended by nature with the intrusion of saltwater, which has forever changed its unique biodiversity. Most of South Florida was never meant to be farmed or inhabited; man has irrevocably destroyed this unique tropical wetland and its ecosystem.

Today, the managed runoff from industrial and residential developments and dairy farms north of Lake Okeechobee void the natural wetlands that filter nutrients and other pollutants. The reversal of flows from nutrient-rich farmland in the Everglades to the south have turned Lake Okeechobee into a virtual cesspool of pollution. Nutrients and minerals have accumulated in Lake Okeechobee, causing seasonal toxic blue-green algae blooms, beginning in the 1960s, monitored and managed throughout the 1970s and exploding in 1983, when the toxic algae covered its entire surface.

The situation in Florida has persisted for too long with little action on the part of state or federal agencies. Discharges from Lake Okeechobee have presented serious ecological and environmental problems for decades. This disaster has significant environmental consequences for the Gulf of Mexico, the Atlantic Ocean, hundreds of miles of coastline, the Florida Everglades, and scores of intercoastal waterways and marshlands.

In July 2018, fourteen Florida Waterkeeper groups, a network of clean water advocates, came together in Tallahassee to meet with the Florida Department of Environmental Protection (FDEP) to discuss the HABs and express their concerns. They submitted a joint request to their local and state leaders asking them to follow these action steps: (1) create a comprehensive audit of infrastructure vulnerability and storm risk to accurately price the cost of inaction; (2) prioritize green infrastructure, and (3) enhance protection of wetlands and mangroves.

The Waterkeepers also submitted a statement about the ongoing impacts of hurricanes and storms on the state's waterways, and specifically that of Hurricane Irma in 2017.

"Hurricanes and major storm events can deteriorate water quality threatening human health and the environment, particularly in Florida. Such storms generate large volumes of flood water, causing sewer and septic systems to fail, and flush large quantities of sewage and pollutants into our oceans, bays, rivers, and lakes. Nutrients, pesticides, fecal bacteria, heavy metals, petroleum products, industrial chemicals, and many other contaminants enter our waterways and make them unsafe for swimming or fishing. Major storm events and the associated pollution can significantly impact local fisheries and tourism-based economies, and the people and livelihoods that depend on them, often taking months or years to recover," the statement said.

The groups also discussed ongoing threats to Florida's water, including excess nutrient pollution from a variety of factors including sewage sludge, failing septic tanks, aging infrastructure, storm water runoff, and agricultural runoff, all of which feed the toxic blue-green algae and red tide. They called on the state to start addressing root causes, stopping pollution at its source.

In addition, they submitted research samples taken in July 2018 of cyanobacteria in the Cape Coral tide canals located on the Caloosahatchee River, which revealed levels of the toxin microcystin (a potent liver toxin) to be nearly 40,000 ppb. The EPA has set safe levels at 4 ppb. The Waterkeeper groups requested the reactivation of the Harmful Algal Bloom Task Force, more testing of the actual bloom to understand its health implications, and better communication from state authorities to residents about toxic outbreaks.

Another group working to raise awareness and push state legislators to take action is Captains for Clean Water, a nonprofit group that started as a group of fishing guides who were fed up with Florida's water mismanagement.

"Given the destruction seen firsthand, we were convinced that if everyone knew what we knew, the problem would have been already fixed," reads a statement on their website. "We discovered, the solution has been delayed for decades because of a lack of political will and public awareness."

Tourism makes up about $67 billion of the state's economy. If visitors are afraid of the water, it has huge consequences for fishing, boating, and other water-related businesses including beachside hotels and restaurants. This group of activists knows firsthand how many Floridians depend on tourism and fishing to make their livings.

Chris Wittman, a co-founder of Captains for Clean Water, who lives and works on the water near Cape Coral, told CNN that he sees the current situation as a breaking point both ecologically and economically.

"This is not the Florida that people move here for. There are people that save all their lives to move to Florida, retire . . . enjoy our natural resources and this is what they're served," he said.

The Captains believe a first step to helping restore the Everglades and Florida's waterways already exists. Congress passed the Comprehensive Everglades Restoration Plan (CERP) in 2000, as a way to "restore, preserve, and protect the south Florida ecosystem while providing for other water-related needs of the region, including water supply and flood protection." It's the largest hydrologic restoration project ever attempted in our country, but the project has wobbled from lack of both funding and political backing.

"As planned, CERP alone will not save the estuaries," according to the Captains' site. "Increased storage, treatment, and conveyance of water south of Lake Okeechobee is essential to stop the damaging discharges and to restore the flow of clean freshwater to Everglades National Park and Florida Bay."

Both Republicans and Democrats running for reelection in Florida have promised to fix the state's water problems and reallocate more resources to projects like CERP, which has not had any projects completed since it was enacted.

"Their constituents are not happy with the current state of their waters, with the current state of their water management system, and they're more engaged than they've ever been," Chris said. "They realize that they aren't going to be able to get around this topic and the citizens are going to hold them accountable."

A similar devastating blue-green algal bloom occurred in the state in 2016. Mike Conner, from the environmental advocacy group Bullsugar.org, told NPR at the time, "This is a man-made—this is a government-sponsored disaster."

That year, Florida governor Rick Scott declared a federal emergency and asked for federal funds, but the White House rejected the request, saying

Florida had the resources to handle the problem itself. Mark Perry, executive director of the Florida Oceanographic Society, an environmental education and research center in Stuart, Florida, said at the time that he thought federal agencies should help manage the algae crisis, but the long-term solution was to restore the natural flow of water and to send the Lake Okeechobee water south through the sugar farmlands.

The root cause for this mess (and so many others like it) is a politically driven process. Months, years, or decades of oversight, mismanagement, or corruption drive these tragedies. We must work to overcome the disconnect between decision makers in government and residents living with these water woes.

More than 1,000 miles of rivers and streams, almost 350,000 acres of lakes, and 900 square miles of estuaries were not meeting the state's water quality standards due to excess nutrients, according to a 2008 FDEP report. Environmental groups in Florida sprang into action, filing a consent decree with the U.S. EPA saying the agency had "failed to perform a non-discretionary duty to set numeric nutrient criteria for the State of Florida," as required by the Clean Water Act. The EPA responded and Florida was on track to become the first state in the nation to set limits for sewage, manure, and fertilizer runoff. But in 2010 three state leaders fought to delay those federal standards for nutrient pollution in state waters, specifically for nitrogen and phosphorus. Once Governor Scott, Agriculture Commissioner Adam Putnam, and Attorney General Pam Bondi were elected, they sent a letter to then EPA administrator Lisa Jackson just ten days into their terms complaining that the pollution limits were an "onerous regulation" by an "overbearing federal government."

The letter continued, "We each ran on the platform of fiscal responsibility and heard from numerous constituents about concerns of an overbearing federal government that's placing burdensome regulations on Florida's families and employers."

The limits meant runoff would have to be cleaned up at the source, and polluters (including Big Ag) did not want to take on those costs. Instead, they hired a high-powered PR firm to help spread the story that these regulations would cost too much and even created a fake "clean water" coalition chock-full of industry leaders.

"According to the Florida Department of Environmental Protection, the EPA mandates set to be finalized this November 14 will impose capital costs of over $4 billion on municipal wastewater treatment utilities and over $17 billion on municipal storm water utilities," state leaders wrote in the letter.

Those figures were based on reverse osmosis, one of the most expensive forms of wastewater treatment, rather than on more affordable systems. The FDEP soon weighed in, asking the EPA for permission to set its own rules. In 2013, the EPA agreed, letting the state manage its own pollution limits for nutrients.

That's not all. Rick Scott also worked to dismantle state programs and reduced budgets intended to help monitor and improve water quality. In 2011, Scott slashed more than $500 million from the budget of the South Florida Water Management District, which was responsible for Everglades cleanup and water quality projects in Lake Okeechobee and the St. Lucie and Caloosahatchee watersheds. That same year, he also fired 270 employees and cut benefits to gouge another $100 million from regional water district budgets. I find it hard to believe these districts could maintain their workload with fewer people and resources.

"Since 2011, when Scott got into office, the critical measures of phosphorus load and nitrogen load into Lake O started to increase, and they are all still on upward trends," wrote Dave Conway in **Florida Sportsman.**

He also contended that the Scott administration has ignored key scientific studies of the nutrient load in Lake Okeechobee. The FDEP disregarded data produced by the South Florida

Water Management District and instead used a computer model to monitor nutrient levels.

Florida has seen the perfect storm of a state, influenced by industry, setting its own water quality standards, taking away valuable resources from those responsible for both protecting the water supply and preventing pollution, and legislators snubbing the science. More lawmakers and environmental advocates need to come together to restore the freshwater flows of the Everglades, set stricter limits on fertilizers and other chemicals from farms and lawns, and work on better plans for flooding and storm water systems.

Hands Along the Water, a nonprofit volunteer organization representing the citizens of Florida, organized an amazing show of unity at Florida beaches across the state in August 2018 to bring attention to the toxic algae crisis.

Regional water issues go beyond one state. The Great Lakes are a mess. The Sacramento Delta is a toilet bowl. The Ohio, Missouri, and Mississippi Rivers are laden with toxins. We need more people and resources focused on solutions for our country's waterways. Now is not the time to walk away from regulations that could help save our most precious resource.

THE EPA VS. THE ECONOMY

Donald Trump's presidency has been marked by his unyielding pursuit of his campaign promises and rallying cries, including one of his most famous slogans, "Drain the swamp!" He promised to "make our government honest again" by getting rid of business as usual in Washington and curbing the influence of lobbyists. Unfortunately, Americans were duped. Draining the swamp for him has been about deregulation and putting into office allies who agree with him.

Another of his talking points was putting coal miners back to work. Trump sees the EPA as an obstacle to stimulating the economy for middle-class Americans.

Two months after he was sworn into office, he visited the headquarters of the EPA in Washington, D.C., for a ceremony and said, "I want to acknowledge the truly amazing people behind me on this stage. Our incredible coal miners."

He then signed an executive order instructing federal regulators to rewrite the Clean Power Plan, rolling back crucial climate and clean air regulations. The Clean Power Plan didn't look to phase out coal, gas, and oil; it didn't ban the use of fossil fuels or require any power stations to close. It simply looked to reduce greenhouse gas emissions by about 30 percent and gave power companies decades to comply. The plan was designed to promote the development of renewable energy sources in our country.

"My administration is putting an end to the war on coal," Trump said at the signing ceremony. "With today's executive action, I am taking historic steps to lift the restrictions on American energy, to reverse government intrusion, and to cancel job-killing regulations."

In the audience that day was Barry Russell, the president and CEO of the Independent Petroleum Association of America. He said in a statement that he welcomed President Trump's "bold decision to tackle the growing regulatory state and identify rules that harm the economy and threaten American jobs."

People outside of the industry had a different perspective on the day.

"President Trump's executive order to roll back

vital climate and clean air protections is the most brazen and transparent assault on the health of Americans in my lifetime," Heather Zichal, former deputy assistant to the president for energy and climate change, told **The Washington Post**.

To be clear, power and water are inextricably linked. Power plants across the country create water stress and are the largest contributors to toxic pollution in U.S. waters. The EPA has studied power plants and in 2013 discovered that they dump more pollutants—mercury, arsenic, and lead—into our drinking water sources than the next nine industries combined.

"Thirsty energy sources like coal can take twenty thousand gallons per megawatt hour to fifty thousand gallons per megawatt hour, while wind power requires almost no water at all," according to the World Resources Institute.

Why do we have to choose between environmental protections and economic development? If we continue to enact policies that are indifferent toward our water resources and climate change, what will be the real cost to our collective livelihood? We need to stop spreading the lie that deregulating the government allows for a thriving economy.

I see regulations not as federal overreach but as effective means for protecting human health. Research compiled by the Cowles Foundation for

Research in Economics at Yale University points to environmental regulations enacted in 1990 that helped reduce toxic emissions for the next twenty years. The study's authors, professors Joseph Shapiro of Yale University and Reed Walker of the University of California, Berkeley, found that regulation of U.S. manufacturing plants contributed to a 60 percent decline in toxic emissions from 1990 to 2008, a time when manufacturing output increased by 33 percent. The researchers used data from both the U.S. Census Bureau and the EPA to track how manufacturers were complying with new requirements of the Clean Air Act.

Studies have also looked at whether regulations hurt the economy and cause people to lose their jobs. One study conducted by economists Eli Berman and Linda T. M. Bui from Boston University looked at the impact of air quality regulations in Los Angeles. The area enacted some of the strictest standards in the '80s. The regulations did not create a decline in employment, and the research suggests that labor demand can increase, as companies have to hire more people to help comply with regulations.

"We find no evidence that local air quality regulation substantially reduced employment," the authors wrote in the study.

Another economist, W. Reed Walker, published research on the impact of workers by the 1990

Clean Air Act amendments that required companies to get operating permits. He found that the average worker from a regulated sector who left their firm (whether they were fired or quit) saw an earnings loss of about 20 percent from their preregulatory earnings. He calculated the total of these workers' losses at about $5.4 billion. The EPA estimated the health benefit of these same regulations to have a value of up to $1.6 trillion.

"In light of these benefits, the earnings losses borne by workers in newly regulated industries are relatively small," he wrote in his 2013 paper, which was published in the **Quarterly Journal of Economics**. "Benefits from environmental policy far exceed the costs."

While regulations may contribute to cuts in certain sectors, they can also create jobs in new ones. Job gains and losses are all part of a healthy economy. New companies are always emerging to keep up with technology and innovation, while older companies can fall out of favor when they don't evolve with the times.

We must remember that the environment is the economy. In 2018, our country experienced fourteen weather- and climate-related disasters, each causing more than $1 billion in damages, for a total of $91 billion. These numbers and costs are the fourth highest since record keeping began in 1980. I'll discuss the impacts of climate change more in depth in the next chapter. In Sarasota County the red tide and blue-green algae drove down hotel occupancy rates by more than 11 percent at the end of 2018. This was one of the steepest declines seen since the September 11 terrorist attack in 2001, during what is usually a busy travel time to the region. It's a sure sign of how environmental disasters can impact business. About 80 percent of hotel owners in Sarasota County also reported that their business looked down for January, February, and March of 2019.

We have all forgotten that the EPA was created by conservatives and many of the laws on the books today were adopted with bipartisan support from our lawmakers. Abraham Lincoln said, "A house divided against itself cannot stand." Let's give the EPA back the tools it needs to do its job and ensure public and environmental health and vitality for years to come. It's time to come together and depoliticize funding and enforcement. Let's put bigger consequences in place for those who don't follow environmental rules. Let's strengthen our resources by helping more credible scientists who care about our country's future work at the federal and state level. Things won't get better if we sideline the science.

ACTION STEPS
Separation of Politics & Water

We need to stop politicizing regulations. Clean water and clean air should not depend on who is sitting in the White House. It's not a "blue" or "red" issue; it's an everyone issue. It's an Earth issue. The best way citizens can impact this process is to stop voting for lawmakers who refuse to talk about water and the environment. It's time to pay better attention to who is funding your candidate's campaign. We need to turn connections to big industry into a political liability. We're already seeing this in Florida. Big Sugar has traditionally funded many campaigns but in 2018 the only person who ran for governor with sugar money was Agriculture Commissioner Adam Putnam. Sugar companies and their cronies gave Putnam's campaign and his PAC $804,000 in direct contributions. He received another $7.6 million from other political action committees funded in part by the industry. It's no surprise that he was the only candidate denying the sugar industry had any part in the nutrient-rich algal blooms happening in the state's waterways. A new crop of candidates running throughout this country are getting their money from crowd-sourced donations. These candidates are truly funded by the people and are the most likely to listen to our environmental concerns. If you want to find out more about who is funding the candidates running in your state, you can use this easy search tool at www.opensecrets.org/states. Open Secrets is run by a nonpartisan, independent, and non-profit organization, the Center for Responsive Politics, the nation's top research group tracking money in U.S. politics and its effect on elections and public policy.

WIFIA: Investing in New Infrastructure Projects

In 2018, the EPA announced a new program that could provide as much as $5.5 billion in loans through the Water Infrastructure Finance and Innovation Act (WIFIA) program, which is intended to generate a source of low-interest financing for large-scale drinking water and waste-water infrastructure projects nationwide. Under WIFIA, states and individual communities that are seeking to finance major water infrastructure projects can apply for loans offered at below-market interest rates that require repayment to begin five years after a project is complete.

As of August 2018, the program received a record number of requests with sixty-two letters of interest, requesting more than $9.1 billion in loans, or more than double what the program has allocated. To date, the EPA has issued over $1 billion in WIFIA credit assistance through loans to King County (Washington), the city of Omaha (Nebraska), the San Francisco Public

Utilities Commission (California), and the Orange County Water District (California). Let's continue to flood this office with requests and put on the pressure to increase its lending capabilities so we can improve our water infrastructure. For more information about the WIFIA program, visit their website: www.epa.gov/wifia.

Becoming Better Advocates

The power of the lobbying industry to influence our political system is enormous. Companies, labor unions, and others spend billions each year to lobby Congress and federal agencies. In 1998, lobbying spending totaled $1.45 billion; today, it's more than $3 billion. Imagine if citizens and groups that represented our public health had those kinds of budgets and sway. Only big industry has the kind of money and power to put a professional in every single meeting and in every congressional office, to weigh in at every comment period, and to be part of every discussion session, so that their voices are heard. It's hard for any politician to resist that kind of power.

But the times are a-changin'. We can become our own lobbyists. The power of the people lies in coming together so that our voices and concerns are at the table, especially when decisions about our future are being made. In the past, people only became involved in real disasters like in Hinkley or Flint. It was during those times that people would pick up their heads and say, "Maybe we need to stop supporting these guys who were telling me everything is okay." In communities throughout the country, people are now working for change and they need your support. It can come in the form of writing letters, calling your senators and representatives, showing up to town hall meetings, or donating to environmental protection foundations. You can check out this great tool at www.townhallproject.com, a website that empowers constituents across the country to have face-to-face conversations with their elected representatives. Another tech venture, www.countable.us, is working to make political engagement easier, and, dare I say, fun. This free app posts clear and succinct summaries of laws Congress is considering and with the click of a button you can contact your lawmakers. You can also see how your elected officials voted on bills so you can hold them accountable in the next election cycle. In 2019, we had 126 women working in the House of Representatives, so let's guide both the freshmen and the more seasoned officials to the issues we care about.

We need more voices chiming in during public comment periods. Part of getting involved is having a better understanding of how the process works. Twice a year, federal agencies like the EPA publish their regulatory agenda, which offers information on the regulations that they plan to issue. When congressional bills become laws, federal agencies are tasked with putting those laws into action through regulations. This process looks like this:

1. An agency initiates a rule-making activity and adds an entry to its regulatory agenda.
2. A proposed rule or other document is published to www.Regulations.gov.
3. The public is given the opportunity to comment on this rule for a specified timeframe.

You can use this tool to get your opinion into the public record and help lawmakers get more input from their constituents. You can visit this website anytime and search for specific rules or see what's trending.

In 2017, the EPA put out a call for public comments about what regulations needed repeal, replacement, or modification. The call came from an executive order issued by President Trump, asking agencies to reevaluate their regulations. More than fifty-five thousand comments came into the EPA full of pleas from Americans to protect our most basic rights to clean water and air and urging the agency to keep enforcing the regulations we have. It was a good start. Now imagine if we had 1 million, 10 million, or 100 million comments. That's democracy.

PART THREE

THE FINAL CALL

Anything else you're interested in is not going to happen if you can't breathe the air and drink the water. Don't sit this one out. Do something.

—Carl Sagan, American astronomer, astrophysicist, astrobiologist, and author

11

DAY ZERO

Early in 2018, Ian Neilson, the deputy mayor of Cape Town, South Africa, announced a cap on the amount of water that could be used by each person in the city. Every resident of the city, he proclaimed, was limited to thirteen gallons of water each—no one could use more than thirteen milk jugs full of water each day.

That might sound like a lot. It's not. As one writer living in South Africa put it, "That's enough for a 90-second shower, a half-gallon of drinking water, a sinkful to hand-wash dishes or laundry, one cooked meal, two hand washings, two teeth brushings and one toilet flush." That writer was on the hunt for a dry-composting toilet, so that her one flush of the toilet could be saved for something else. One less toilet flush, which represented a third of the daily allotment, could mean another cooked meal, or the opportunity to wash dishes **and** laundry on the same day. That thirteen-gallon cap isn't arbitrary: it's the United Nations guideline for a human being's minimum daily requirement. (By contrast, the federal government estimates that the average American uses up to a hundred gallons per day.)

Throughout Cape Town, citizens were having to figure out how to make the most of the little water they had left. Things looked dire—it was the sort of crisis that wasn't supposed to happen in one of the wealthiest cities on the continent. As South African resource-management expert Anthony Turton put it, "I'm afraid we're at the 11th hour. There is no more time for solutions. We need an act of God. We need divine intervention."

It's one thing when we read about parched, arid desert towns or cities in conflict zones running out of water. We might feel bad about their misfortune, but it makes sense. In places where disease is rampant, where electricity is limited, where warfare is constant, it isn't too surprising to us that they are **also** running out of water. That's what makes the story of Cape Town's water shortage so astonishing. This isn't some war-torn village in the middle of nowhere, nor is it a landlocked, sunbaked desert. This is a vibrant coastal city of 4 million people, a place that hosts tourists in the millions every year. It's the home of world-class art museums and dining, a city that, less than a decade earlier, had helped to host 3 million soccer fans for a successful World Cup tournament.

And in its disastrous water shortage, Cape Town is also an early look at one of our planet's probable futures. Cape Town's residents gave the day that the city would run entirely out of water an appropriately ominous-sounding name: Day Zero. On Day Zero, when emergency water reserves would reach their lowest point, the city would shut off the majority of its pipes, and faucets at homes and businesses across Cape Town would run dry. To meet the bare needs of survival, citizens would line up each day to collect just 6.6 gallons each— half the UN minimum. Originally, the water was supposed to run dry at some point in 2018. But thanks to almost unheard-of efforts on the part of the city's leadership and its residents, Cape Town was able to push Day Zero back. To do that, they had to enact water taxes, reduce water pressure, and institute the water caps described above. City officials made it illegal to use a water tap to wash your car, fill a pool, or water a garden. Shipments of bottled water sold out as soon as they hit store shelves. A black market in river water cropped up online. Thousands of Capetonians lined up in the predawn hours to fill jugs and jerry cans at natural springs. Sometimes, fights broke out in the lines, and a "water police force" was mobilized to help. The mayor even took to making unannounced public visits to households that were using too much water—an effort to shame them and everyone else into reducing their personal water usage.

Maybe you noticed a story about Cape Town's impending water disaster sometime in 2018. And maybe, after clicking on it or scrolling past it, you never saw a follow-up. It wouldn't be surprising, given the notoriously short attention span of the international news cycle. It would be natural to think that, somehow, Cape Town solved its problem and that the water shortage was averted or was a false alarm. Otherwise, you would've heard something, right?

The remarkable efforts of Cape Town's citizens didn't avert Day Zero. They only pushed it further out into the future. The problem hasn't gone away. It has only been delayed. For the first time in human history, a city of millions of people came within a hairs-breadth of running out of water completely. And Day Zero is still coming.

SHRINKING WATER SUPPLIES, SHIFTING CLIMATE

What happened in Cape Town? The same thing that threatens so many cities around the world. The population of the city increased rapidly. Its government deferred building sewage-recycling plants to increase the usable water supply, and it waited too long to implement aggressive conservation policies. Above all, the environment that produces the city's water changed entirely. Cape Town had hotter weather, less rainfall, and emptier streams—all of which led to a shortage that got worse and worse over time. Then, starting in 2014, came three years of drought, which emptied out Cape Town's reservoirs and led to the 2018 near–Day Zero moment.

Cape Town isn't alone. The 21 million people who live in Mexico City regularly have their domestic supplies of running water cut off. The same thing has happened in São Paulo, Brazil. In 2015, the Brazilian city's water reserves hit terrifying lows, and some of the emergency trucks brought in to help were looted. By one estimate, São Paulo had only twenty days of water left—less than three days removed from its own Day Zero.

Bangalore, Beijing, Istanbul, Moscow, Cairo, Jakarta—these cities of millions of people, around the world, could be at serious risk for running out of water soon. Perhaps some part of you thinks that this sort of crisis doesn't happen in wealthy "Western" countries. But the climate crisis is worldwide, and it makes no such distinctions. Melbourne, Australia, is a city on the edge of a desert continent, at a time when deserts are expanding around the world. The city's authorities predict that its Day Zero may come in the next decade. California recently emerged from a record-breaking five-year drought; its major cities, Los Angeles and San Diego, were down to less than a year's supply of water in reserve. Other American cities, like Miami and Salt Lake City, are running the same perilous risks. If and when these cities run out of water, we may be looking at an unprecedented kind of political unrest. One driven by a loss of one of the two substances, along with air, that human beings cannot live without. The struggle for water, under those conditions, would be a struggle for survival. And there is no telling what people pushed to such an extreme of desperation would do to satisfy their bodies' thirst for another day.

I've spent a lot of this book talking about what happens when our water becomes contaminated—and discussing what we can do about it as individuals and communities. But there's another threat to our water supply, one that affects not the quality of the water we rely on, but its quantity—in fact, its existence. There would be no water crisis in Cape Town—no looming Day Zeros from China to California—without global warming. There is no greater existential threat to our future on this planet. Perhaps it is cold comfort, then, that we now understand the looming threat better than ever.

—

Many, many volumes published by thoughtful people have covered the ways in which man-made carbon emissions are changing the environment and the planet we live on. I have no interest in reciting what is settled science. And the truth is, you don't need to study the science to see its effects. In nearly every place I travel in the United States, people come up to me and discuss how different the weather has become, even in the last decade.

That difference in the lived experience of our climate isn't your imagination, your nostalgia, or your faulty memory talking. It's real, and it's backed up by hard data. **The New York Times** has a nifty tool that quantifies climate changes over our lifetimes in our most familiar places: you can try it for yourself at www.nytimes.com/interactive/ 2018/08/30/climate/how-much-hotter-is-your-hometown.html. Enter your hometown and year of birth (or, if you prefer, the year you moved there), and observe how much the climate has changed from then to now. I chose Hinkley, California, the town where I first studied drinking water contamination, and 1982, the year I first moved to the state. In 1982, Hinkley experienced 129 days with temperatures above 90 degrees Fahrenheit. In 2017, it experienced 143 such days—or an extra two weeks of scorching heat. And lest you think that 2017 was an exception, you can enter the same data and look at the steadily rising trend line for yourself. In the world's great population centers, the outlook is even worse. By the end of the century, Jakarta is expected to experience six months of 90-degree heat each year, and New Delhi is expected to suffer through eight months.

Consider the charred wreckage left behind by the 2018 California wildfire season, which burned more than 1.8 million acres and did an estimated $9 billion in damage. Consider Hurricane Maria in 2017, which killed thousands in Puerto Rico and left parts of the island in a months-long blackout. Or set aside the spectacular damage caused by an unbalanced planet and look out your back door. Were summers this hot when you were a kid? Wasn't there less torrential rain? Don't you remember more snow on the ground in winter? However we measure the facts, people are waking up and seeing that the climate is fundamentally different now.

We can't escape the facts—2018 was the fourth hottest year on record and the last five years have been the hottest climate researchers have observed. The year 2018 was also the wettest year in the last thirty-five years. Scientists attribute the higher rainfall to a warmer atmosphere, which causes more evaporation, along with warming oceans, which add to the intensity of storms and hurricanes. As

I mentioned in the last chapter, 2018 was also one of the most intense years for natural disasters with more than fourteen events in the U.S. alone, including two Atlantic hurricanes causing severe rains.

"Climate change" is an umbrella term for a global set of processes taking shape in innumerable, interconnected ways, ranging from the dwindling of glaciers in the Andes to the increased outbreaks of prairie fires in the American Midwest, to the increasing prevalence of disease-carrying mosquitoes. It would take a much longer book to address the ways in which averting, mitigating, and adapting to climate change is going to affect our lives in the years to come. So, rather than doing that, I'm going to focus on the impact of climate change on the thing I know best: the water we drink. I'm focusing on water because "What do I do when I turn on the faucet and nothing comes out?" is a far more compelling, visceral, and, I hope, action-motivating question than "What do I do if the average global sea level is a meter higher in 2100?"

This isn't some distant problem that your children's children will have to deal with. Unless you are at death's door right now, this is something that **you**—the person reading this book—are going to have to deal with. Climate change is reducing the amount of drinkable water on the earth's surface—not in some projected future, but right now—and we need to understand the scope and scale of the problem so we can take immediate action to fix it.

In October of 2018, the United Nations Intergovernmental Panel on Climate Change (IPCC) released a report that made no bones about how bad things were. We have, they argued, a dozen years left to keep temperatures in check, or else we face drastic consequences. A team of ninety-one scientists from forty countries came together to study and review nearly every research paper written on this subject, and they all came to one incontrovertible conclusion: we need to act. Now. Climate change is happening, and it's having a direct effect on millions of people around the world. Unchecked, it could lead to worse forest fires than we've seen, massive food shortages, and the death of many coral reefs around the world— among many, many other catastrophes.

Before I get into the substance of the report, let me tell you a bit about its authors. The IPCC is chaired by Hoesung Lee, a South Korean scholar who is an international expert on the economics of climate change and the world's most trusted authority on the state of the climate. Rather than conducting its own research, the organization assembles and digests the most up-to-date research in the fields of climate science and meteorology into reports that the world's governments can use to inform their actions. Thousands of scientists have contributed to this process. The IPCC has been at it for three decades, and by 2007, its global reputation was such that it won that year's Nobel Peace Prize, along with Al Gore. If there's a knock on the IPCC, it's that, given the organization's consensus-oriented process, it produces findings that **understate** the threat of climate change. If you read the IPCC's reports, you'll notice that nearly every sentence they write and every conclusion they reach comes with a confidence assessment— low, medium, high. They are their own harshest critics.

As climate journalist David Wallace-Wells explains, "Almost since the panel was convened, in 1988, it has been criticized for being too cautious in its assessment of the problem—a large body of temperamentally cautious scientists zeroing on those predictions they can all agree on (and which, they may have hoped, policymakers might find workable). The panel's Wikipedia page has separate subsections for 'Outdatedness of reports' and 'Conservative nature of IPCC reports.'" So take what you're about to read with a grain of salt: not because it exaggerates the threat but because it quite possibly downplays it.

The report's full name is "Global Warming of 1.5°C, an IPCC special report on the impacts of global warming of 1.5°C above pre-industrial levels and related global greenhouse gas emission pathways, in the context of strengthening the global response to the threat of climate change, sustainable development, and efforts to eradicate poverty." But the full title gives the reader important context. The IPCC focused on outlining, in a painstaking, numbers-based, hundreds-of-pages-of-thinking level of detail, what happens if we keep the warming of the planet to 1.5 degrees Celsius above pre-industrial levels.

Planet-wide, we're already 1 degree above pre-industrial levels, and what this report makes clear is that controlling climate change to limit warming to only 1.5 degrees is both hugely difficult—and important. If half a degree of difference doesn't seem like much, think again. When these scientists are speaking about degree-level differences, they aren't talking about this or that unseasonably warm or cold day. They are talking about the planetary temperature on average. In this context, a difference of a half degree Celsius reflects a fundamental change to the planet's climate, a delicate system on which human civilization, and our way of life, depend.

As Hans-Otto Pörtner, co-chair of IPCC Working Group II, put it, "Every extra bit of warming matters, especially since warming of 1.5°C or higher increases the risk associated with long-lasting or irreversible changes, such as the loss of some ecosystems." Temperature differences that look small on the printed page translate, in fact, to questions of life or death for millions.

Some of these changes are already taking place. The report's authors found that climate change of 1°C above pre-industrial levels has already taken place. "One of the key messages that comes out very strongly from this report is that we are already seeing the consequences of 1°C of global warming through more extreme weather, rising sea levels and diminishing Arctic sea ice, among other changes," said Panmao Zhai, a climatologist who co-chaired one of the report's working groups. Among other things, the report's authors found that climate change has led to both "an increase in the frequency and duration of marine heatwaves" and more heat waves on land. It's also led to an increase in the incidents and the intensity of heavy rainfall—and at the same time, increased the risk of droughts in the Mediterranean region.

But the primary work of the report wasn't to tell us what we already know—that there have been changes to our environment that are a direct cause of things we've done—but to look ahead, to point us to what might happen if we aren't more careful stewards of the planet.

If we pass 1.5 degrees Celsius, we can expect more extreme weather: "The strongest warming of hot extremes is projected to occur in central and eastern North America, central and southern Europe, the Mediterranean region (including southern Europe, North Africa and the Near East), western and central Asia, and southern Africa (medium confidence). The number of exceptionally hot days are expected to increase the most in the tropics, where interannual temperature variability is lowest; extreme heatwaves are thus projected to emerge earliest in these regions, and they are expected to already become widespread there at 1.5°C global warming."

The report also explores what happens if we exceed 1.5 degrees Celsius and hit 2 degrees of increase above pre-industrial temperatures. And again, while half a degree of difference can seem minuscule to us, the report reminds us just how much is at stake. At 2 degrees, warming and related ocean acidification will destroy most of the world's coral reefs. Flooding could endanger coastal cities around the world, such as Guangzhou, China; Mumbai, India; Osaka, Japan; New Orleans; and New York City. The property damage, displacement of millions of people, and costs required to protect low-lying areas from increased flooding would help cut global GDP per capita by more than a tenth. And even the most monumental efforts to protect urban centers from flooding will, by necessity, remain incomplete. As Wallace-Wells points out, Manhattan is wealthy enough that policymakers will almost certainly consider it worth protecting from rising waters with a massive seawall; in fact, such efforts started soon after Superstorm Sandy in 2012. But such an undertaking costs hundreds of billions of dollars, is likely to take more than thirty years to complete, and still leaves neighboring Long Island exposed. How would local and state governments deal with the millions of internal climate refugees who would have to abandon their homes under that scenario?

Already, we're learning that the U.S. isn't exempt from the displacement of populations caused by climate change. A "climate refugee" isn't a distant, foreign figure on the evening news. It's a family driven out of their home by the Camp Fire in California or Hurricane Florence in the Carolinas. "The survivors of the disasters," writes environmental reporter Alleen Brown, "have resorted to camping in tents in retail parking lots, sleeping on friends' couches, parking trailers on the lawns of their destroyed homes, or renting overpriced apartments in communities where housing has become increasingly scarce. Safety nets like flood and fire insurance or the Federal Emergency Management Agency (FEMA) routinely fall far short of providing the support needed to keep survivors housed, fed, and on their feet."

Even more seriously, how would governments

across the world deal with influxes of climate refugees at their borders or within their borders? That is not a hypothetical question, either. Keep in mind that many of the refugees arriving at America's southern border have been displaced by drought in Central America. One of them is Davíd, a farmer who joined the migrant caravan from Honduras to the U.S. border. Asked by Brown why he had made an almost unthinkably dangerous trek across much of Central America and Mexico on foot, he responded, "I'm here because of the drought."

In fact, none of the potential consequences of unchecked warming hit as close to home as the prospect of massive droughts. The number and scale of droughts will be "substantially larger at 2°C than at 1.5°C in the Mediterranean region (including southern Europe, North Africa, and the Near East) and southern Africa." Like flooding, water scarcity is expected to be worse at 2 degrees than at 1.5 degrees—with socioeconomic differences also affecting which populations are made worse off by the effects. Unsurprisingly, the most impoverished will suffer the worst effects. But none of us will be exempt: at 2 degrees of warming, up to 400 million people will suffer from water shortages like, or worse than, the one just experienced in Cape Town.

Keep in mind, though, that even 2 degrees of warming is an "optimistic" target, because without dramatic reductions in emissions, we are projected to blow right through it by the end of the century. Without a change to the emissions status quo, 3 or 4 degrees of warming by the end of the century are in fact more likely. Three degrees could mean multi-year droughts in southern Europe and Africa. Four degrees could cut worldwide grain production by half, meaning regular economic crises and famines around the globe. Read enough of the report and a mere 1.5 degrees of warming, even taking into account the devastation that it would bring, starts to sound like some sort of happy ending.

ACCESS TO CLEAN WATER

I read this report with great interest, and even greater trepidation, because climate change around the world is tied to what I have made my life's work here in the United States: making sure people have access to clean water. But just weeks after this UN report landed, another report dropped that hit much closer to home. In late November 2018, thirteen federal agencies got together and released their own report showing that if America did nothing about climate change, we risk losing 10 percent of our economy. You read that right: climate change poses a direct and active threat to one-tenth of the entire GDP of our country. As **The New York Times** reported, that kind of loss would represent "more than double the losses of the Great Recession a decade ago." Just like the IPCC report, the domestic version pointed out that the crises we can already see playing out around us—devastating annual wildfires in the West, crops failing in the Midwest, and record-breaking hurricane seasons on the Atlantic and Gulf coasts—can be traced to the single source of climate change.

The 1,656-page report isn't remarkable just for its findings but for the fact that it was published at all. In fact, thirteen federal agencies (including NASA and the EPA) banded together to release a report that directly contradicted the views of President Trump, who has, among his other remarks, celebrated "beautiful, clean coal" and dismissed climate change as a "Chinese hoax." It's the most comprehensive data published to date in our country determining that "there is no convincing alternative explanation" for global warming other than human causes. Needless to say, Trump didn't agree with the report's conclusions, and he's directed the EPA to take actions that will make things substantially worse for the climate, the environment, and, by extension, our water supply by—to take one example—rolling back vehicle emissions standards. His administration also directed scientists to finalize their research and release the report two weeks early on "Black Friday," a day when most Americans are distracted with holiday shopping and not checking the headlines. When asked about it the following Monday, Trump told reporters, "Yeah, I don't believe it."

"There is a bizarre contrast between this report, which is being released by this administration, and this administration's own policies," Philip B. Duffy, president of the nonprofit climate change research organization Woods Hole Research Center, told **The New York Times**. But here at least I want to dwell on the positive. Even as the climate change denier-in-chief dominates the headlines, we should never forget that scientists and policy professionals continue to work behind the scenes to alert us to the reality of climate change, and to help us meet its challenge before it's too late. When exactly is too late? Keep in mind that the IPCC tells us that 1.5 degrees of warming will likely be locked in by 2040.

What's to be done about a problem that's as big as climate change? I'll end this chapter with some practical suggestions, but before we get there, I think that there's one suggestion that takes precedence. Meeting the challenge of climate change begins with looking the facts squarely in the face. That's why I'm glad that the federal report pulled no punches in its conclusions: "More frequent and intense extreme weather and climate-related events, as well as changes in average climate conditions, are expected to continue to damage infrastructure, ecosystems, and social systems that provide essential benefits to communities. Future climate change is expected to disrupt many areas of life, exacerbating existing challenges to prosperity posed by aging and deteriorating infrastructure, stressed ecosystems, and economic inequality."

And when it comes to water, the report is downright bracing: "Rising air and water temperatures and changes in precipitation are intensifying droughts, increasing heavy downpours, reducing snowpack, and causing declines in surface water quality."

It's worth diving into the details. Part of what climate change does is change weather patterns—more intense snow, not enough rainfall, areas that become warm when they should be cold. When that happens, it leads to unpredictability in how much water is available relative to what communities have needed in the past. Climate change also leads to sea levels rising, and when salty ocean water rises and gets mixed in with a drinkable water supply, that further reduces how much water is available for people to drink. It doesn't help, of course, that U.S. water infrastructure is in about as bad a shape as the rest of our infrastructure, and that many of the water and waste-treatment plants we rely on were built for different weather conditions than we are experiencing today. Estimates show that updating our water infrastructure alone—dams, levees, wastewater systems, and so on—will cost some $1 trillion in the next twenty-five years.

And it isn't just potable water that's at risk either. It's the water that's integral to all aspects of our lives and economies. Water cools power plants, for instance, and the report notes that we may face energy issues if our power plants can't cool themselves. Some energy is derived from water directly, in the form of hydroelectric plants. When the total volume of available water decreases because of fluctuations in the environment, that energy source is also put at risk, potentially driving consumers to fossil fuels and their emissions. It's a vicious circle. Our farm animals need water to drink, and thus agriculture is hit by the changes in water that stem from the changes in our environment. And, of course, the crops we depend on for food depend, in turn, on water. A 2012 drought brought the Mississippi River to record low levels, holding up shipping and leading to harvest failures in the Midwest. The extreme floods and droughts that we've become accustomed to seeing on the nightly weather reports often mask deeper, systemic changes and shocks—the implications of which can last for decades.

The report makes an additional point about water that I want to emphasize: "Water systems face considerable risk even without anticipated future climate changes." Even if climate change were magically resolved tomorrow, dams and levees aren't as well maintained as they ought to be, and as a result, "several recent heavy rainfall events have led to dam, levee, or critical infrastructure failures."

One of the most notorious of these failures was the breach of the levees protecting New Orleans during 2005's Hurricane Katrina, which led to disastrous flooding. But similar water infrastructure failures have become the background noise of American life. For instance, in 2015 and 2016, a total of seventy-five dams failed in South Carolina under the pressure of unusually high rainfall. And in 2017, the emergency spillway of the Oroville dam in Northern California collapsed, leading to the evacuation of some 180,000 residents. These are just the acute failures. The infrastructure that makes your tap work and releases clean water is sorely in need of an upgrade. "Across the Nation," the report finds, "much of the critical water infrastructure is aging and, in some cases, deteriorating or nearing the end of its design life, presenting an increased risk of failure. Estimated reconstruction and maintenance costs aggregated across dams, levees, aqueducts, sewers, and water and wastewater treatment systems total in the trillions of dollars based on a variety of different sources." Here's a truly frightening conclusion for many people in the United States who live close to a dam: "More than fifteen thousand dams in the United States are listed as high risk due to the potential losses that may result if they failed."

But what has climate change, you might be asking, done specifically to drinking water? Here's what has happened: as temperatures rise in different parts of the country, the total amount of snowfall is reduced. (As the report notes, this has been especially true in the western United States.) Melting snow eventually populates the freshwater bodies we rely on for drinking water. Less snow means less melt, which means lower water levels. Won't that be offset, though, by increased rainfall? Not enough to solve the problem. First, the rainfall isn't expected to be concentrated in the parts of the country that most need water. As the federal report points out, for instance, "the 2011–2016 California drought was characterized by low precipitation combined with record high temperatures." Second, where heavy rainfall does occur, it often "mobilize[s] pollutants," washing them into the water supplies we depend on. You may remember the viral photos of hog manure spilling out of storage lagoons in North Carolina during Hurricane Florence in 2018. Add to these facts that the timing of the melting is happening earlier, and the fact that melting glaciers change aquatic ecosystems, and you have what the report calls "a risk of decreased and highly variable water supplies for human use and ecosystem maintenance."

Climate change affects the demand for water, as well as the supply. In many ways, the impact of climate change on water can be a vicious circle: not only does a warming climate deplete our usable water supplies, but the hotter it gets, the more water humans need to use. There is, of course, the obvious way in which that works: when it's hotter, we consume more water. But there's also the fact that water used to irrigate crops evaporates faster, prompting farmers to use more water to make up for the loss and, therefore, to deplete precious supplies like underground aquifers at even higher rates. In other words, as temperatures rise, farms have to consume more water just to maintain their operations.

The quality as well as the quantity of water is affected when the climate changes. When there are massive floods or other events that shift how water flows in our country, it means that new substances, pathogens, microbes, sediment, and saltwater, can infiltrate our drinking water supplies. Rising sea levels and deteriorating infrastructure means that "saltwater intrusion" is a serious threat to drinking water on islands from the Caribbean to the Pacific, and even in Miami.

Miami already faces "chronic flooding," even on days when the sun is out. But its water problems are likely to prove even more immediate than sea level rise. As the seas rise, saltwater seeps into the supplies of groundwater that Miami relies on for drinking water. At the same time, increased rain and flooding connected to climate change threaten to pollute drinkable groundwater with toxic waste from local Superfund sites and with human feces from septic tanks. Currently, Miami draws its water from an easy-to-tap aquifer. But, reports **Bloomberg Businessweek**, "without this abundant source of freshwater, made cheap by its proximity to the surface, this hot, remote city could become uninhabitable." If anything, the headline on the story is even more harrowing: "Miami will be underwater soon. Its drinking water could go first."

Another major degradation of drinking water took place in Toledo, Ohio, in August 2014. A toxic algae bloom developed in Lake Erie, as the microorganisms turned much of the water that Toledo residents rely on into a viscous green soup. The algae didn't just discolor the water; they released toxins that can cause vomiting in humans and death in domestic animals and livestock, and local water treatment plants were unable to keep up. Half a million residents were left without drinking water. As the recent federal report recognizes, this was no one-off incident but another impact of climate change:

"Warmer temperatures and heavy precipitation associated with climate change contribute to the development of HABs [harmful algal blooms]." In fact, such blooms have been trending upwards in Lake Erie for the past decade. It's not just a problem for Ohio. In the summer of 2018, another toxic bloom, the worst in more than a decade, was responsible for the deaths of thousands of marine animals in Florida.

For all of these reasons, the warming of the planet can degrade the quality of our water both directly and indirectly. Keep in mind that all of these stresses on our water systems are interconnected. In that way, they're not unlike the interconnected changes in our planet's climate—for instance, the way that rising temperatures threaten to melt Arctic permafrost, releasing methane emissions that raise the temperature even more, or the ways that carbon emissions filter into and acidify the oceans. The built water systems we rely on can be almost as complex, and almost as prone to unexpected shocks.

Consider the case of Toledo again. The temporary loss of the city's drinking water was an inconvenience rather than a tragedy because residents could rely on bottled water for as long as the algal bloom lasted. But bottled water doesn't magically appear on shelves—collecting it just depletes water supplies somewhere else. Not only does the process of bottling and shipping it contribute to the emissions that make events like Toledo's loss of drinking water more likely; more to the point, a bottled water solution is only practicable to the extent that drinking water problems are localized and temporary. When a water shortage lasts too long or affects too many people, then we're no longer in Toledo, we're in Cape Town, where bottled water couldn't stay on the shelves long enough to meet demand.

Or consider the 2012 Midwest crop failures. Centuries ago, crop failures like that would have starved entire regions, bringing mass death in their wake. We're fortunate that such famines are far rarer today, because the global food system is generally flexible and resilient enough to make up for local shortages. You might have experienced the 2012 crop failures yourself in higher prices at the grocery store, but not in the agonizing realization that you can't feed your family. But the very reason the 2012 crop failures had a limited impact is the same reason that the increased severity of droughts is so worrisome: the interconnectedness of global food and water systems. Those systems are resilient enough to adapt to localized crop failures. But as the pace of droughts picks up and the likelihood of crop failures increases, those shocks can reverberate through the global system. Remember, a consequence of 4 degrees of warming could mean that worldwide grain outputs are cut in half. A drought in Ukraine or Zimbabwe could mean empty shelves at the grocery store in Rhode Island.

In a way, all of these interlocking facets of our lives that might suddenly go wrong point to one of the biggest tragedies of climate change. It helps us see the interdependence and the beautiful complexity of the natural and human systems we have unthinkingly relied on, at the moment those systems are threatening to fall apart.

And yet, all of this can still feel a bit abstract. When I turn on the tap in my kitchen, I don't think about global water systems, at least not very often. I think about water, about the life-giving substance that pours out of the faucet with a flick of my wrist. If I'm in a grateful mood, I think of how fortunate I am to live in a place where clean, drinkable water is a utility, not a luxury; how much I depend on the infrastructure that channels water from melting snow, through reservoirs and filtration systems and into my tap, and on the people who work every day to maintain it; how my cup of water depends on a set of precarious environmental conditions that are eroding every day. I hope you'll think about those things too from time to time. But it might help, instead, to think once again about what will happen on the day when you turn on the faucet and nothing comes out.

Lori Paup doesn't have to imagine that. Soon after she and her family moved to a new home in southeastern Arizona in 2014, she found brown water running out of her kitchen tap. When she ran her hand under it, she felt grains of sand. Soon the dishwasher and laundry machine stopped working, and a local water driller confirmed her fears: "You're running out of water." Her house relied on a well dug three hundred feet deep to tap into an underground aquifer but suddenly it went dry. So did her neighbors' wells. About a hundred families in the Sulphur Springs Valley where Paup lived experienced similar water shortages.

The immediate culprit was large-scale industrial farming in the valley. Backed by overseas investors, massive agricultural operations had sprung up over the previous decade, digging up to two thousand feet deep in search of the water needed to grow pecans and pistachios. Groundwater extraction in Arizona was, and still largely is, unregulated, so if agribusiness siphoned off the water that families like the Paups and their neighbors relied on, there was no recourse. But the larger problem is that the industrial farms are extracting more and more of a dwindling resource. As **The New York Times Magazine** reports, "Aquifers across the globe are beginning to quietly dry up under the compound strain of increased food production and a two-decade stretch that now includes the ten warmest years in recorded history."

Aquifers take thousands of years to accumulate, as precipitation gradually seeps into the earth, but humans can deplete them in a fraction of that time. In the past decades, residents and farms in the Sulphur Springs Valley were extracting more than ten times the amount of water from the local aquifer than percolated in each year; in other words, they were withdrawing from a generational savings account at a rate that would soon leave them bankrupt. Around the world, the same pattern is repeating itself, as climate change and more intensive agriculture deplete water supplies on both the input and output ends.

"Of the planet's thirty-seven major aquifer systems," NASA scientists found, "twenty-one were on the verge of collapse. In the Great Plains, farmers had exhausted a third of [the Ogallala aquifer's] potable water in just thirty years. In California, the Central Valley aquifer was showing signs that it could drop beyond human reach by the middle of this century. But the worst declines were in Asia and the Middle East, where some of the planet's oldest aquifers were already running out of water."

For people like Lori Paup, running out of water isn't an abstraction they read about in the news, or in climate projections, or in international reports.

It's a reality that's already here. Her family has been unable to sell their home, but they were lucky enough to move to a nearby ranch as caretakers; for now, they can draw from a well with sufficient water. But for Lori, the act of opening a faucet will never be the instinctual, indifferent act it is for so many of us: "You're wondering what might happen when you turn on the sink. What it could mean."

None of this is a secret. It's public knowledge that the aquifers are drying up. It's common sense that you can't practice water-intensive farming in a desert and expect the water to last forever. It makes headlines when a dam fails in California, or freshwater turns slimy green in Ohio, or the Mississippi River gets so low that boats have to stop sailing it. You can read the IPCC report, or our federal government's report online, for free. We can't say we haven't been warned.

I started this chapter describing the harrowing story of Cape Town's Day Zero, and its temporary delay. But I didn't mention the part of the story that strikes me as the saddest. It's a headline from April 26, 1990, in the **Cape Times** newspaper: "City will run out of water 'in seventeen years.'" The prediction was a bit premature, but in essence, it was right on. Cape Town was warned. Cape Town knew what was coming. And despite some truly impressive efforts, it couldn't take the warning seriously enough because if you really believe a warning that you're going to run out of water, the source of life, you'd do anything, pay any cost, and implement any policy to avert it. Cape Town didn't, and the prediction came true.

We are getting all of the same warnings today, except on a far larger, more dramatic, more unignorable scale. The lights are flashing red. Are we going to heed the warnings? Climate change can be our problem—ours to face and ours to solve. Just as I don't want to understate the scale of the crisis, I don't want to understate what facing it will require of us. As one of the scientists involved in the drafting of the UN report put it, "Limiting warming to 1.5°C is possible within the laws of chemistry and physics but doing so would require unprecedented changes." We'd need those changes to achieve the required 45 percent reduction in carbon emissions from 2010 levels by 2030—and we'd still have to remove some CO_2 from the air manually.

Yet the mere fact that the UN report offers the possibility of fixing this problem should be reason enough to try: we're not too far gone yet to do something about the dramatic effects of climate change generally, and the effects it has on our water supply specifically. As you know, I'm not a believer in standing on the sidelines. The thousands of people I meet with and talk to every year come to me because they want to do **something**. They want to take action. They want to make their voices heard. And perhaps most important, they want to make sure that their kids, families, and neighbors are able to drink safe, clean water—for a long time.

So how can we make that happen? How can we take real, concrete action for the sake of our planet and our water? Here are some suggestions:

VOTING COUNTS

In addition to turning the EPA over to polluting industries and gutting fuel efficiency standards, one of the things that the Trump administration did that has had profound consequences for the future of the environment was pulling America out of the Paris Agreement. That was a set of agreements that the U.S. helped to negotiate back in 2016, intended to help the entire world band together and figure this problem out. Taking us out of the agreement told the world that we're not serious about fighting climate change, even as the report released by Trump's own administration points out that a changing climate will hit our economy twice as hard as the Great Recession. Along with China, the U.S. leads the world in carbon emissions— and it's impossible to imagine a solution to the problem of climate change that doesn't include American action.

So, what to do with a problem that seems as difficult and big as global warming? Start with your vote. Make sure that the next time an election comes around, the candidates know that you, their constituents, are paying attention to their votes and messages on global warming. If you don't like what your representatives have to say, tell them so. Write in. Call in. Demand answers. The next time there's an election, see where your local and national candidates stand on the Paris Agreement and then vote. Tell your friends to vote too.

Let me say again: this isn't about taking political sides or choosing a political party. I've been disappointed by both Democrats' **and** Republicans' approach to these issues. And in truth, they aren't political issues, or they shouldn't be. These are reality issues, scientific issues, and as the IPCC report illustrates, there's a well-established, well-researched, agreed-upon set of conclusions— and we need to begin taking them seriously. I am encouraged by recent elections: in 2018, a new crop of men and women were elected to Congress who are sounding the right notes on these subjects. They are introducing solution-oriented legislation like the Green New Deal, which would work to reduce U.S. carbon emissions and create new jobs to boost the economy. At a minimum, they are making issues like climate change a central subject of discussion, and that itself is important.

Probably the most important element of the IPCC's report is the one that the media underplayed: that there is still time to do something about the problem of global warming. In other words, things look bad, but there's hope. We nurture that hope when we turn it into action, when we stand up and say, "Enough is enough. This is a global problem, and the United States of America needs to lead on this." I've ended every chapter of this book by telling you things you can do, and this chapter is no different. You need to pay attention to problems that seem remote and unsolvable like global warming, because they affect the water you drink and the water your children will drink. In fact, if we don't take action, our taps will run dry sooner than we may think.

WATCH BUSINESS LEADERS

There are leaders in the private sector in the United States who have been vocal and outspoken on the issue of climate change. While Elon Musk is a controversial figure, I applaud what he did as soon as President Trump pulled out of the Paris Agreement: Musk stepped down from the White

House advisory councils he was a part of. As he tweeted, "Am departing presidential councils. Climate change is real. Leaving Paris is not good for America or the world."

If you can imagine a situation designed for flak, this was it: politics, climate change, and Elon Musk, all in one very public moment. But Musk knows what he's talking about. He's not a tree-hugger or an environmental activist; he's the head of a car and rocket company, and he's also scientifically literate enough to understand that climate change isn't just a spooky-sounding phrase.

Why does his story matter? Because when a CEO of a company has the courage of their convictions, when they endure the flak they're bound to receive for making a statement like that, we ought to applaud them and support them. Bob Iger, the CEO of Disney, announced that he too was leaving a White House advisory council after the Paris decision. Amazon CEO Jeff Bezos has announced plans to fight climate change; Apple CEO Tim Cook has been a trailblazer for sustainable business practices and has called other leaders to action.

We need to make sure that the leaders of companies that make the products and services we use every day know that we're watching their moves on these subjects. It's one thing for a random person to tweet their disapproval about the Paris decision; it's another when a Musk or a Cook goes out on a limb and tells the White House that they've done something wrong.

TAKING DIRECT ACTION

But what can **you** do, personally? If someone like Musk or Cook can't force the White House to accept the reality of climate change, what can you hope to accomplish?

Quite a lot, actually, but only if you join forces with others around the country and around the world who share your convictions. The good news is that, thanks to the internet and social media, it's easier to find people who share your convictions than it ever has been. Throughout our history, tools like boycotts and civil disobedience have succeeded in bringing much-needed change to pass. Consider the Standing Rock protests in 2016 and 2017, in which thousands came together to resist a pipeline in North Dakota that threatened Native Americans' land and drinking water. In the short run, the protesters were unable to block the pipeline, but their stand inspired and mobilized ordinary people across America, a few of whom ran for and won public office in the 2018 midterm elections.

Stopping the worst of climate change will take many more brave stands like that, from many more ordinary people who have decided to make their voices heard. Connecting with climate activists near you only takes a few clicks, but it can make a world of difference.

REDUCE YOUR FOOTPRINT

Climate change is the result of millions of small decisions we make every day, whether to eat meat for lunch, book a trans-Atlantic flight, or bike to work instead of drive. My choices and yours are part of climate change. I point that out to make you feel empowered. Climate change isn't happening to us, it's something that we are all participating in, and it's something that we can choose to change, if we act in time. The scary thing about climate change is that our small and seemingly inconsequential choices turn out, over time, to add up to effects of such magnitude that they can radically disrupt our way of life. But that's the fortunate thing about climate change too: the solution isn't, at base, any more complicated than those small choices. The solution starts right now, right where you are at this moment.

In 2017, a team of researchers reviewed the results of thirty-nine studies to identify the most effective steps individuals can take to lower their share of carbon emissions.

Here are the top twelve actions:

1. Have one fewer child
2. Live car-free
3. Avoid one round-trip trans-Atlantic flight
4. Buy green energy
5. Buy a more efficient car
6. Switch from an electric car to car-free
7. Eat a plant-based diet
8. Replace a gasoline car with a hybrid car
9. Wash clothes in cold water
10. Recycle
11. Hang-dry clothes
12. Upgrade lightbulbs

Of course, even if you take every step on that list—even if you're a childless, car-free vegan without a dryer—you will only make an infinitesimal dent in the total amount of carbon pumped into our atmosphere every minute. So why bother?

First, because it's the right thing to do. I don't want to be part of a problem on the scale of climate change, period—sometimes, we're called to do the right thing whether or not we can be sure of the results. But in this case, doing the right thing shows us that, together, we don't have to be powerless in the face of climate change. We don't have to sit passively as water dries up and is poisoned all around us. We can start by taking action in our

own lives, and then reaching out to others who
share our commitments and building movements
that can reach those in power before it's too late.
Just as learning about water helps us appreciate it
more, I hope that addressing climate change and
its impact on our lives can help drive your future
choices.

If you need any more motivation to act
now: While this book was going through edits,
another climate change headline caught my eye
about the Colorado River. A study published in
February 2020 confirmed the dire water situation
in the West. It's not news that for years drought
and warming temperatures have taken a toll on
the river's flow. But computer simulations and
historical data helped piece together that about
1.5 billion tons of water from the river has been
lost, thanks to an ever-shrinking snowpack, according to researchers from the U.S. Geological Survey.
That amount of water is equivalent to the annual
water consumption of about 10 million Americans.
The Colorado River is the largest and most vital
one in the Southwest, supplying drinking water to
40 million people, supporting $1 trillion in eco-
nomic activity each year, and irrigating millions of
acres of farmland.

Here's the thing. While these numbers sound
alarming, evaporation is not new. Scientists have
been monitoring and warning us about these

problems for years. In 2015, researchers called evaporation "a large and continuing problem in the Colorado River basin, including Lake Mead and Lake Powell, where about 500 billion gallons of water evaporate annually." These are the two largest man-made water reservoirs in the country. Once this water is gone, it's gone. I even have a study looking at water loss in Lake Powell from 1986. The time to find new water management strategies is here. The time to act on climate change is now.

Global warming, like many of the issues we've highlighted in the book, can seem distant, theoretical, and impossible to solve. But as you've seen with water pollution and the threat posed by toxins to our communities, there's **always** something that can be done. I am, and have always been, a big believer in the idea that no problem caused by people can't be fixed by people. Global warming is no different. If I've learned one thing in my career, it's that each of us can change the world.

12

TIME TO ACT!

Dr. Seuss's classic children's book **The Lorax** is a story about responsibility and the natural environment. The author said it was one of his personal favorites and that he had written it out of anger about what he saw as corporate greed ruining our natural world. We all know the famous quote, "Unless someone like you cares a whole awful lot, nothing is going to get better. It's not."

Having read this to my granddaughters recently, I felt so much anger thinking about the drinking water crisis we find ourselves in today. Most of the people contacting me each day share these feelings of frustration. They see the devastation firsthand, knowing there's been a breakdown in the regulations meant to protect them. Many have reached out to their local officials to no avail. Frankly, they don't know what to do or where to turn.

I want to continue to offer my encouragement and motivation to stay strong in the face of uncertainty like we've never seen before. You've learned about the role of policy, the toxic chemicals, the laws, the regulatory agencies, the roles of local, state, and federal government, the scientific fraud, and the communities rising. This book did not cover in depth many other pressing water issues including water shortages (nearly every region of the U.S. has experienced shortages since 2008), increased flooding, and the growing problem of pipeline ruptures and explosions throughout the country that dump oil directly into our drinking water supplies, but these issues are also critically important.

"Is my water safe?" people ask. It's a question I get asked at least a thousand times a day. It's a question authorities and regulators struggle to answer when communities have concerns. Even after pollution has been discovered and drinking water issues get addressed, many people still refuse to drink their tap water because of possible or ongoing health concerns.

More than 60 million Americans have been exposed to unsafe drinking water more than once in the past decade, thanks to industrial dumping, farm pollution, and aging infrastructure. Problems with drinking water systems typically take up to two years to get resolved, while many water treatment plants simply can't afford the equipment to filter out contaminants. Water system upgrades are desperately needed throughout the country, including replacing millions of lead service lines. We have a huge problem with the approximately four hundred coal-fired power plants that produce millions of pounds of toxic industrial pollution—including arsenic, lead, and mercury—which get dumped into rivers and streams throughout our country. Years of political strife, along with industry dollars influencing the regulatory process, have overwhelmed and stalled action from the EPA. Recent executive orders and proposed budget cuts are causing damage that could take decades to undo.

Millions of Americans have been exposed to chemicals like PFOA and PFOS, which most systems still do not regulate or regularly test for. These chemicals have been linked to cancer, thyroid disease, suppressed immunity, and many other health problems. When I began writing this book in 2016, the Environmental Working Group (EWG) reported that 16 million Americans had been exposed to these fluorine-based chemicals, collectively referred to as PFAS. In May 2018, the EWG reported that more than 1,500 water systems may be contaminated with these chemicals, affecting up to 110 million people across the country. The EPA held a summit that same month to address PFAS chemicals. The agency mandated national testing for PFAS chemicals in public water systems from 2013 to 2015, but results from these taxpayer-funded assessments were hidden from the public for months. While the EPA did identify municipalities with the highest concentrations of contamination, the names of utilities with detectable levels of PFAS contamination below 90 ppt were not released, meaning millions of people are still not aware that their water supply is tainted. As I'm writing, more communities are discovering health problems connected to these chemicals in their water, including in Satellite Beach, Florida, where high rates of cancer among young alumni from the local high school caught the eye of Dr. Julie Clift Greenwalt, an oncologist and also a cancer survivor, who noticed an article about carcinogens that had been found in the water at nearby Patrick Air Force Base. After Dr. Greenwalt posted about it on her personal Facebook page, she got hundreds of messages from others who had been diagnosed with cancer and is now working to raise awareness, get further investigation about these chemicals in the drinking water, and save the next generation of students from this environmental exposure.

We cannot ignore these problems any longer. The biggest barrier to clean water in our country today is not chemical, physical, or financial, it's political. Our political system has run amok and is taking down our most precious resource—water. This is not business as usual. We are at a turning point where we all need to fight before there's not a drop of water left to drink. Our issues are about right versus wrong, not left versus right. From the crisis in Flint, Michigan, to the toxic waste discharges from Lake Okeechobee in Florida, the root cause is always a politically driven process. When the community and the consumers are actively involved and armed with the knowledge of what's truly happening with their water and allowed to participate in the process, real change and progress can happen. More often than not, decisions are made by those who have the most to gain or the most to lose. The community that will ultimately be dumped on or the consumers who are forced to drink dangerous water are often not part of the process, cut out by powerful corporations and big lobby dollars. In almost all of these cases, facts get twisted and misinformation campaigns are launched. Yes, these issues are complicated, but all of us in the United States must take notice, become educated, and become engaged. We cannot wait around any longer while our government continues to pander to special interest groups. This is not a partisan issue, it's a human rights issue.

"What can we do to help?" is easily the second-most-asked question I get and it's what gives me hope for our future. People want to be part of the solution. My role has been to shine a spotlight on what's happening with our water and to help educate, inform, and empower others with the truth. Facts are our best weapon in the fight for clean water.

To start, we need to ask the fundamental question: Who does our government work for? We cannot stand for elected officials who don't respond to the facts or to the concerns of their constituents. I've been working to inspire action across America at the national and local levels so that our communities and leaders are armed with the strongest weapons in politics: truth, answers, and solutions. No more mayors on TV telling their constituents the water is safe to drink, just as former Flint, Michigan, mayor Dayne Walling did during the Flint water crisis; he also tweeted that he and his family were drinking the water every day. No more governors ignoring the crisis, just as former Florida governor Rick Scott did for years in Florida, causing toxic algae blooms to harm the water, the wildlife, and the people. It's time to storm these local offices, flood them with calls, and fund more independent research and testing so that we can work toward solutions to these issues.

Our environmental policies have been seriously forgotten, rolled back, and de-prioritized during these disruptive political years. While this baffles me beyond belief, I feel that these times are teaching us something. We are waking up and realizing that the protections we thought were in place are not. The agencies we thought were looking out for us have been looking the other way. As we recognize more about the impacts on our water, our environment, and our health, we now have a window of opportunity to refocus our attention on the serious issues we face.

With more information and awareness, we can become more vigilant and outspoken about what is happening in our own backyards. As we begin to recognize the enormous cutbacks to the EPA and the tremendous burden of too many contaminated places, we must rise up town by town, city by city, and state by state. Together, we must speak out for the future and for change.

HOUSTON, WE HAVE A PROBLEM

The first step in solving this national crisis is admitting we have a problem. Just as we've seen the rise of #MeToo and Time's Up, the pioneering anti-sexual-assault and women's empowerment movements and the #NeverAgain movement to raise awareness and curb gun violence in schools, we need a powerful water movement too. You are more powerful than you think. I see pockets of people who care deeply about water throughout the country, and they are working to bring aware- ness about clean, safe water for everyone. I would love to see more people join them and harness the energy of citizen power. We've seen this kind of momentum before. In 1963, 250,000 people gathered outside the Lincoln Memorial in Washington, D.C., for the March on Washington to draw attention to the continued inequalities faced by African Americans. In 1982, close to 1 million people demonstrated in Central Park against nuclear arms and to ask for an end to the tensions created by the Cold War. Millions more have turned out for women's issues in the last few years. These movements have shown us all that marches are only the beginning. Can we find enough passionate people to sustain a water movement that will address these systematic failures? I'm not just calling on young people or those living in communities already affected. I'm calling on heads of industry, mayors and senators, moms and dads, scientists, students, real estate agents, healthcare workers, water utility operators, veterans, and more. Ultimately, our community drinking water systems belong to us. We pay for the water and without us, these systems can't continue. We need to step up and take an interest in our drinking water systems, our infrastructure, our government, and our regulatory agencies.

Just as better communication skills can help companies grow and individual relationships thrive, we need to develop effective ways to exchange information when it comes to issues with our water supply. Utility and treatment managers along with city officials need to learn how to properly address water contamination issues, listen to their constituents, and work to rebuild trust in communities. Corporations need to take responsibility for toxic dumping, create more robust testing and monitoring systems, and stop using chemicals known to have negative impacts on public health. Companies need to become leaders for environmental protection, focusing on innovation that does not harm people or the environment, and be better neighbors to the communities they reside in. Medical providers and health professionals need to understand and become informed about toxic chemicals and how exposure to them can affect their patients. Everyday people need to trust their instincts, speak up when they see environmental issues impacting their community, and know that their voices matter. Because when we know, we can rise.

Almost every week, a new community discovers that its drinking water is no longer safe. Clean water is something most of us have taken for granted, relying on it for drinking, cooking, bathing, irrigation, washing our vegetables, making coffee and tea, and more. Without much thought, we take showers, flush toilets, and fill up our glasses from the tap throughout the day. But the time has come to open our eyes and see what's really happening with our water—and get involved. We have to put an end to this ever-growing crisis, step up our investment in vital infrastructure, and see greater enforcement of both the Clean Water Act and the Safe Drinking Water Act. As I've said, we have good laws on the books, but we need stricter enforcement to keep our waterways safe for all.

You might be feeling overwhelmed by these issues—the cover-ups, the mishaps, the lack of regulations, the shady politics—and that's why I'm so passionate about waking everyone up to this idea that we need to be the ones to save ourselves. You can become your own superhero simply by waking up the hero within you. Yes, the situation is huge and overwhelming, but you can't eat a whole apple at once. You need to take it bite by bite.

SEVEN STEPS CITIZENS CAN TAKE IN A WATER CRISIS

Think your drinking water might be toxic? Let's review your action plan to address it.

Step 1: Get Curious

Have you noticed a change in your water in color, smell, or pressure? Request a copy of your water quality report, also called a Consumer Confidence Report. Once you've got it, look for any contaminants that have exceeded legal limits or any other warnings about chemicals in your water. If you have recently read an article about a contaminant of concern that might be in your water supply, skip ahead to step 2.

Step 2: Separate Fact from Fiction (and Deception)

Talk to your water treatment operators and utility managers and show up to meetings with your public officials to voice your concerns. Take photographs, write observational notes, use news reports or whatever evidence you can gather that will support your case. Let both sides talk to discuss the issue(s) and create steps to move forward.

Step 3: Speak the Truth and Publicize It

Rally support in your community to get changes enacted. Many times, this step begins by hosting a town meeting and/or starting a Facebook group. Find allies such as scientists, lawyers, public relations firms, nonprofit groups, and other changemakers who can help lend credibility to your case.

Step 4: Put the Pressure On

If you are not getting a response from those in charge, then kick your efforts into high gear. Start a petition, engage your local media, make signs, and keep garnering support for the cause.

Step 5: Shield Yourself

Protect your family while you are working on solutions. Don't drink contaminated water. Request (or purchase) home water filters or bottled water in the interim until the problem is resolved.

Step 6: No More Nos

Keep going, continue to press elected officials to be honest and keep the lines of communication open, keep asking questions, and take on a never-give-up attitude.

Step 7: Celebrate!

No matter what happens or how long it takes to enact change, honor your journey and the courage and effort it takes to speak up and work to make a difference in your community. Keep putting attention on the message of clean water and remember how many people will benefit from your continued effort.

NATIONAL PRIORITIES

Clean water is a national priority that virtually no one is working on—not Congress, not corporations, not many local or state agencies. But as Americans, we deserve a water supply that we can trust. We need to demand vital updates to our infrastructure that will sustain us for years to come. In a 2016 article investigative reporter T. Christian Miller wrote about the safety of our drinking water, commenting, "Perhaps, what is needed are crowd-sourced water projects—an army of citizen water sleuths rising across the country to document the safety of water from the tap." I love this idea! Whether you like the term "water sleuth," "water warrior," or "water-keeper," people like you can and need to get involved. Let's become a collective energy that's so strong, we can make real changes with our water and in our world. It's a human need we cannot live without. You have the facts, so now the question becomes "What are you going to do about it?"

One of the most powerful tools I've developed over the years is **RAM**, which stands for Realization, Assessment, and Motivation. It's a process I teach to help individuals, companies, and cities to get empowered, check their instincts, and take action.

R: Realization is the epiphany and the response.

It's easy to blame others, but the moment of realization comes when you decide to get honest and take responsibility for your actions. On a personal level it means taking ownership or looking at how you have impacted a situation. Admitting there's a problem is the first step and it's shocking how many people are unwilling to begin. When it comes to communities, it may look like hosting a press conference or creating a task force to study a problem. Don't wait for your health and well-being and even your survival to be on the line. Begin now. Open your eyes and take an honest look at the drinking water in your community.

A: Assessment is taking stock and being accountable to yourself.

Assess your skills, your attitudes, your beliefs, and if you don't like what you see, don't be afraid to remodel. Tear things down and start over if you need to. Give yourself an appraisal and allow yourself to see who you are—and then trust who you are. To apply this principle to a city, officials might need to seek outside consultants or call on experts to find out the source of the problems. We need more systems in place to evaluate safety plans and contamination levels, and to stay on top of the issues at hand. Once a system has been assessed, you're ready to move to the next step.

M: Motivation and mindfulness are what keep you going.

You can probably think of at least one or two people in your life who have plenty of talent but aren't successful. And vice versa: you probably know plenty of people who aren't all that talented but are exceptionally successful. In this case, success is defined by being able to fix the problem and create something better. The key to finding success is to find your motivation. Your motivation is the fuel that will keep you going. Most public utilities should be motivated by the sheer fact that their job is to deliver safe, clean drinking water to the residents of the area. But as you can see in many places, this motivation has not been effective. That's where you come in. You need to make sure that those in charge can see your faces, hear your problems, and know that you care. We've forgotten how much power we really have. It's time to use it. We also need to take time away from our screens to stop and reconnect with the planet. There's so much chatter these days that it becomes hard to hear your own voice and even harder to tune in to what's happening around you. Are the streams looking more polluted or cloudy? How does the air smell? What does the water look like when you fill up your tub? Keep observing the world around you and be mindful of the details, and particularly when conditions change. You are your own best ally.

REBUILDING TRUST

All water treatment systems have choices and no single test is available to determine whether or not the water is safe to drink. Before deciding on the method of treatment, our water operators must know the quality of the source water and continue to monitor it for changes. If they receive complaints from consumers, they need to LISTEN, just as our colleague Randy Alstadt did in Poughkeepsie.

When the city of Wilmington, North Carolina, found itself in a water crisis, the initial response from officials was silence—followed by claims that the drinking water met all state and federal standards. That statement was true on a technicality as GenX, the toxic chemical of concern found in the drinking water, was not covered under any regulations. Researchers found that DuPont/Chemours was discharging GenX into the Cape Fear River just a hundred miles upstream from Wilmington. The local water utilities couldn't filter it out of the river, which hundreds of thousands of people were depending on as their water source. I'd like to use this community to offer lessons and recommendations for each stakeholder in how to handle such situations.

Utilities

Thanks to mounting pressure from consumers, the Cape Fear Public Utility Authority and Brunswick County Utilities started testing their raw and treated drinking water for GenX and similar compounds. Both utilities have started taking bids and working toward implementing additional treatment protections, one with a new granular-activated-carbon system and the other with a reverse osmosis system. Both utilities are also pursuing legal action against Chemours in hopes that the company, not consumers, will pick up the bill for these million-dollar projects.

One approach that Wilmington and other municipalities can consider for future use is text alerts. Text messages have a 99 percent open rate and about 90 percent get read within three minutes of receipt. You can use this technology to send helpful alerts and notifications and provide status updates, advisories, and more, helping provide information to residents in a way that people are already using to communicate. Instead of saying nothing or insisting that the water meets all guidelines, cities can improve their communication plans so that citizens are not stirred into a frenzy. In the case of Wilmington, most people learned about the contamination from their local paper, but the research was public knowledge. We need more treatment facilities staying up-to-date with new contaminants of concern and paying attention to other risks to their drinking water sources. It's not about maintaining the status quo but about becoming watchdogs and leaders for the health and well-being of their customers.

Public utilities should be aware of new research from the University of Missouri. Scientists there conducted a nationwide survey and found that members of the public are willing to pay for improved water quality.

"People in different areas of the country have different priorities, and that's hard to coordinate at a national level," Francisco Aguilar, one of the survey's authors and associate professor of forestry in the university's School of Natural Resources, said in a statement. "Still, people from around the nation consistently seem to be willing to pay for water quality improvements."

Business

Chemours representatives were quick to meet with town officials in Wilmington after news broke about GenX, vowing to work with local, state, and federal officials on next steps. Yet, they did not stop producing the compound and received three notices of violations along with lawsuits by residents, even after the bad press. Once the

Department of Environmental Quality (DEQ) issued a sixty-day notice in April 2018 threatening to revoke the company's air permit, they announced plans to stop all emissions by 2020 (including dumping GenX into the water supply) and invest $100 million to do it.

My message to industry is simple: The truth always comes out. Start with ethical business practices and then you don't have to deal with legal or regulatory repercussions. Become a leader in your field and be a good neighbor in your community. You can be the ones to stop this legacy of pollution and corruption.

Let me give you another example from my work. Rocketdyne was a rocket engine design and production company, originally located not far from my home in a suburb of Los Angeles. It was part of Rockwell International from 1967 through 1996, and eventually became Aerojet Rocketdyne. For years, the company launched rocket engine tests over the area, which generated many questions about violating air pollution regulations and created concerns about spills of toxic materials into nearby communities. Two class-action lawsuits were filed against the company, and my former boss Ed Masry led one of them. I still have the documents related to the case: in one, a former employee testified that he tried to discuss his uncertainties about the company's practices with management. The response to him was "It doesn't matter if we kill a few people with our testing, because Rockwell has a large legal staff that can take care of that kind of thing." Sadly, this attitude is still rampant in big business. To Rockwell and others, don't forget that people who have suffered with illnesses or lost relatives due to this kind of pollution and corporate misdeeds have more tenacity than you think. Why not trim the budget of your legal defense fund and spend more money on innovation that is good for all of us?

Business can and must become a force for good in the world. One option is to join the ranks of companies like Kickstarter, Ben & Jerry's, Cascade Engineering (a plastics manufacturer), New Belgium Brewing, Natura (the largest cosmetics maker in Latin America), and Eileen Fischer, which have become certified B Corporations. These businesses meet the highest standards of third-party-verified social and environmental performance, public transparency, and legal accountability to balance profit and purpose. They are measured on everything from carbon emissions to diversity and agree to share the results. The private sector has more resources than government agencies and can easily take the lead on reducing waste, increasing efficiency, and helping to solve environmental problems rather than create them.

Science & Health Experts

Science is such a critical part of the equation in environmental cases. When GenX first became an issue, the North Carolina Department of Health and Human Services (NCDHHS) set a health goal of 71,000 ppt. But experts quickly lowered the level to 140 ppt, after gaining access to additional studies, having consultations with the Centers for Disease Control and Prevention and other national health organizations, and considering the health impacts of similar compounds.

We need more information about all the chemicals found in the marketplace today, and we need more scientists and experts to take a bolder stand. Let's not make humans into guinea pigs but instead take a more cautionary approach about releasing these toxins into the environment. I've seen it time and again that once the science is in, the health goals get lowered. We need to increase budgets for science and health advisory boards so that they can keep up their important public health work.

Regulators

Many contaminants found in our drinking water, including pharmaceuticals and industrial chemicals, are not regulated. How do so many unregulated chemicals get into our water? Chemicals in this country are considered safe until they have been proven to be toxic. It's time to turn that around. We need to assume a chemical may be harmful until it is proven to be safe. In Europe, a regulation was enacted in 2007 to help improve the protection of human health and the environment from the risks posed by chemicals; it's called REACH, which stands for Registration, Evaluation, Authorization, and Restriction of Chemicals. The regulation puts the burden of proof on companies, which have to register their substances, then identify and manage the risks of the chemicals they manufacture and market in the European Union and communicate any risk-management measures to users. If risks can't be managed, officials can restrict or ban the use of those substances. If our friends across the pond can enact this commonsense legislation, surely we can too.

GenX was such a mysterious chemical that no one knew who was responsible for regulating it. Local regulatory agencies felt unable to act because the EPA stated it didn't have regulations for the compound. It essentially left Chemours to evaluate the toxicity of its own product, a standard practice. Regulatory agencies need peer-reviewed toxicological information in order to provide public health advisories, but the process of obtaining that data can take time, partially because funding for these kinds of studies is in short supply. The

EPA has been unable to adopt a single new standard in the last twenty years.

In addition, we need to find advanced and inventive ways to regulate industry that don't allow loopholes and that enforce steeper fines for those who cheat regulations. We need to make sure that regulators are not former employees of the industry being regulated.

Lawmakers

Often, contamination cases quickly turn political. People point fingers at the other side of the table, but clean water is not a Democrat or Republican issue. Lawmakers can play a vital role in protecting the people and environment when toxins are discovered in the water supply. We need support from our lawmakers to increase and approve budgets for water infrastructure, strengthen safeguards, and enforce regulations, regardless of your (or their) political affiliations. Oftentimes, citizens suffer while policymakers disagree on how to best handle the situation.

During Wilmington's crisis, Democratic governor Roy Cooper attempted to establish a Water Health and Safety Division to continue monitoring levels of GenX and add staff to the DEQ, but his requests were denied by a Republican-led General Assembly. The case quickly became divided as

Republicans proposed a bill that would put more money into research and testing on GenX. Both the state house and the state senate have established special committees on GenX, but real action has been stalled, as lawmakers continue to propose bills that don't pass. The 2018–19 state budget did not provide additional funding for the N.C. Department of Health and Human Services' water health safety unit. Without proper resources, how can state agencies handle their regular workload and help when environmental tragedies strike?

At the local level, none of Wilmington's local officeholders attended a public forum in August 2017 hosted by a community group called Wilmington Stop GenX in Our Water Supply. The online version of this group had about ten thousand members. Local legislators can do better by listening and engaging with citizens and finding ways to communicate about how to move forward during a contamination crisis.

Here are some good questions for local leaders to ask themselves:

- What can we do to be more transparent?
- How can we better protect our water sources from contamination in the first place?
- How can we work to restore confidence with our constituents?

- What can we learn from other
  communities that have seen similar
  problems and how can we implement
  changes faster?

People

No one asks for pollution in their water. When you
find out your tap is tainted, it's natural to have questions and concerns. Part of why I've hosted hundreds
of town hall meetings throughout the country is to
offer facts and information to the people. Usually,
my presence in a small town drums up interest and
local media will cover the issue. I show up so that
people can become informed and educated about
how to come together and take action to clean up
the water. I want to remind you it's okay to ask
questions when it comes to your drinking water.
Don't let anyone tell you otherwise or put you off.
When I was in town to discuss the water situation
in Wilmington, we handed out index cards to the
hundreds of people who attended the town hall
meeting. They had great questions for the panel of
experts we assembled, including these:

- Why can't we make companies prove
  something is safe before they can dump it?
- Is there any reason our elected officials
  did not stop this earlier? Is there no
  accountability?

- Is GenX in our air and if so, is it toxic to us?
- What's the best way to approach our schools about ensuring our children have safe drinking water?
- Is showering and bathing in the water harmful?
- When will the water be safe to drink again?
- How do we empower our wastewater treatment operators who are on the front lines of defense?
- Is there any hope of the CFPUA [Cape Fear Public Utility Authority] being able to install equipment to effectively remove all concerning PFCs for a reasonable cost in a reasonable time frame?
- When will politicians have the courage and creativity to develop processes to incentivize business to bring jobs to states like North Carolina but also demand that public health be priority #1?

Officials might try to underestimate you, but in every community I've visited people ask good questions and are extremely well versed in their understanding that something's gone wrong with the water. When communities come together, they have all the passion, fortitude, and smarts to create positive solutions. Don't stand for anything less than the truth of what's really happening. It's your backyard, it's your tap, it's your children. You can protect yourselves by keeping your elected officials accountable and staying conversant on these issues. My best advice is **don't give up**. Keep the energy building and find more allies who can support you in making changes. With enough people, you can truly make a difference.

IS BOTTLED WATER A SOLUTION?

I'd like to talk about the double-edged sword of the bottled water industry. Yes, it can be a lifesaver in an immediate crisis, and it has been a lifeline for many communities with undrinkable water, but you need to know what you are drinking. Americans tend to think that bottled water is cleaner and safer than what's coming out of the tap. In some communities, that's very true, but bottled water labels can be confusing. They portray an illusion of virtue, with images and messages printed on the bottles saying they are filled with water from pure mountain springs, while many of these bottles contain tap water in a fancy-looking to-go package.

The bottled water industry began to take off when beverage giants like Coca-Cola and Pepsi launched the product as a means to maintain profits when soda sales began declining in the early 2000s. Bottled water outsold soda in 2016 and is now the largest beverage category by volume.

"When Perrier first entered the country in the 1970s, few would have predicted the heights to which bottled water would eventually climb," Michael Bellas, chairman and CEO of Beverage Marketing Corp., said in a statement. "Where once it would have been unimaginable to see Americans walking down the street carrying plastic bottles of water or driving around with them in their cars' cup holders, now that's the norm."

Today, Americans spend about $16 billion a year on bottled water. The biggest brands in the industry are Nestlé Pure Life, Coca-Cola-owned Dasani, and PepsiCo's Aquafina, according to **Beverage Digest**. Water municipalities can't possibly compete with these companies when it comes to advertising, so it's no surprise why bottled water sales have taken off. Both Pepsi and Coca-Cola's bottled water is water from public sources (tap water) that is then filtered.

Bottled water is not regulated by the EPA, which is responsible for the quality of water that comes out of your tap. Instead, the U.S. Food and Drug Administration is responsible for the safety of bottled water sold nationally. States regulate water that is packaged and sold within their state lines, which is most of the market.

If you are in a situation where you need to buy bottled water, always read the fine print on the label and look for brands that treat the water with reverse osmosis, distillation, granular activated carbon, micron filtration, or water sourced from pure spring water, which the EPA defines as groundwater collected "at the point where water flows naturally to the earth's surface or from a borehole that taps into the underground source." If the label says from "a municipal source" or "from a community water system," that means tap water.

Bottled water is also a lot more expensive than tap. At first glance it might seem like paying $1 to $3 for a bottle isn't so bad, but about 4,787 bottles of water can be filled with tap water for $2.10. Each bottle of water you buy costs more than two thousand times what you would pay for fresh tap water.

Here's the breakdown:

Water municipalities typically measure water
  in centum cubic feet (CCF).
1 CCF = 748 gallons of water
748 gallons of water = 95,744 ounces
95,744 ounces = 4,787 bottles of water
Cost of 1 CCF = $2.10

Of course, you may buy bottled water in bulk and get a better deal, and water bill rates vary throughout the country, but you get the idea.

In addition to cost, bottled water creates a ton of waste. The industry used about 4 billion pounds of plastic in 2016 alone. Many of those bottles don't get recycled and clog up landfills and public trash bins. Plus, plastic manufacturing plants that make the bottles have been known to pollute local drinking water sources.

Bottled water may be a useful short-term strategy for drinking water in an emergency, but it shouldn't be a permanent solution. The National Guard assisted with door-to-door distribution of bottled water in Flint, Michigan, starting in January 2016 during the city's water crisis. The city established free bottled water stations throughout the city, giving away millions of cases of water at a cost of about $22,000 per day. The program was part of a $450 million state and federal aid package, though taxpayers certainly footed some of that bill. It's no question that the bottled water program helped reduce harm in Flint, but it came at quite a cost for everyone.

THE ENVIRONMENTAL MOVEMENT IS FOR EVERYONE

I've met a lot of people in my travels and most of them would not identify as "environmentalists" or "activists." However, people's perspectives change rapidly when they can't drink their water. One of the most contentious talking points I've heard from the Trump administration is the idea that the environmental movement is a product of rich elites and that regulations hurt working-class people. I speak with these same people every day and I can tell you that they are not suffering because of regulations. Instead, they have been harmed by neglected infrastructure updates, corporate misdeeds, and bureaucratic hurdles. The American Dream is dissolving. Our country is cluttered with forgotten towns, and these communities need our attention.

Just ask Paula Jean Swearengin, a single mom to four boys, born and raised in Mullens, West Virginia—the heart of coal country. She's a coal miner's daughter and a coal miner's granddaughter. Like so many from her region, her family has seen the negative impacts of working for the coal industry. Her grandfather died from coal workers' pneumoconiosis (also known as black lung). Her uncles have also been diagnosed with the disease. The streams and rivers in her town have become toxic thanks to runoff from the mines. She has seen entire communities turn into ghost towns after a mine shuts down and miners struggling with disease for years after the work has ceased. A whole generation of West Virginians is looking to get back to work, and it's no wonder that Trump's campaign message spoke to them. But these people want reliable, safe jobs and there's no indication that the coal industry, as it stands today, can deliver that to them.

Paula Jean is paving a new path for herself, working for the people and running for a U.S. Senate seat in West Virginia.

"The question we face today is: What are we going to do when the coal is gone?" her website said. "And make no mistake it's going. No one has given us an answer that doesn't require the sacrifice of our health and our environment. I believe our future is in building a 21st-century, clean economy."

Paula Jean did not win in the much-watched race against incumbent Joe Manchin in the 2018 Democratic primary, but she did garner 30 percent of the vote. And she was not the only person running for political office based on environmental and water contamination concerns. In fact, a whole crop of 2018 midterm candidates ran to help clean up the toxic water in their towns. I believe we will see more of these candidates running for state and national seats, as we've already seen this happening for years at the local level with city council seats.

Matt Morgan ran for Michigan's 1st Congressional District, and sent out a campaign email about PFAS compounds, which have been found in the water of several nearby military bases in his district.

"As a retired Marine who was personally involved in the closure and environmental remediation of two 60-year-old Marine Corps air bases, I know firsthand the responsibility our military departments have to fully address environmental issues to the standards of surrounding communities," he wrote in a May 2018 campaign email.

Morgan retired from the Marine Corps in 2013 as a lieutenant colonel after more than twenty years. The forty-seven-year-old did not win against incumbent Republican Jack Bergman but he did receive 44 percent of the vote, for a seat where an incumbent hasn't lost since 1966.

Not surprisingly, North Carolina's 7th Congressional District, which includes Wilmington, had another interesting race. Dr. Kyle Horton, a female physician, ran as a Democrat for the seat against Republican incumbent David Rouzer, whose campaign was funded in part by DowDuPont, which created GenX. She, on the other hand, had a firm policy of not taking money from the chemical or fossil fuel industries.

Kyle comes from a working-class family with a long history of military service, and is a champion of health care for women, children, and families, as well as veterans. She knew water was on the minds of many people in her state, and one of her campaign promises was to "protect our water."

In regard to the GenX situation, she told a

local news site, "Our children really should not be guinea pigs at the hands of a Fortune 500 company. We need policies that make sense to protect our children from essentially being poisoned by these corporate polluters who get all kinds of breaks and tax incentives. Right now, as they are dismantling and defunding the Environmental Protection Agency, they can really do whatever they want, including recklessly risking our health and the health of future generations with these emerging compounds in our water, including many fluorocarbons."

Kyle ran a great campaign and in a concession message she wrote, "We set out to build a grassroots movement for the people of the 7th District—and we did! We put the Washington establishment insiders, career politicians, and big money special interests on notice! We accomplished all this ourselves without the corporate PACs, big polluters, and the dark, dirty money of corrupt cronies. While we weren't able to overcome THIS time in an unconstitutional district, we brought people together to help heal our divides. We united so many folks with a vision of a government that is 'of the people, by the people, and for the people'— a vision that respects our most fundamental founding values and traditions to preserve our democracy."

Kyle has also been involved in grassroots advocacy work, organizing more physicians to get involved in water issues and garnering attention for environmental public health tracking in her state. She helped pass bipartisan legislation for lead and copper, noting that North Carolina was one of a few states in the country not routinely submitting lead and copper results to the Centers for Disease Control and Prevention. The state is now regularly submitting that data.

Another important piece about this new crop of political candidates is that polluters and waste sites are typically situated in places that are not expected to push back. It's a chicken-and-egg situation: Once pollution strikes, property values go down, but usually it's communities that are already hurting that are most vulnerable to toxic dumping. For example, in Flint, Michigan, 45 percent of residents live below the federal poverty level. More than 50 percent of the population is African American. It's hard not to see their plight as environmental racism in action.

In his book **Dumping in Dixie: Race, Class, and Environmental Quality**, Professor Robert D. Bullard writes, "The problem of polluted black communities is not a new phenomenon. Historically, toxic dumping and the location of locally unwanted land uses (LULUs) have followed the 'path of least resistance,' meaning black and poor communities have been disproportionately burdened with these types of externalities."

There's a "class of hyper-polluters—the worst-of-the-worst—that disproportionately expose communities of color and low-income populations to chemical releases," according to a 2016 study published in **Environmental Research Letters**. In other words, polluters are excessively found near communities of color. One of the worst examples is Cancer Alley, the stretch between Baton Rouge and New Orleans in Louisiana that is peppered with more than 150 industrial facilities. It's no surprise that cancer cases and other health issues are notoriously high in this community.

The color of your skin, the amount of money in your bank account, and your zip code should not determine whether or not you have clean water. We can and must do better. Seeing political candidates run on the issue of contaminated water is something we've rarely seen before, but I'm hopeful that they can break up the existing state of affairs in our political system—and that more people will pay attention to candidates with pro-environment platforms.

WE NEED MORE DISRUPTORS

At the beginning of this book I told you about my own struggles with dyslexia as a child. Well, there's more to the story. When I was a kid, my father would take me every weekend to Watson Park, my favorite place because it was home to Locomotive Engine 1073. It was a real steam engine that sat on real railroad tracks. I loved to play on it, running up and down and in and out of all the compartments, as my imagination ran wild pretending to be the conductor.

One day while running around on top of the train, Dad yelled out that it was time to go. As I headed toward the ladder where he was standing, I started to climb down when I suddenly got scared and said, "I can't do this." My father replied, "Sure you can honey," as he grasped his hands together and said, "I'm right here, just come down, step into my hand, I've got you."

I slipped and fell all the way down, hitting my head on each rung of the ladder, right past my dad, landing facedown on the railroad track. I later learned that both my dad and my brother felt terrified when they saw me tumble. They weren't sure I was going to make it. I had a terrible concussion, to say the least, and I was in and out of consciousness for days, with two solid black eyes that lasted about a year. I miraculously recovered with what seemed to be no long-term effects, yet my mother did notice a few changes in me. I began to put my shoes on the wrong feet. I couldn't remember how to tie my shoes. I went right when I meant to go left. I lost my sense of direction, yet strangely you couldn't beat me at a game of Go Fish.

Once I started school many other changes were noted. I could memorize anything. I relied on visual acuity and stored that information rather than reading it. I loved anything visual, especially maps, and I needed to see everything. I was always asking for a full discussion and demonstration for projects in the classroom. My teachers thought I was being argumentative, but I was full of questions and I became extremely observant. I could see other people's frustration with me by how they looked at me and I learned how to read people's emotional cues.

Suddenly, I was the difficult child. Throughout the years I was labeled lazy, dumb, careless, low-attention-span, and was told I needed special classes. I couldn't comply with the so-called standard of conformance of the education system. It wasn't until my formative educational years that I received the diagnosis of dyslexia, something experts didn't know much about at that time. Years later, it was called trauma-induced dyslexia.

I was so frustrated by being labeled and judged. Maybe I didn't learn it the "right" way. But who set these standards and rules? I didn't know we all had to act and think alike. It felt like I couldn't catch a break. Just because I was different didn't mean I was inferior. Even though some people called me disruptive, I didn't have to see disruption as a bad thing. In fact, some would say I've made my career out of disruption.

Most people think of the term "disruptor" as a bad label. It conjures up ideas of being troublesome, rowdy, or chaotic. In school, any student who talks out of turn might be punished and girls especially are rewarded for obedient behavior, but life doesn't work this way. You don't get awards later in life for maintaining the status quo. We need to take risks. My high school teacher was a disruptor, as a teacher who took a risk by giving me my tests orally. She didn't ask permission to do that; she relied on her instinct instead. In the business world, being disruptive means being innovative and original. Politically, we are seeing disruption throughout the halls of Congress and in the highest levels of government. The world is transforming faster than we could have ever imagined and so more than ever we need disruptors who can lead the charge.

Dealing with early life challenges pushed me out of my comfort zone and opened me to new ways of expressing myself. I also learned that if I let others define who I was, then I would never be able to succeed in my life. What seemed like my biggest flaw became my superpower. It's time for you to start looking within to wake up your own superpowers. It's time to move from feeling confused and frustrated to being empowered and ready to take action. I want you to join me in disrupting business as usual and start making much-needed changes to our water system. It's time to become a disruptor to this broken system.

THE SENSATIONAL MOMENT

I know we are living in times where much of our media coverage is dubbed "fake news." From my perspective, the media can be helpful, though they miss a lot of the stories that come into my inbox. They usually cover an environmental story once it hits a sensational moment. After they leave, the people who live in that town are left with the problem and that's the trouble. I'll never forget when I traveled to southern Louisiana during the BP Deepwater Horizon oil spill in the Gulf of Mexico in 2010. I had reporters chasing me around, begging me to talk to them and give them a soundbite for their nightly news coverage. I was there to work and help people on the ground who were sorting out the developing legal and environmental issues. Oil doesn't just go away; it takes years to clean up. We saw devastation to people's lives and livelihoods, wildlife, and fisheries throughout the region. Who could forget the images of pelicans and gulls covered in heavy oil, dead sea turtles washing ashore, or marsh grasses covered in that thick, black oil? I finally said to them, "You are here for the sensational moment. You will report the story and go away, but these people still have to live with this mess for years to come."

I bring up this story not to pick a fight with the media or put down the hardworking people who choose to cover these important stories (I've used many, many well-reported news stories as references in this book), but to discuss the real destruction that takes place from these toxins. The scope of the issue can't possibly be covered in a 2:26 clip—two minutes, twenty-six seconds is the typical length of a national TV news story. Even Walter Cronkite once called the evening news a "powerful headline service" and recommended that his audience keep reading newspapers and dive deeper into these issues. I know many people have been inspired by the **Erin Brockovich** movie, but it was years and years of work reduced to two hours and twelve minutes of legal drama. It focused on one contaminant and one town. Five years after the Gulf spill, dolphins were still dying from it. A 2015 study from the National Oceanic and Atmospheric Administration found that more than a thousand bottlenose dolphins had died off the Gulf coast since the spill in 2010. The spill lasted for almost three months with millions of gallons of oil and chemicals pouring into the Gulf of Mexico. The dangerous contamination marred businesses, tourism, and commercial fishing along the coast.

One of the ways media can help rebuild trust with its viewers is to continue to cover stories even after the dramatic moment has passed. We all need to be vigilant and listen to the news and read the local paper to understand what's happening in our communities. But we can't just skim the headlines and then sink into a feeling of overwhelm and inaction. We need to get involved and help one another. We need to be the ones to say, "How can I help?"

THE WATERSHED MOMENT

A **watershed** is a piece of land that catches the rain and snow that then seeps into streams, rivers, and lakes. Colloquially, we use the term "watershed" to define a turning point. We have reached the watershed moment that I've been waiting for my whole career. Disruption is in the air. When I first started working in Hinkley, California, the people of Hinkley and I felt like a lone voice. Would anyone care about this small town and its devastating pollution problems? Those voices rose without a platform or social media, and when the movie came out, viewers supported their story.

Now, Hinkleys are happening everywhere all the time. Will we be the people who can care enough about each of these communities to take action? Like waves rushing to the shore, it's time to use this momentum, get off the couch, and realize the potential we have to shape our future—for us, for our kids, for our grandkids, and for so many generations to come. The solution rests in our hands. The technology is available. With enough funding, science can help us get through this crisis. No one has a right to destroy our water and it's up to every one of us to protect it.

In a country that seems to be more and more split on the issues we face today, we need to remember how our humanness unites us. Ask anyone what they do to relax, renew, and unwind, and I will bet you that 99.9 percent of people say they go outside. They feel the sun on their face, the wind blow through their hair; they garden; they golf; they go swimming in a nearby lake or at the ocean; they walk with a friend at a nature preserve; or take a weekend away in the great outdoors.

Now imagine for a moment that all that was gone for good. We can't live without these natural resources—our water, air, or soil. What would happen if that very livelihood, and the most necessary elements to sustain life, were too polluted or simply vanished? I know some people think this scenario could never happen. The message of this book is clear: We are in trouble and we need to be the ones to save our water, and ourselves.

Now is not the time to fight against one another; it's a time to come together for a greater good. I've seen too much waste, selfishness, greed, hidden agendas, and finger-pointing. Sharing information and working together is our only hope. The solution lies with people in their communities, and at the local and state level, working for change throughout our great nation. We don't need to wait for anyone else to come save us. We can start small, start in our neighborhoods, and work to make significant changes that will impact generations to come. I've been inspired to devote my life to this work and I hope you will join me.

APPENDIX: RESOURCES

GET INVOLVED

Many amazing organizations are working on water contamination issues. You can get involved by giving them your support, joining in to call your legislators, or signing up for a day of action in your community or at a national level. If you can't find a group working on a cause near you, then start your own. It's as easy as doing some research, starting your own online group, and finding a few like-minded people to help.

Here's a roundup of the top national organizations working to help communities clean up their water.

Americans Against Fracking
www.americansagainstfracking.org

Their goal is to ban fracking, by supporting federal, state, and local efforts to ban fracking, enact moratoriums, and stop practices that facilitate fracking like natural gas exports, frac sand mining, and the construction of pipelines.

American Rivers
www.americanrivers.org

The mission of this organization is to protect healthy rivers, restore damaged rivers, and conserve clean water for people and nature.

Citizens Concerned About Chloramines
www.chloramine.org

This nonprofit organization's mission is to raise the public's awareness about chloramine and its health effects when used as a disinfectant in the water.

Clean Water Action
www.cleanwateraction.org

Created in 1972 during the campaign to pass the landmark Clean Water Act, this grassroots advocacy group works to protect the environment and safeguard public health, promote passage of strong environmental laws, and help communities address local environmental problems affecting them.

The Clean Water Fund

www.cleanwaterfund.org

Since 1974, the Clean Water Fund has helped people campaign successfully for cleaner and safer water, cleaner air, and protection from toxic pollution in homes, neighborhoods, and workplaces.

Earth Justice

earthjustice.org

The nation's original and largest nonprofit environmental law organization leverages its expertise and commitment to fight for justice and advance the promise of a healthy world for all.

Environmental Working Group

www.ewg.org

This nonprofit, nonpartisan organization is dedicated to protecting human health and the environment with a mission to empower people to live healthier lives in a healthier environment.

Environment America

environmentamerica.org

This organization researches the challenges confronting our environment and works to educate the public about what's at stake.

Environmental Integrity Project

www.environmentalintegrity.org

The Environmental Integrity Project is a nonpartisan, nonprofit watchdog organization that advocates for effective enforcement of environmental laws.

Food and Water Watch

www.foodandwaterwatch.org

Food and Water Watch champions healthy food and clean water for all, with a mission to stand up to corporations that put profits before people, and advocate for a democracy that improves people's lives and protects our environment.

The Union of Concerned Scientists

www.ucsusa.org

The scientists and engineers at UCS puts rigorous, independent science to work to solve our planet's most pressing problems. The organization was founded in 1969 by scientists and students at the Massachusetts Institute of Technology.

National Association of Clean Water Agencies
www.nacwa.org

The National Association of Clean Water Agencies (NACWA) has been a leader in legislative, regulatory, and legal advocacy on the full spectrum of clean water issues, as well as a top technical resource for water management, sustainability, and ecosystem protection interests for more than forty years. NACWA represents public wastewater and stormwater agencies of all sizes nationwide.

The National Wildlife Federation
www.nwf.org/Home/Our-Work/Waters

The National Wildlife Federation has been advocating for improvements in our nation's water quality since their first annual meeting in 1937.

Waterkeeper Alliance
waterkeeper.org

This nonprofit is focused solely on clean water. They preserve and protect water by connecting local Waterkeeper organizations and affiliates worldwide with a goal of drinkable, fishable, and swimmable water everywhere.

ACKNOWLEDGMENTS

I'm so grateful to everyone in my life who has supported my work, especially:

Bob Bowcock, for your friendship and expertise, and for driving around so many towns with me all these years.

Suzanne Boothby, for writing this book with me, translating countless conversations to the page and bringing these stories to life, along with putting in immense hours of research and dedication to this project.

Jimmy Soni and Rob Goodman, for your additional help with research and writing on climate change.

Victoria Wilson, for championing this book from the moment we met and for your careful edits and attention throughout the process.

Laura Yorke, for your vision, support, and cheerleading from start to finish.

Dave Kass, for your years of friendship and for always connecting me with the right people.

To all the water warriors and communities I've worked with for your strength and dedication to the cause. Thank you for sharing your stories in this book. I applaud all communities working hard to improve their water, including those whose stories didn't make it into this book. You are creating the change we all want to see. Thank you for inviting me to your towns, into your homes, and for the incredibly long hours you have spent spreading awareness about these important issues.

NOTES

INTRODUCTION

xix We've got more than forty thousand: "EPA Releases First Major Update to Chemicals List in 40 Years," U.S. EPA press release, February 19, 2019.

1. HOW DID WE GET HERE?

7 The Federal Water Pollution Control Act: History of the Clean Water Act, U.S. EPA.

7 "Potential cancer-causing chemicals": James L. Agee, "Protecting America's Drinking Water: Our Responsibilities Under the Safe Drinking Water Act," **EPA Journal**, March 1975.

8 "We can no longer afford": Richard Nixon, Annual Message to the Congress on the State of the Union, January 22, 1970.

9 He set up an Environmental Quality Council: Jack Lewis, "The Birth of the EPA," **EPA Journal**, November 1985.

9 The purpose of the act: "What Is the National Environmental Policy Act," U.S. EPA, https://www.epa.gov/nepa/what-national-environmental-policy-act.

10 This led to the creation: EPA Mission Statement, U.S. EPA website.

11 nonpoint source pollution: "Basic Information about Nonpoint Source (NPS) Pollution," U.S. EPA website.

11 urban runoff: "Nonpoint Source: Urban Areas," U.S. EPA website.

11 half a million times: Charles Duhigg, "Clean Water Laws Are Neglected, at a Cost in Suffering," **The New York Times**, September 12, 2009.

12 In **Rapanos v. United States**: The United States Department of Justice, "Rapanos v. U.S.," U.S. Department of Justice website.

12 the Clean Water Rule: "Waters of the United States (WOTUS) Rulemaking," U.S. EPA website.

12 However, the rule: Timothy Cama, "Federal Judge Blocks Obama's Water Rule," **The Hill**, August 27, 2015.

13 the order wasn't enough: Coral Davenport, "Trump Plans to Begin E.P.A. Rollback with Order on Clean Water," **The New York Times**, February 28, 2017.

13 on December 23, 2019: "Current Implementation of 'Waters of the United States,'" U.S. EPA website.

13 "challenged in court": "NRDC: Trump Moves to Deny Americans Clean Water," September 12, 2019, National Resources Defense Council.

13 the Safe Drinking Water Act: "Summary of the Safe Drinking Water Act," U.S. EPA website.

14 The agency sets: "How EPA Regulates Drinking Water Contaminants," U.S. EPA website.

17 While the company tried to argue: Technical Report Summary, made available in **Palmer v. 3M**, https://www.documentcloud.org/documents/4592747-PFAS-in-Tennessee-River-Fish.html.

17 the compounds were toxic: Sharon Lerner, "3M Knew About the Dangers of PFOA and PFOS Decades Ago, Internal Documents Show," **The Intercept**, July 31, 2018.

17 2016 health advisory: "Toxicological Profile for Per-fluoroalkyls," Draft for Public Comment, Agency for Toxic Substances and Disease Registry website, June 2018.

18 in the womb: "Teflon Chemicals Harmful at Smallest Doses," Environmental Working Group, August 20, 2015, http://www.ewg.org/research/teflon-chemical-harmful-at-smallest-doses/pfoa-pollution-worldwide-and.

18 the Lead and Copper Rule: "Lead and Copper Rule," U.S. EPA website.

19 Since early 2019, thirteen state and local officials: Curt Guyette, "A Deep Dive into the Source of Flint's Water Crisis," **Detroit Metro Times**, April 19, 2017.

19 More than 80 percent: Kate Taylor, "Most New York City Schools Had High Lead Levels, Retests Find," **The New York Times**, April 28, 2017.

19 The bill's author: George Lavender, "Bill Would Force CA Schools to Test Drinking Water for Lead," KPCC, April 6, 2017.

22 the average American uses: "Water Questions & Answers," USGS, http://water.usgs.gov/edu/qa-home-percapita.html.

23 Some estimates show: Stephen A. Hubbs, "Facts About Chloramine Drinking Water Treatment," Water Quality & Health Council, February 19, 2016, https://waterandhealth.org/safe-drinking-water/facts-chloramine-drinking-water-treatment.

24 That's the estimated number: "Cancer Statistics,"

National Cancer Institute, https://www.cancer.gov
/about-cancer/understanding/statistics.

24 15 million U.S. households: "American Housing
Survey for the United States: 2007," U.S Department of Housing and Urban Development, September 2008.

24 **Legionella** outbreaks: Lena H. Sun, "Legionnaires'
Outbreaks Cases Nearly Quadrupled in 15 Years,"
The Washington Post, June 7, 2016.

2. IT BEGAN IN HINKLEY ... AND
IT'S EVERYWHERE NOW

30 By 2016, a report: David Andrews and Bill Walker,
"'Erin Brockovich' Carcinogen in Tap Water of
More Than 200 Million Americans," Environmental Working Group, September 20, 2016,
http://www.ewg.org/research/chromium-six-found
-in-us-tap-water.

41 Even after all these years: Jim Steinberg, "Milestone
Reached in Cleanup of Polluted Hinkley Water
Made Famous in 'Erin Brockovich,'" **San Ber-
nardino Sun**, April 20, 2017.

42 Groundwater in Hinkley tested as high as 580 ppb:
Marla Cone, "Chromium in Drinking Water Causes
Cancer," **Scientific American**, February 9, 2009.

42 It's estimated that it will take: David Danielski,
"Spreading Pollution Spawns More Worries in Hinkley," **The Press-Enterprise**, December 12, 2010.

43 In 2006, PG&E paid: Genevieve Bookwalter,
"Pending Chromium 6 Limits Worry Small Water
Company," California Health Report, November 12,
2011.

43 Lockheed Martin: Andrew Blankstein and Jean Guccione, "Lockheed Linked to Chromium 6 Pollution," **Los Angeles Times**, January, 21, 2001.

43 coal ash dump sites: Lisa Evans, "EPA's Blind Spot: Hexavalent Chromium in Coal Ash," Earth Justice Report, February 1, 2011.

44 A spokesperson from the company: Sedina Banks, "The 'Erin Brockovich Effect': How Media Shapes Toxics Policy," University of California, Davis School of Law, 2003.

44 PG&E also sent an internal memo: Ibid.

45 "Between 1996 and 2008": "Industry Groups Used Cherry-Picked Science to Avoid Regulation of Chromium," Union of Concerned Scientists, Disinformation Playbook.

46 Dennis Paustenbach: David Heath, "How Industry Scientists Stalled Action on Carcinogen," Center for Public Integrity, March 13, 2013.

46 The scientists sat in a hot tub: Corbett, Finley, Paustenbach, and Kerger, "Systemic Uptake of Chromium in Human Volunteers Following Dermal Contact with Hexavalent Chromium," **Journal of Exposure Analysis and Environmental Epidemiology**, April-June 1997.

47 They also drank jugs of water: Kerger, Finley, Corbett, Dodge, and Paustenbach, "Ingestion of Chromium(VI) in Drinking Water by Human Volunteers," **Journal of Toxicology and Environmental Health**, January 1997.

47 ChemRisk earned: Egilman and Scout, "Corporate Corruption of Science—the Case of Chromium(VI)," **International Journal of Occupational and Environmental Health**, April–June 2006.

47 While funding: "OECD Science, Technology and Industry Scoreboard 2015," Organisation for Economic Co-operation and Development, 2015, p. 156.

48 She responded by saying: Cynthia McFadden, "Town Plagued with Contaminated Water," ABC News, 1996.

50 Court papers later revealed: Peter Waldman, "Study Tied Pollutant to Cancer; Then Consultants Got Hold of It," The Wall Street Journal, December 23, 2005.

50 The consultants were from ChemRisk: Ibid.

51 They made it look: Zhang and Li, "Cancer Mortality in a Chinese Population Exposed to Hexavalent Chromium in Water," Journal of Occupational and Environmental Medicine, April 1997.

51 retracted the paper: Melissa Lee Phillips, "Journal Retracts Chromium Study," The Scientist, June 7, 2006.

51 John Stossel: John Stossel, Give Me a Break (New York: HarperCollins, 2004), p. 84.

51 A 2012 UCS report: "Heads They Win, Tails We Lose: How Corporations Corrupt Science at the Public's Expense," Union of Concerned Scientists, February 2012 Report.

54 Gary and I both testified: Senate Hearing of the Senate Health & Human Services Committee, "Possible Interference in the Scientific Review of Chromium VI Toxicity," February 28, 2003, Los Angeles, California.

56 "The caution I'd give anybody": Chip Jacobs and Kevin Uhrich, "Troubled Waters," LA CityBeat, April 22, 2004.

56 In July 2014, California: "Frequently Asked Questions About Hexavalent Chromium in Drinking Water," California Water Boards, September 25, 2015.

57 The National Toxicology Program studies: "Hexavalent Chromium," National Toxicology Program Fact Sheet, February 2018.

58 The Superior Court of Sacramento County: Sara Jerome, "California Drops Tough Chromium-6 Standard," **Water Online**, August 16, 2017.

58 "As if the current challenges": Ryan McCarthy, "State Panel Removes Water Standard Opposed by Vacaville, Taxpayers Group," **Daily Republic**, August 2, 2017.

59 While the MCL: "Chromium-6 Drinking Water MCL," California Water Boards.

3. CONNECTING THE DOTS & BUILDING A MAP

77 In general, we see: "Cancer Statistics," National Cancer Institute, April 27, 2018.

81 Cancer is the second leading cause: "Child Health," National Center for Health Statistics, Centers for Disease Control and Prevention.

81 Yet, forty-six American children: "About Us," Trevor's Trek Foundation.

82 Trevor's Law: "Frank R. Lautenberg Chemical Safety for the 21st Century Act," Public Law 114-182, June 22, 2016.

4. FLOATING IN A SEA OF CHEMICALS

89 The first thing: "How Much Water Is There on, in, and Above the Earth?" U.S. Geological Survey.

90 We've specifically seen: Lena H. Sun, "Legionnaires' Outbreaks Cases Nearly Quadrupled in 15 Years," **The Washington Post**, June 7, 2016.

90 "public health enemy number 1": Stephen A. Hubbs, "Addressing Legionella: Public Health Enemy #1 in U.S. Water Systems," Water Quality & Health Council, August 29, 2014.

91 We have more: "Drinking Water Requirements for States and Public Water Systems," U.S. EPA.

92 Last amended in 1996: "President Clinton Signs Legislation to Ensure Americans Safe Drinking Water," U.S. EPA press release, August 6, 1996.

93 Rates of chronic disease for children: "Percentage of U.S. Children Who Have Chronic Health Conditions on the Rise," American Academy of Pediatrics, April 30, 2016.

93 Nearly half of U.S. adults: "About Chronic Diseases," National Center for Chronic Disease Prevention and Health Promotion, Centers for Disease Control and Prevention, September 5, 2018.

93 more than eighty-five thousand chemicals: "EPA Releases First Major Update to Chemicals List in 40 Years," U.S. EPA press release, February 19, 2019.

93 We have studied: CNN Wire Staff, "Everyday Chemicals May Be Harming Kids, Panel Told," CNN, October 26, 2010.

93 In 1975 John Quarles: "Quarles Testifies on the Need for Toxic Substances Act," U.S. EPA press release, July 10, 1975.

94 Today, about two thousand: "Emerging Chemicals of Concern," California Department of Toxic Substances Control, State of California, https://www.dtsc.ca.gov/assessingrisk/emergingcontaminants.cfm.

94 Congress passed the Toxic Substances Control Act (TSCA): "Summary of the Toxic Substances Control Act," U.S. EPA.

94 It also gave the EPA authority: "TSCA Chemical Substance Inventory," U.S. EPA.

95 In 2009 testimony: John Stephenson, "Chemical Regulation: Observations on Improving the Toxic Substances Control Act," Testimony Before the Committee on Environment and Public Works, U.S. Senate, December 2, 2009.

96 Meanwhile, the list: "NTP: Known to Be a Human Carcinogen," Toxic Substances Portal, Agency for Toxic Substances and Disease Registry, March 3, 2011.

98 presence of plastic fibers: Chris Tyree and Dan Morrison, "Invisibles: The Plastic Inside Us," **Orb**.

98 We produce more: Emily J. North and Rolf U. Halden, "Plastics and Environmental Health: The Road Ahead," **Reviews on Environmental Health**, January 22, 2013.

98 One thing we do know: Rolf U. Halden, "Plastics and Health Risks," **Annual Review of Public Health**, January 13, 2010.

99 still in dispute: Warren Cornwall, "In BPA Safety War, a Battle over Evidence," **Science**, February 9, 2017.

100 The **Los Angeles Times** reported: Ken Broder, "It's Never Too Late to Test the Air Around Toxic Superfund Sites," **AllGov.com**, March 10, 2015.

101 The property was declared: "Montrose & Del Amo Superfund Sites Update Fact Sheet," U.S. EPA Region 9, Spring 2018.

101 By the 1990s, discoveries: Tony Barboza, "Shell to Spend $55 Million to Clean Soil at Old South Bay

Rubber Plant," **Los Angeles Times**, September 30, 2015.

102 About 53 million Americans: "Population Surrounding 1,836 Superfund Remedial Sites," U.S. EPA, October 2017.

104 But the EPA provides a map: Consumer Confidence Reports (CCR), U.S. EPA, https://ofmpub.epa.gov /apex/safewater/f?p=ccr_wyl:102.

105 Get to know your watershed: "Surf Your Watershed," U.S. EPA.

5. THE TOP TOXINS

108 A 2016 analysis: David Andrews and Bill Walker, "'Erin Brockovich' Carcinogen in Tap Water of More Than 200 Million Americans," Environmental Working Group, September 20, 2016.

110 toxic air contaminant (TAC): "Understanding the History, Usage, and Regulation of Hexavalent Chromium," Pantheon Enterprises.

110 This MCL: "Chromium in Drinking Water," U.S. EPA.

110 carcinogenic after oral exposure: Matthew D. Stout, Ronald A. Herbert, Grace E. Kissling, Bradley J. Collins, Gregory S. Travlos, Kristine L. Witt, Ronald L. Melnick, Kamal M. Abdo, David E. Malarkey, and Michelle J. Hooth, "Hexavalent Chromium Is Carcinogenic to F344/N Rats and B6C3F1 Mice After Chronic Oral Exposure," **Environmental Health Perspective**, May 2009.

111 recommended for regulation: Julia Lurie, "Remember That 'Erin Brockovich' Chemical? There's a Good Chance It's in Your Water," **Mother Jones**, September 22, 2016.

112 The process to establish: "Public Health Goals," California Office of Environmental Health Hazard Assessment (OEHHA).

112 annual Consumer Confidence Reports: "Consumer Confidence Reports (CCR)," U.S. EPA.

112 A chemical's MCL is required: "Comparison of MCLs and PHGs for Regulated Contaminants in Drinking Water," California Water Boards, November 19, 2018.

112 The California Department of Public Health: Michael S. Feely and John A. Heintz, "Calif. to Make Waves with New Drinking Water Standard," **Law360**, February 28, 2014.

113 Coal ash: "New Report Reveals Toxic Coal Ash Contamination Threatens Public Health," NJ Sierra Club press release, August 26, 2010.

113 the Drinking Water Quality Institute: "Meeting Minutes," Drinking Water Quality Institute, September 10, 2010.

113 In North Carolina, residents: Michael Biesecker, "Testimony: Health Director Covered Up Cancer-Causing Water in North Carolina," **PBS NewsHour**, August 2, 2016.

114 Hexavalent chromium: "Public Health Goal for Hexavalent Chromium (Cr VI) in Drinking Water," Pesticide and Environmental Toxicology Branch, California Office of Environmental Health Hazard Assessment (OEHHA), July 2011.

115 In 1974, scientists discovered: J. J. Rook, "Formation of Haloforms During Chlorination of Natural Waters," **Journal of Water Treatment Examination**, 1974.

116 haloacetic acids (HAAs): "Disinfection By-Products," Centers for Disease Control and Prevention, December 2, 2016.

117 But it is also a known carcinogen: J. K. Dunnick and R. L. Melnick, "Assessment of the Carcinogenic Potential of Chlorinated Water: Experimental Studies of Chlorine, Chloramine, and Trihalomethanes," **Journal of the National Cancer Institute**, May 1993.

125 According to Hach: "Monochloramine Treatment Not as Effective in Protecting Drinking Water," **Chemical Online**, March 2, 2007, the American Society for Microbiology and ASM Biodefense and Emerging Disease Research Meeting.

126 Genetic damage occurs: Jim Barlow, "Byproduct of Water-Disinfection Process Found to Be Highly Toxic," University of Illinois press release, September 14, 2004.

126 In Washington, D.C., chloramines: Katherine Shaver and Dana Hedgpeth, "D.C.'s Decade-Old Problem of Lead in Water Gets New Attention During Flint Crisis," **The Washington Post**, March 17, 2016.

127 The maximum residual disinfectant level (MRDL): "National Primary Drinking Water Regulations," U.S. EPA.

127 Chloramines are known: "Water Treatment Process: Chloramination," PWC & Partnership for Safe Water, Fayetteville, NC.

128 Studies have demonstrated: J. M. Wright, J. Schwartz, and D. W. Dockery, "Effect of Trihalomethane Exposure on Fetal Development," **Occupational and Environmental Medicine**, March 2003.

129 more than 6 million lead service lines: Rachel Layne, "Lead in America's Water Systems Is a National Problem," CBS News, November 21, 2018.

129 The U.S. Agency for Toxic Substances and Disease Registry reported: "ATSDR Public Health Statement: Lead," ATSDR, August 2007.

129 ordered stringent testing: Amy Zimmer, "83 Percent of City Schools Found with Too Much Lead in Water, Data Shows," **DNAinfo**, April 28, 2017.

129 waited more than two months: Kelly House, "Portland Schools Lead: Superintendent Carole Smith Vows to 'Take Responsibility,'" **OregonLive.com**, June 5, 2016.

129 New Jersey governor Chris Christie ordered: Susan K. Livio and Claude Brodesser-Akner, "Christie: All N.J. School Water Fountains to Be Tested for Lead," **NJ.com**, May 4, 2016.

130 Schools and childcare facilities: "Drinking Water Requirements for States and Public Water Systems: Lead in Drinking Water in Schools and Childcare Facilities," U.S. EPA.

130 not regulated under federal law: Ibid.

130 From a health perspective: "Study: Improvement Needed to Accurately Detect Precise Levels of Lead in Blood," American Academy of Pediatrics, July 17, 2017.

131 The rule then established: "Drinking Water Requirements for States and Public Water Systems: Lead and Copper Rule," U.S. EPA.

131 The EPA published: "Lead and Copper Rule Revisions White Paper," U.S. EPA Office of Water, October 2016.

132 A January 2016 investigation: Oliver Milman, "U.S. Authorities Distorting Tests to Downplay Lead Content of Water," **The Guardian**, January 22, 2016.

132 A 2016 Reuters report: M. B. Pell and Joshua Schneyer, "The Thousands of U.S. Locales Where Lead Poisoning Is Worse Than in Flint," Reuters, December 19, 2016.

132 Another recent report: Oliver Milman, "U.S. Authorities Distorting Tests to Downplay Lead Content of Water," The Guardian, January 22, 2016.

133 the Safe Drinking Water Act Amendment: H.R. 1068—Safe Drinking Water Act Amendments of 2017.

133 the first major overhaul of the LCR: "EPA Proposes Updates to Lead and Copper Rule to Better Protect Children and At-Risk Communities," U.S. EPA website, October 10, 2019.

134 cities would only be required: Miranda Green and Rebecca Beitsch, "EPA to overhaul rule on testing for lead contamination," The Hill, October 10, 2019.

134 said in a statement: "AWWA Statement on Revised Lead and Copper Rule," American Water Works Association, October 10, 2019.

134 In 2016, New York: "Governor Cuomo Signs Landmark Legislation to Test Drinking Water in New York Schools for Lead Contamination," New York State press release, September 6, 2016.

135 But environmental groups: Joan Leary Matthews, "Grade F to A? Getting Rid of Lead in School Drinking Water," Natural Resources Defense Council, April 12, 2018.

135 California state assemblywoman Lorena Gonzalez Fletcher: California Assembly Bill No. 746, October 13, 2017.

135 It is also associated: "Lead and Copper Rule Revisions White Paper," U.S. EPA Office of Water, October 2016.

137 Scientists have found: "Public Health Statement: Perfluoroalkyls," ATSDR Division of Toxicology and Human Health Sciences, August 2015.

137 Researchers at Johns Hopkins: "PFOA and PFOS Detected in Newborns," Johns Hopkins University Bloomberg School of Public Health press release, April 24 2007.

137 In 2017, the Environmental Working Group: Bill Walker and Soren Rundquist, "Mapping a Contamination Crisis: PFCs Pollute Tap Water for 15 Million People, Dozens of Industrial Sites," Environmental Working Group, June 8, 2017.

137 "We earn our place": "Our Approach," DuPont company website, 2018.

138 profits from PFOA that year: Nathaniel Rich, "The Lawyer Who Became DuPont's Worst Nightmare," **The New York Times Magazine**, January 6, 2016.

140 In 2006, eight major companies: "Assessing and Managing Chemicals Under TSCA: Fact Sheet: 2010/2015 PFOA Stewardship Program," U.S. EPA.

141 As of 2017, DuPont and Chemours Co.: Arathy S. Nair, "DuPont Settles Lawsuits over Leak of Chemical Used to Make Teflon," Reuters, February 13, 2017.

141 $30 billion in sales in 2016: "3M Reports Fourth-Quarter and Full-Year 2016 Results," 3M press release, January 24, 2017.

141 "PFOS is persistent": "Co-operation on Existing Chemicals Hazard Assessment of Perflurooctane Sulfonate (PFOS) and Its Salts," Joint Meeting of the Chemicals Committee and the Working

Party on Chemicals, Pesticides, and Biotechnology, Organisation for Economic Co-operation and Development, November 21, 2002.

142 The U.S. Department of Defense knew: Kyle Bagenstose, "Dangers of Firefighting Foam Discussed in 2001, Document Shows," **The Intelligencer**, June 9, 2017.

142 Communities near bases from Washington State: "Baron & Budd Investigating Potential Lawsuits Regarding PFOS and PFOA Contamination of Drinking Water," **Business Wire**, May 17, 2017.

142 New York: Tiffany Kary, "Hamptons Tainted Water Lawsuit Adds to Slew of 3M Complaints," **Bloomberg News**, June 14, 2017.

142 In 2016, Harvard researchers: Karen Feldscher, "Unsafe Levels of Toxic Chemicals Found in Drinking Water of 33 States," **Harvard Gazette**, August 9, 2016.

142 3M makes water filters: "Water Quality: About 3M Residential Water Filtration Products," 3M company website.

143 billions of dollars in legal fees: Annie Snider, "Exclusive: Trump EPA Won't Limit 2 Toxic Chemicals in Drinking Water," **The Hill**, January 28, 2019.

144 In 2013, a Harvard School of Public Health study: "U.S. Standards for 'Safe' Limits of PFCs in Drinking Water Appear Too High for Children," Harvard T. H. Chan School of Public Health press release, January 2013.

145 Fourteen other states: Claire Condon, "EPA Targets PFAS—but Is Your State Ahead of the Game?" **EHS Daily Advisor**, January 2, 2018.

145 DuPont scientists have concluded: Arathy S. Nair,

"DuPont Settles Lawsuits over Leak of Chemical Used to Make Teflon," Reuters, February 13, 2017.

145 "Studies indicate that exposure": "Fact Sheet: PFOA & PFOS Drinking Water Health Advisories," U.S. EPA, November 2016.

146 Research has linked PFOS exposure: "Perfluoro-octane Sulfonic Acid," TOXNET Toxicology Data Network, National Library of Medicine, October 25, 2016.

146 80 percent of New Hanover County's: Tim Buckland, "So Where Does Your CFPUA Water Come From?" **StarNews Online**, June 12, 2017.

146 now owned by Chemours has been dumping: Laura Leslie, "NCSU Scientist: GenX Not Only Toxic Chemical in Cape Fear River," WRAL.com, July 28, 2017.

147 The EPA also issued: Sharon Lerner, "New Teflon Toxin Found in North Carolina Drinking Water," **The Intercept,** June 17, 2017.

147 tumors and reproductive problems in lab animals: "N.C. Drinking Water Tainted with Chemical Byproduct for Decades?" CBS News, June 26, 2017.

148 By 2013, almost four thousand public water systems: "Hydraulic Fracturing for Oil and Gas: Impacts from the Hydraulic Fracturing Water Cycle on Drinking Water Resources in the United States," Executive Summary, U.S. EPA, December 2016.

149 The EPA reports: "Analysis of Hydraulic Fracturing Fluid Data from the FracFocus Chemical Disclosure Registry 1.0," U.S. EPA.

149 They include chemicals: Michael Greenwood, "Chemicals in Fracking Fluid and Wastewater Are Toxic, Study Shows," **Yale News**, January 6, 2016.

149 We have more than a thousand documented cases: Abrahm Lustgarten, "Buried Secrets: Is Natural Gas Drilling Endangering U.S. Water Supplies?" ProPublica, November 13, 2008.

149 More than 17 million Americans: Eliza D. Czolowski, Renee L. Santoro, Tanja Srebotnjak, and Seth B. C. Shonko, "Open Access Toward Consistent Methodology to Quantify Populations in Proximity to Oil and Gas Development: A National Spatial Analysis and Review," **Environmental Health Perspectives**, August 23, 2017.

150 "activities in the hydraulic": "Hydraulic Fracturing for Oil and Gas: Impacts from the Hydraulic Fracturing Water Cycle on Drinking Water Resources in the United States," Executive Summary, U.S. EPA, December 2016.

150 The following activities and factors: "Questions and Answers About EPA's Hydraulic Fracturing Drinking Water Assessment," U.S. EPA.

151 The Ohio Supreme Court: Robert Higgs, "Ohio Supreme Court Rules Munroe Falls Regulations on Oil and Gas Drilling Are Improper," Cleveland .com, February 17, 2015.

151 The Colorado Supreme Court: Bruce Finley, "Colorado Supreme Court Rules State Law Trumps Local Bans on Fracking," **Denver Post**, June 23, 2016.

151 a local paper reported: John Boyle, "Did Energy Group Bus Homeless In to Support Fracking?" **Citizen Times**, September 15, 2014.

151 In March 2017, Maryland: Pamela Wood, "Maryland General Assembly Approves Fracking Ban," **Baltimore Sun**, March 27, 2017.

152 People who live near fracking wells report: Beth

Weinberger, Lydia H. Greiner, Leslie Walleigh, and David Brown, "Health Symptoms in Residents Living near Shale Gas Activity: A Retrospective Record Review from the Environmental Health Project," **Preventive Medicine Reports**, December 2017.

152 Researchers at Johns Hopkins University: Stephanie Desmon, "Study: Fracking Associated with Migraines, Fatigue, Chronic Nasal and Sinus Symptoms," **The Hub**, Johns Hopkins University, August 25, 2016.

152 University of Colorado School of Public Health researchers found: Lisa M. McKenzie, William B. Allshouse, Tim E. Byers, Edward J. Bedrick, Berrin Serdar, and John L. Adgate, "Childhood Hematologic Cancer and Residential Proximity to Oil and Gas Development," **PLOS One**, February 15, 2017.

152 Further research has found:"Endocrine-Disrupting Activity Linked to Birth Defects, Infertility Found near Drilling Sites," Endocrine Society press release, 2013.

153 In 2011, total estimated commercial production of TCE: "Background and Environmental Exposures to Trichloroethylene in the United States," Draft Toxicological Profile for Trichloroethylene, Agency for Toxic Substances and Disease Registry.

153 fungicides and insecticides: "Report on Carcinogens, Fourteenth Edition: Trichloroethylene," National Toxicology Program, National Institutes of Health.

154 It was added to the list of substances: "14th Report on Carcinogens," U.S Department of Health and Human Services, National Toxicology Program, November 3, 2016.

154 TCE and its health effects: Alexander Nazaryan,

"Camp Lejeune and the U.S. Military's Polluted Legacy," **Newsweek,** July 16, 2014.

154 TCE was found in the drinking water: Eric Pianin, "The US Military Is Facing Another Polluted Drinking Water Scandal," **Business Insider**, April 26, 2017.

155 The EPA set the MCL: "What Are EPA's Drinking Water Regulations for Trichloroethylene?" U.S. EPA Fact Sheet.

155 These proposals: "Fact Sheet on Trichloroethylene (TCE)," U.S. EPA.

155 Health problems associated: "What Are Trichloroethylene's Health Effects," U.S. EPA Fact Sheet.

155 "carcinogenic to humans": "Background and Environmental Exposures to Trichloroethylene in the United States," Draft Toxicological Profile for Trichloroethylene, Agency for Toxic Substances and Disease Registry.

6. THE COMMUNITIES RISING

159 A water main breaks: "America's Infrastructure Receives Poor Assessment," **PBS NewsHour**, March 11, 2017.

160 Records showed: Ken Silverstein, "Clean Up Chemical Leaks and Put Safety First, Activist Tells West Virginians," **Forbes**, January 14, 2014.

161 Even with a robust carbon filtration system: "Report on the National Toxicology Program Response to the Elk River Chemical Spill," Division of the National Toxicology Program, National Institute of Environmental Health Sciences, National Institutes of Health, June 16, 2015.

161 Many residents remained: "Investigation Report: Chemical Spill Contaminates Public Water Supply in Charleston, West Virginia," U.S. Chemical Safety and Hazard Investigation Board, September 2016.

162 sold out of bottled water: John Raby, "Chemical Spill into River Shuts Down Much of Charleston, W.Va.," **The Ledger**, January 10, 2014.

163 "We don't know": Trip Gabriel, "Thousands Without Water After Spill in West Virginia," **The New York Times**, January 10, 2014.

163 The agency set: Deborah Blum, "Our Toxicity Experiment in West Virginia," **Wired**, January 18, 2014.

163 "There are unknowns": Elizabeth Shogren, "The Big Impact of a Little-Known Chemical in W.Va. Spill," NPR, January 13, 2014.

164 dodged questions from local reporters: Amy Goodman and Aaron Maté, "Erin Brockovich: After Chemical Spill, West Virginians Organizing 'Stronger Than I've Ever Seen,'" **Democracy Now!**, January 14, 2014.

164 The damage had been done: Emily Atkin, "What Freedom Industries' Bankruptcy Really Means for Those Harmed by the Chemical Spill," **ThinkProgress**, January 22, 2014.

165 people refused to drink the water: Matt Pearce, "Many Reported Sickened After West Virginia Chemical Spill, Survey Says," **Los Angeles Times**, May 21, 2014.

165 a federal judge fined: Ken Ward Jr., "Freedom Fined $900,000 for Elk Spill, but Unlikely to Ever Pay," **Charleston Gazette-Mail**, February 4, 2016.

165 Southern did go to court: "Summary of Criminal Prosecutions," U.S. EPA, 2016.

165 Southern was later accused: Associated Press, "Freedom Industries Pleads Guilty to Pollution Charges in West Virginia Chemical Spill Case," Fox News, March 23, 2015.

165 Booth Goodwin, the lead prosecutor: Raf Sanchez, "British Executive Admits Spilling Chemicals into West Virginia Drinking Water," **The Telegraph**, August 19, 2015.

166 In 2017, the $151 million settlement: Joseph Fitzwater, "Settlement Reached in Freedom Industries MCHM Class Action Lawsuit," WOWK-TV, May 12, 2017.

166 Both companies issued statements: Rebecca Hersher, "$151 Million Settlement Deal Reached over West Virginia Water Poisoning," NPR, November 1, 2016.

166 to help further regulate chemical storage: Joanna M. Foster, "West Virginia House Passes Chemical Storage Bill in Effort to Prevent Future Spills," **ThinkProgress**, March 6, 2014.

167 The state completed all inspections: Brian Clark Howard, "A Year After West Virginia Chemical Spill, Some Signs of Safer Water," **National Geographic**, January 10, 2015.

167 in 2015 scientists detected: Emily Atkin, "New Analysis Shows West Virginia's Chemical Spill Traveled into Kentucky," **ThinkProgress**, January 12, 2015.

167 West Virginia legislators passed: "WV Bill Would Exempt O&G Industry from Storage Tank Law," **Marcellus Drilling News**, March 13, 2017.

168 EPA administrator Gina McCarthy said: Gina McCarthy, "U.S. EPA's Cabinet Exit Memo," U.S. EPA, January 5, 2017.

168 "The implications of deteriorating infrastructure":
Jim Gebhardt, "The Time to Invest in America's
Water Infrastructure Is Now," **The EPA Blog**,
July 12, 2016.

169 President Lyndon Johnson visited: Pam Fessler,
"Kentucky County That Gave War on Poverty a
Face Still Struggles," NPR, January 8, 2014.

169 the poverty rate: "QuickFacts: Martin County,
Kentucky," U.S. Census Bureau.

170 A coal slurry spill: Nina McCoy, "A Victim of
Official Abuse, Martin County Says 'Time's Up,'"
Lexington Herald-Leader, February 11, 2018.

171 More than one in ten households: Christian Detisch,
"How Many People Can't Afford Their Water Bills?
Too Many," Food & Water Watch, March 21, 2017.

171 "Two years after Flint": "Martin County Could See
Huge Rate Increase Despite Failing System," Food
& Water Watch press release, January 24, 2018.

176 Baum once said about his work: James A. Fussell,
"Meet L. Frank Baum, The Man Behind the Curtain," **Kansas City Star**, August 31, 2014.

177 Led by both the oil and steel industries: Kenneth G.
McCarty, "Farmers, the Populist Party, and Mississippi (1870–1900)," **Mississippi History Now**, July
2003.

177 according to the U.S. Department of Agriculture:
Ibid.

178 In an essay: Henry Littlefield, "The Wizard of Oz:
Parable on Populism," **American Quarterly** 16,
no. 1 (Spring, 1964), pp. 47–58.

182 Americans eat more chicken: "Broiler Chicken Industry Key Facts 2018," National Chicken Council.

182 Each year, the chicken industry: Ibid.

182 leads in the production of ready-to-cook poultry products: Amanda Little, "Tyson Isn't Chicken," **Bloomberg Businessweek**, August 15, 2018.

182 Tyson was the second-biggest polluter: "America's Next Big Polluter: Corporate Agribusiness," Environment America Research & Policy Center.

184 By 1999, up to one-third of underground wells: Peter S. Goodman, "An Unsavory Byproduct: Runoff and Pollution," **The Washington Post**, August 1, 1999.

184 unless they have this permit: "National Pollutant Discharge Elimination System (NPDES)," U.S. EPA.

184 In 2003, Tyson pleaded guilty: "Tyson Pleads Guilty to 20 Felonies and Agrees to Pay $7.5 Million to Clean Water Act Violations," Department of Justice press release, June 25, 2003.

185 Despite several citations: Ibid.

185 Tyson and five other poultry companies: Sheila Stogsdill, "Animal Waste Caused Pollution, Study Shows," **The Oklahoman**, November 22, 2003.

185 Tyson paid the maximum fine: Lynn LaRowe, "Tyson Foods to Pay $500,000," **Texarkana News**, June 13, 2009.

186 The Justice Department fined: Bryan Salvage, "Tyson Fined $2M for Animal Waste Discharging Violation," **Meat + Poultry**, August 21, 2009.

186 Tyson paid another $5.2 million: Tom Schoenberg, "Tyson Foods to Pay $5.2 Million over Mexican Bribes," **Bloomberg News**, February 10, 2011.

186 Tyson paid $32 million to settle: Dan Rivoli, "Tyson Settles Donning, Doffing MDL for $32M," **Law360**, September 6, 2011.

186 The company settled: "Tyson Foods $7.75 Million Settlement Approved by Judge," WATTAgNet.com, July 23, 2014.

186 In 2016, Oxfam America released a report: "No Relief: Denial of Bathroom Breaks in the Poultry Industry," Oxfam America, 2016.

186 "We believe sustainability": "Tyson Foods Commits to New, Sustainable Approach to a Better Workplace," Tyson Foods press release, April 26, 2017.

189 "The continued presence": Erica Shaffer, "Tonganoxie City Council Tanks Proposed Tyson Plant," **Meat + Poultry**, October 4, 2017.

189 revoked its decision: Megan Durisin and Shruti Singh, "How Tyson's Chicken Plant Became a $320 Million Turkey," **Bloomberg Businessweek**, October 11, 2017.

190 National regulations: "Chromium in Drinking Water," U.S. EPA.

192 In a **New York Times** article: Jeremy P. Jacobs, "Another Pollution Battle Looms in Erin Brockovich's Town," **The New York Times**, August 18, 2011.

193 But a feasibility study: "Hinkley Chromium Clean-Up Could Take More Than a Century," **Trager Water Report**, November 29, 2010.

193 three hundred more properties in Hinkley: Paloma Esquivel, "15 Years After 'Erin Brockovich,' Town Still Fearful of Polluted Water," **Los Angeles Times**, April 12, 2015.

193 The company still admitted: Molly Peterson, "PG&E Makes $3.6 Million Settlement with Hinkley, Its Second in 20 Years," KPCC, March 16, 2012.

194 Hinkley's school shut down: Jim Steinberg, "Hinkley Residents Angered at Decision to Close Town's Only School," **The Sun**, February 27, 2013.

194 "It's a very complex project": Miles O'Brien, "Protecting Americans from Danger in the Drinking Water," **PBS NewsHour**, March 13, 2013.

194 Reports from the water board: Letter to Kevin Sullivan, "Conditional Acceptance of Plan to Improve Lower Aquifer Chromium Remediation and Modification to Agricultural Treatment Unit Permit Monitoring and Reporting Program . . . ," Lahontan Regional Water Quality Board, December 22, 2014.

194 cleanup and abatement actions: "Cleanup and Abatement Order NO. R6V-2015-0068," California Regional Water Quality Control Board Lahontan Region, November 4, 2015.

196 PG&E's top environmental executives: Jim Steinberg, "Milestone Reached in Cleanup of Polluted Hinkley Water Made Famous in 'Erin Brockovich,'" The Sun, April 20, 2017.

197 a 1964 letter from the U.S. Department of the Interior: Donna Foote, "Erin Fights Goliath," Newsweek, March 12, 2000.

197 In 2002, PG&E spokesman Jon Tremayne: David Lazarus, "Erin Brockovich Going After PG&E Again," SF Gate, January 13, 2002.

197 market manipulations spearheaded by Enron: Richard A. Oppel Jr. and Jeff Gerth, "Enron Forced Up California Prices, Documents Show," The New York Times, May 7, 2002.

198 rolling blackouts throughout the state: Rene Sanchez and Peter Behr, "California Utility Declares Insolvency," The Washington Post, April 7, 2001.

198 But California's governor, Gray Davis: David Lazarus, "PG&E Files for Bankruptcy / $9 Billion in Debt, Firm Abandons Bailout Talks with State," SF Gate, April 7, 2001.

198 Consumer advocates: "Bankruptcy Reorganization

Plan Violates State Law," Consumer Watchdog, 2001.

198 $335 million in 2006: Laura Roberts, "BP Oil Disaster: Major Compensation Payouts from Other Global Corporations," The Telegraph, June 17, 2010.

198 In a twenty-two-page decision: David Lazarus, "Erin Brockovich Going After PG&E Again," SF Gate, January 13, 2002.

198 "Clearly, this situation": David Pierson and Hemmy So, "PG&E Will Pay Residents Who Sued over Groundwater Pollution," Los Angeles Times, February 4, 2006.

198 In 2016, a federal jury: Associated Press, "PG&E Is Found Guilty of Obstructing Investigators After Deadly 2010 Pipeline Blast," Los Angeles Times, August 9, 2016.

199 Ultimately, PG&E: George Avalos, "PG&E Gets Maximum Sentence for San Bruno Crimes," Mercury News, January 27, 2017.

199 This was after the company spent: Taryn Luna, "PG&E Spends More Than $1 Million to Lobby California Officials on Wildfire Laws," Sacramento Bee, August 1, 2018.

199 huge safety failures: Russell Gold, Katherine Blunt, and Rebecca Smith, "PG&E Sparked at Least 1,500 California Fires. Now the Utility Faces Collapse," The Wall Street Journal, January 13, 2019.

199 The company's equipment allegedly sparked: Cleve R. Wootson Jr., "The Deadliest, Most Destructive Wildfire in California's History Has Finally Been Contained," The Washington Post, November 26, 2018.

200 Meanwhile, BlueMountain Capital Management LLC: Tomi Kilgore, "PG&E Shareholder Blue-Mountain Says Bankruptcy Filing Would Be 'Utter Abdication' of Duty to Shareholders," January 17, 2019.

201 "Rather than spend the money": Jeff Daniels, "'Pretty Overwhelming' Evidence Against PG&E in Deadly Paradise Fire, Says Attorney Suing CA Utility," CNBC, November 14, 2018.

202 said California governor Gavin Newsom: Phil Willon, "Newsom Tested Right Out of the Gate with Teachers' Strike and PG&E Crisis," **Los Angeles Times**, January 28, 2019.

202 In addition, he said: J. D. Morris, "Does PG&E Need to File for Bankruptcy? Erin Brockovich Doubts It," **San Francisco Chronicle**, January 22, 2018.

202 30 percent live below the poverty line: "American Community Survey 5-Year Estimates," U.S. Census Bureau, 2017, **Census Reporter Profile** for Kettleman City, CA.

203 For years, residents have suspected: Jacques Leslie, "What's Killing the Babies of Kettleman City?" **Mother Jones**, July/August 2010.

204 Back in 2008, EPA tests: Allen Martin, "California Town's Water Tainted with Arsenic for Decades," KPIX 5 San Francisco, May 19, 2016.

204 research from the Environmental Integrity Project: "Drinking Water for 55,000 Californians Has Illegal Levels of Arsenic," Environmental Integrity Project press release, September 12, 2016.

204 The notices mailed to consumers: Ibid.

205 The California state government: Lewis Griswold,

"Environmentalists, State Settle Differences over Hazardous Waste Site," **Fresno Bee**, September 6, 2016.

207 About 15 percent of Americans: Jennifer LaVista, "Contamination in U.S. Private Wells," U.S. Geological Survey (USGS), March 2009.

207 from this kind of contamination: "Learn About Private Water Wells," U.S. EPA.

208 In a statement: "Brockovich: Midland, Texas Water Sullied," CBS News, June 10, 2009.

209 The TCEQ maintains: Kathleen Thurber, "Residents File Lawsuit Against Companies in Relation to Hexavalent Chromium Contamination," **Midland Reporter-Telegram**, April 9, 2011.

7. SAYING NO TO "UNINTENDED CONSEQUENCES"

213 General Electric (GE) dumped: "Hudson River PCBs," Riverkeeper.

213 Exposure to these odorless man-made chemicals: "Learn About Polychlorinated Biphenyls (PCBs)," U.S. EPA.

214 The EPA and GE have worked together:"EPA Expands Scope of Hudson River Cleanup Analysis," U.S. EPA press release, January 29, 2018.

214 list of "Most Miserable Cities": "America's Most Miserable Cities 2013," **Forbes**.

219 In a paper: Djanette Khiari, "The Role and Behavior of Chloramines in Drinking Water," Water Research Foundation. June 2018.

220 a suspected carcinogen: "Technical Fact Sheet: N-Nitroso-dimethylamine (NDMA)," U.S. EPA, January 2014.

220 When exposed at high levels: "Public Health Statement: What Is N-Nitrosodimethylamine?" Agency for Toxic Substances and Disease Registry.

220 "NDMA is preferentially": Stuart W. Krasner, "Controlling Nitrosamines: A Balancing Act," **American Water Works Journal**, June 2017.

220 A 2007 study: John Tibbetts, "Chloramine Catch: Water Disinfectant Can Raise Lead Exposure," **Environmental Health Perspectives**, February 2007.

221 Even the U.S. EPA: Sara Jerome, "EPA Considering Change in Chloramine Rules," **Water Online**, August 12, 2016.

221 A 2009 EPA report: "Chloramines-Related Research: What Does EPA See as the Disadvantages of Using Monochloramine?" U.S. EPA, February 24, 2009.

221 said the lead author of the study: Kris Maher, "Use of a Water Disinfectant Is Challenged," **The Wall Street Journal**, August 9, 2016.

222 In 2011 officials in Tulsa, Oklahoma: Emily Baucum, "Major Changes Coming to Tulsa Drinking Water," **News on 6**, October 14, 2011.

222 "Most Livable Cities": Zack O'Malley Greenburg, "America's Most Livable Cities," **Forbes**, April 1, 2009.

224 Here's the statement: Michael Bates, "Chloramine Controversy: Safe for Tulsa's Water?" BatesLine website, October 17, 2011.

230 By the summer of 2012: "Other Major Accomplishments," Tulsa Metropolitan Utility Authority.

232 In May 2016 a two-week citywide order: Kim Womack, "City Manager Ron Olson Resigns," City of Corpus Christi Newsroom, May 17, 2016.

232 An estimated 1,550 boil-water advisories: Associated Press, "Boil-Water Alerts on the Rise in Texas," **CBS DFW**, May 29, 2016.

233 Corpus Christi has 225 miles: Asher Price, "Corpus Christi Facing Water Crisis amid Contamination Concerns," **Austin American-Statesman**, December 16, 2016.

233 "We historically have not replaced": Matt Woolbright, "What Led to Corpus Christi's Water Crisis? Depends Who You Ask," **The Caller-Times**, May 21, 2016.

234 In total, the ban lasted four days: Associated Press, "Corpus Christi Lifts Drinking Water Ban," **The Wall Street Journal**, December 18, 2016.

236 "In our view, chloramines": Kris Maher, "Use of a Water Disinfectant Is Challenged," **The Wall Street Journal**, August 9, 2016.

238 ninety-one confirmed cases: Elisha Anderson, "Genesee County Confirms Its First Case of Legionnaires,'" **Detroit Free Press**, July 6, 2016.

238 suspected deaths still in question: Oona Goodin-Smith, "More Deaths May Be Tied to Flint Legionella Outbreak Than Reported, Expert Says," MLive .com, September 21, 2017.

238 Another outbreak at California's Disneyland: Tony Barboza, "Disneyland Shuts Down 2 Cooling Towers After Legionnaires' Disease Sickens Park Visitors," **Los Angeles Times**, November 11, 2017.

238 CDC research: Mike Stobbe, "Most Legionnaires' Deaths Tied to Spray from Shower, Faucet," **Business Insider**, August 13, 2015.

245 Before the election, the **Hannibal Courier-Post** interviewed her: "Meet the Candidates: 2 Vying

to Represent Ward 3 on Hannibal City Council," **Hannibal Courier-Post**, March 21, 2017.

248   On April 4, 2017, voters showed up: Ashley Szatala, "Use of Ammonia in Hannibal Drinking Water Will Cease," **The Herald-Whig**, April 5, 2017.

254   a granulated-activated-carbon system for the city: Ashley Szatala, "Hannibal BPW Directors Choose Carbon Filtration System to Filter Drinking Water," **The Herald-Whig**, February 20, 2018.

255   Since 2009, Columbia Water and Light: Alyssa Casares, "Columbia's Water Disinfection Method Switched from Chlorine to Chloramine," KBIA 91.3FM, November 6, 2014.

256   In a 2016 letter: David J. Lamb, Letter to Mayor Brian Treece, September 21, 2016, https://www.como .gov/utilities/wp-content/uploads/sites/20/2017/04 /DNRwaterColumbiaSept2016.pdf.

258   "We feel it's very short-sighted": Yehyun Kim, "Residents Explore Alternatives for Columbia Water Treatment," **Columbia Missourian**, January 25, 2018.

8. LOCAL POLITICS RUN AMOK

266   The new law: Michigan House Bill No. 4214, March 16, 2011.

266   In his first few days: Oona Goodin-Smith, "Flint's History of Emergency Management and How It Got to Financial Freedom," MLive.com, January 16, 2018.

267   At the time, the city's: City of Flint: Comprehensive Annual Financial Report, June 30, 2011.

267   Brown's salary: Kristin Longley, "State-Appointed Emergency Managers Make Six Figures at Local

Community's Expense," MLive.com, December 27, 2011.

267 increasing its rates: Jeff Wright, "The Flint Water Crisis, DWSD, and GLWA," Michigan Civil Rights Commission & Flint Water Crisis Committee, November 22, 2016.

268 In addition, the Flint River: Susan J. Masten, Simon H. Davies, and Shawn P. McElmurry, "Flint Water Crisis: What Happened and Why?" **Journal of the American Water Works Association**, December 2016.

268 The river flows: David Rosner, "Flint's Toxic Industrial Legacy," Columbia University Mailman School of Public Health, January 26, 2016.

269 "The expedited time-frame": Susan J. Masten, Simon H. Davies, and Shawn P. McElmurry, "Flint Water Crisis: What Happened and Why?" **Journal of the American Water Works Association**, December 2016.

269 April 2014 email: Ibid.

270 Flint mayor Dayne Walling: Merrit Kennedy, "Lead-Laced Water in Flint: A Step-by-Step Look at the Makings of a Crisis," NPR, April 20, 2016.

270 The company negotiated: Ron Fonger, "General Motors Shutting Off Flint River Water at Engine Plant over Corrosion Worries," MLive.com, October 13, 2014.

270 GM was one of the largest: Lindsey Smith, "How People in Flint Were Stripped of a Basic Human Need: Safe Drinking Water," Michigan Radio, December 15, 2015.

271 The results: Lindsey Smith, "This Mom Helped Uncover What Was Really Going On with Flint's Water," Michigan Radio, December 14, 2015.

271 the following statement: Ron Fonger, "Emergency Manager Calls City Council's Flint River Vote 'Incomprehensible,'" MLive.com, March 24, 2015.

273 Officials at the MDEQ: Paul Egan, "Fired DEQ Official Pleads Fifth in Flint Water Probe," **Detroit Free Press**, June 16, 2016.

275 Within a year: Mark Brush and Sarah Hulett, "EPA Region 5 Administrator Susan Hedman to Resign in Wake of the Flint Water Crisis," Michigan Radio, January 21, 2016; Paul Egan, "DEQ Director Wyant Resigns over Flint Water Crisis," **Lansing State Journal**, December 29, 2015.

281 So far, fifteen officials: Paul Egan, "These Are the 15 People Criminally Charged in the Flint Water Crisis," **Detroit Free Press,** June 14, 2017.

281 Nick Lyon: Ed White, "Flint Official Faces Manslaughter Trial over Deaths Possibly Caused by Tainted Water," **Time**, August 20, 2018.

281 On average, Flint residents: Ron Fonger, "Flint Water Prices Almost Eight Times National Average, Erin Brockovich Associate Says," MLive.com, March 17, 2015.

282 LeeAnne offered her testimony: LeeAnne Walters testimony to the House Oversight and Governmental Reform Committee, February 3, 2016.

283 Marc told the **Detroit News**: Jim Lynch, "EPA Stayed Silent on Flint's Tainted Water," **Detroit News**, January 12, 2016.

283 these Virginia Tech scientists: Dr. Marc Edwards et al., "Lead Testing Results for Water Sampled by Residents," Flint Water Study, September 2015.

283 In their report: Dr. Marc Edwards et al., "Our Sampling of 252 Homes Demonstrates a High Lead in Water Risk: Flint Should Be Failing to Meet the

EPA Lead and Copper Rule," Flint Water Study, September 8, 2015.

284 Elin said in an interview: Ryan Grimes, "High School Friend Sounded First Alert to Flint's Dr. Mona Hanna-Attisha," Michigan Radio, February 16, 2016.

286 Her study was eventually published: Mona Hanna-Attisha, Jenny LaChance, Richard Casey Sadler, and Allison Champney Schnepp, "Elevated Blood Lead Levels in Children Associated with the Flint Drinking Water Crisis: A Spatial Analysis of Risk and Public Health Response," **American Journal of Public Health**, February 2016.

287 "Our data is just a snapshot": Dr. Mona Hanna-Attisha testimony to House Democratic Steering and Policy Committee, "The Flint Water Crisis: Lessons for Protecting America's Children," February 10, 2016.

288 a $100 million grant: "EPA Awards $100 Million to Michigan for Flint Water Infrastructure Upgrades," U.S. EPA press release, March 17, 2017.

288 Virginia Tech scientist Marc Edwards: "Gov. Rick Snyder Announces Comprehensive Efforts to Strengthen Flint," Office of Governor Rick Snyder press release, January 27, 2016.

289 his former colleagues: Robby Korth, "Virginia Tech's Flint Research Professor Accuses Ex-Colleagues of Defamation," **Roanoke Times**, July 26, 2018.

289 other Flint researchers: "Mackinac Center and Virginia Tech Professor Dr. Marc Edwards Sue Wayne State over Flint Water Documents," Mackinac Center for Public Policy press release, June 13, 2018.

289 Virginia Tech has been awarded: "EPA Awards $4 Million in Grants to Research Lead in Drinking Water," U.S. EPA press release, April 25, 2018.

289 the city clerk's office: Jiquanda Johnson, "More than 50 petitions Taken Out for Seats on Flint City Council," MLive.com, February 3, 2017.

289 His top three policy priorities: "Meet the 17 Candidates Running for Flint City Council," MLive.com, October 25, 2017.

290 they have repealed a law: Oona Goodin-Smith, "Flint Emergency Manager Order Repealed, City Officially in Control of Finances," MLive.com, January 22, 2018.

291 "I noticed articles": Adele Peters, "This 11-Year-Old Invented a Cheap Test Kit for Lead in Drinking Water," **Fast Company**, July 13, 2017.

292 More than 18 million Americans: Erik D. Olson and Kristi Pullen Fedinick, "What's in Your Water? Flint and Beyond," Natural Resources Defense Council, June 28, 2016.

293 The Philadelphia Water Department is facing a class action lawsuit: Jessica Glenza, "Philadelphia Water Department Faces Class Action Lawsuit over Water Testing," **The Guardian**, June 3, 2016.

294 the world's largest oil-storage tank farm: Catherine Ngai, "Cushing Hub's Crude Storage Shell, Working Capacity Edges Lower: EIA," Reuters, May 31, 2017.

294 "pipeline crossroads of the world": Jessica Resnick-Ault, "Oil Glut Up Close: How Cushing Copes with Full Crude Tanks," Reuters, April 5, 2016.

294 earthquake capital of the world: Jessica Miller, "Oklahoma World's No. 1 Earthquake Area," **Enid News & Eagle**, November 10, 2015.

294 hundreds of earthquakes per year: USGS-NEIC ComCat & Oklahoma Geological Survey, Preliminary as of December 3, 2018.

295 drilling competes with farming: Michael Klare, "How Obama Became the Oil President," **Mother Jones**, September 12, 2014.

295 19 billion gallons of freshwater: Elizabeth Ridlington, Kim Norman, and Rachel Richardson, "Fracking by the Numbers: The Damage to Our Water, Land and Climate from a Decade of Dirty Drilling," Environment America Research & Policy Center and Frontier Group, April 2016.

295 triggering the tremors: Thea Hincks, Willy Aspinall, Roger Cooke, and Thomas Gernon, "Oklahoma's Induced Seismicity Strongly Linked to Wastewater Injection Depth," **Science**, March 16, 2018.

295 The water cycle has five parts to it: EPA's Study of Hydraulic Fracturing and Its Potential Impact on Drinking Water Resources: The Hydraulic Fracturing Water Cycle, U.S. EPA.

296 in a 2015 statement: Michael Wines, "Oklahoma Recognizes Role of Drilling in Earthquakes," **The New York Times**, April 21, 2015.

296 Scott Pruitt: Robinson Meyer, "Could Scott Pruitt Have Fixed Oklahoma's Earthquake Epidemic?" **The Atlantic**, January 18, 2017.

296 Oklahoma governor Mary Fallin: Michael Wines, "Oklahoma Recognizes Role of Drilling in Earthquakes," **The New York Times**, April 21, 2015.

297 In an aptly titled 2015 lecture: Justin Rubinstein, "Yes, Humans Really Are Causing Earthquakes," USGS Monthly Evening Lecture Series, U.S. Geological Survey, August 27, 2015.

298 more than a thousand earthquakes: Rivka Galchen, "Weather Underground: The Arrival of Man-Made Earthquakes," **The New Yorker**, April 13, 2015.

298 produced water: Jessica Morrison, "Earthquakes

and Fracking Activities Linked in Environmental Protection Agency Report," **Chemical & Engineering News**, February 13, 2015.

299 landowners and farmers alike: Forum News Service, "Saltwater Spills Can Cause Lasting Damage," SOS Environmental, October 29, 2015.

299 dozens of earthquakes: Robinson Meyer, "Could Scott Pruitt Have Fixed Oklahoma's Earthquake Epidemic?" **The Atlantic**, January 18, 2017.

299 Since 2011, well operators: Thea Hincks, Willy Aspinall, Roger Cooke, and Thomas Gernon, "Oklahoma's Earthquakes Strongly Linked to Wastewater Injection Depth," **ScienceDaily**, February 1, 2018.

299 These disposal wells: Susan Phillips, "Could Fracking Earthquakes Shake Pennsylvania?" StateImpact Pennsylvania, January 23, 2012.

299 Arkansas lawmakers banned: Ibid.

300 Earthquakes also impact drinking water: Michelle Sneed, Devin L. Galloway, and William L. Cunningham, "Earthquakes—Rattling the Earth's Plumbing System," U.S. Geological Survey Fact Sheet 096-03.

300 the largest earthquake: "Magnitude 5.8 Earthquake in Oklahoma," USGS press release, September 3, 2016.

300 The earthquake occurred: "Geophysicist Says Pawnee Earthquake Happened on Newly Discovered Fault," KWCH12, September 6, 2016.

300 "That was the one earthquake": Ross Kenneth Urken, "Native Americans Sue Frackers over Manmade Earthquakes," **National Geographic**, July 6, 2017.

301 since 1875: "Pawnee History," Pawnee Nation of Oklahoma website, http://www.pawneenation.org /page/home/pawnee-history.

301 a multi-year study: "Hydraulic Fracturing for Oil and Gas: Impacts from the Hydraulic Fracturing Water Cycle on Drinking Water Resources in the United States (Final Report)," U.S. EPA, December 2016.

301 Some of its main points: Ibid.

304 one of the largest shale formations: "How Much Gas Is in the Marcellus Shale?" U.S. Geological Survey.

306 Kramer told the town board: Glynis Hart, "Dryden Takes First Step to Ban Fracking," **Ithaca Times**, April 21, 2011.

307 according to research: "Local Resolutions Against Fracking," Food & Water Watch, https://www .foodandwaterwatch.org/insight/local-resolutions -against-fracking.

307 a permanent moratorium: CNN Wire Staff, "Vermont First State to Ban Fracking," CNN, May 17, 2012.

307 Cuomo banned fracking: Thomas Kaplan, "Citing Health Risks, Cuomo Bans Fracking in New York State," **The New York Times**, December 17, 2014.

307 a bill banning fracking: Brian Witte, "Maryland Governor Signs Fracking Ban into Law," AP News, April 4, 2017.

307 a ten-year ban on fracking: Zack Burdryk, "Oregon House Approves 10-Year Fracking Ban," **The Hill**, March 19, 2019.

309 the EPA offers guidelines: "3Ts for Reducing Lead in Drinking Water in Schools and Child Care Facilities," U.S. EPA.

9. HEROES FIGHTING POLLUTION AT MILITARY BASES

312 with toxins spread: Abrahm Lustgarten, "Open Burns, Ill Wounds," ProPublica, July 20, 2017.

312 The EPA has identified: Corinne Roels, Briana

Smith, Adrienne St. Clair, and News21 staff, "Military Bases' Contamination Will Affect Water for Generations," Center for Public Integrity and Carnegie-Knight News21 program, August 22, 2017.

313 Retired Michigan congressman and veteran John D. Dingell: Alexander Nazaryan, "Camp Lejeune and the U.S. Military's Polluted Legacy," Newsweek, July 16, 2014.

313 McClellan Air Force Base: McClellan Air Force Base, U.S. Nuclear Regulatory Commission, November 2, 2018.

313 Wright Patterson Air Force Base: "City of Dayton Demands Wright-Patterson Air Force Base Stop Contaminating Water Source," City of Dayton, Ohio, press release, February 8, 2018.

313 Fort McClellan: "Public Health: Potential Exposure at Fort McClellan," U.S. Department of Veterans Affairs.

313 The EPA has found: "Superfund Site: Hill Air Force Base, Hill AFB, UT," U.S. EPA.

314 "to fulfill President Lincoln's promise": Mission Statement, U.S. Department of Veterans Affairs.

314 the Feres Doctrine: Feres v. United States, 340 U.S. 135 (1950).

315 a collection of three cases: Rachel Natelson, "The Unfairness of the Feres Doctrine," Time, February 25, 2013.

316 CTS Corp.: "Cleanup to Begin at the CTS Superfund Site in Asheville, N.C," U.S. EPA press release, November 17, 2017.

316 The CTS Corp. v. Waldburger case: CTS Corp. v. Waldburger, 573 U.S. No. 13-339 (2014).

316 the Department of Justice: Ibid.

318 a 2017 report: "Report to Congressional Com-

mittees: Military Base Realignments and Closures," U.S. Government Accountability Office, January 2017.

320 about three thousand children are diagnosed with ALL: David A. Siegel, S. Jane Henley, Jun Li, Lori A. Pollack, Elizabeth A. Van Dyne, and Arica White, "Rates and Trends of Pediatric Acute Lymphoblastic Leukemia—United States, 2001–2014," **Morbidity and Mortality Weekly Report (MMWR)**, Centers for Disease Control and Prevention, September 15, 2017.

320 The American Cancer Society states: "What Are the Risk Factors for Childhood Leukemia?" American Cancer Society.

323 in a 2012 interview: Brian Lamb, "Q&A with Jerry Ensminger and Rachel Libert," C-SPAN transcript, March 15, 2012.

323 The Marine Corps said: Manuel Roig-Franzia, "Water Probe Backs Marine Corps Defense," **The Washington Post**, October 7, 2004.

324 This letter: Carey P. McCord, "Toxicity of Trichloroethylene," **Journal of the American Medical Association**, July 30, 1932.

326 researchers from the Harvard School of Public Health published: S. W. Lagakos, B. J. Wessen, and M. Zelen, "An Analysis of Contaminated Well Water and Health Effects in Woburn, Massachusetts," **Journal of the American Statistical Association**, vol. 81 (1986).

326 A 1994 analysis: P. Cohn, J. Klotz, F. Bove, M. Berkowitz, and J. Fagliano, "Drinking Water Contamination and the Incidence of Leukemia and Non-Hodgkin's Lymphoma," **Environmental Health Perspectives**, June-July 1994.

326 the EPA did not classify TCE: "Toxicological Review of Trichloroethylene," U.S. EPA, September 2011.

326 250 million pounds: "Risk Management for Trichloroethylene (TCE)," U.S. EPA.

326 The EPA has proposed: Ibid.

326 "Baby Heaven": Alexander Nazaryan, "Camp Lejeune and the U.S. Military's Polluted Legacy," Newsweek, July 16, 2014.

327 a Superfund site: ATSDR Public Health Assessment for Camp Lejeune Drinking Water, U.S. Marine Corps Base Camp Lejeune, North Carolina, January 20, 2017.

329 worst and largest water contamination: "A Few Good Men, a Lot of Bad Water," Dan Rather Reports, October 21, 2008.

330 court documents: CTS Corp. v. Waldburger, 573 U.S. No. 13-339, Brief of Jerry Ensminger, the Estate of Christopher Townsend, Mike Partain, Kris Thomas, and the Estate of Rosanne Warren as Amici Curiae in Support of Respondents.

330 Mike Partain, "Marine Corps Base Camp Lejeune Chronology of Significant Events Concerning Contamination of the Base Drinking Water Supply," Tftptf.com, Part 1, 1941–October 1989, http://tftptf .com/Misc/Timeline_Linked_March_2012.pdf.

332 A Condensed Timeline: Associated Press, "Key Events in Camp Lejeune's Water Contamination," San Diego Union-Tribune, April 28, 2009.

335 A new PHA: "ATSDR Releases Public Health Assessment of Drinking Water at Camp Lejeune," Agency for Toxic Substances and Disease Registry, January 26, 2017.

336 introduced a bill: Amanda Greene, "Justice for Janey," Star-News, August 26, 2007.

336 Honoring America's Veterans: H.R.1627—Honoring America's Veterans and Caring for Camp Lejeune Families Act of 2012, Public Law No: 112-154, August 6, 2012.

337 In 2017, the VA passed a rule: "New Rule Establishes a Presumption of Service Connection for Diseases Associated with Exposure to Contaminants in the Water Supply at Camp Lejeune," Official Blog of the U.S. Department of Veterans Affairs, January 13, 2017.

340 The manufacturers of these chemicals: Sharon Lerner, "3M Knew About the Dangers of PFOA and PFOS Decades Ago, Internal Documents Show," The Intercept, July 31, 2018.

340 Despite a deal: Tom Roeder and Jakob Rodgers, "Toxic Legacy: Air Force Studies Dating Back Decades Show Danger of Foam That Contaminated Local Water," The Gazette, October 23, 2016.

340 The Union of Concerned Scientists reported: Michael Halpern, "Bipartisan Outrage as EPA, White House Try to Cover Up Chemical Health Assessment," Union of Concerned Scientists Blog, May 16, 2018.

340 "The public, media, and Congressional reaction": Annie Snider, "White House, EPA Headed Off Chemical Pollution Study," Politico, May 14, 2018.

341 The EPA estimates: Technical Fact Sheet— Perfluorooctane Sulfonate (PFOS) and Perfluorooctanoic Acid (PFOA), U.S. EPA, November 2017.

341 "It is unacceptable": "NH Delegation Calls on Trump Administration to Immediately Release Study About Health Impacts of PFOA and PFOS," Office of U.S. Senator Maggie Hassan of New Hampshire press release, May 15, 2018.

342 Groundwater in western Michigan: Dan Kildee et al., Letter to Scott Pruitt, December 5, 2017.

342 National Defense Authorization Act: H.R. 2810—National Defense Authorization Act for Fiscal Year 2018, Public Law No: 115-91, December 12, 2017.

342 Federal lawmakers approved a budget: Kyle Bagenstose, "Federal Budget Bill Includes $10M for PFAS Health Study, $85M for Cleanup," **The Intelligencer**, March 23, 2018.

343 In a bipartisan letter: Carol A. Clark, "Udall, Heinrich Call on EPA to Set Federal Drinking Water Standards for PFOA and PFOS," **Los Alamos Daily Post**, February 7, 2019.

344 the military has been investigating: Maureen Sullivan, "Addressing Perfluorooctane Sulfonate (PFOS) and Perfluorooctanoic Acid (PFOA)," U.S. Department of Defense, March 2018.

344 the DoD tested another 2,688: Tara Copp, "DoD: At Least 126 Bases Report Water Contaminants Linked to Cancer, Birth Defects," MilitaryTimes.com, April 26, 2018.

345 ulcerative colitis: Kyle Steenland, Liping Zhao, Andrea Winquist, and Christine Parks, "Ulcerative Colitis and Perfluorooctanoic Acid (PFOA) in a Highly Exposed Population of Community Residents and Workers in the Mid-Ohio Valley," **Environmental Health Perspectives**, June 2013.

345 low birth weights: Kellyn Betts, "PFOS and PFOA in Humans: New Study Links Prenatal Exposure to Lower Birth Weight," **Environmental Health Perspectives**, November 2007.

346 Testing for Pease: Testing for Pease website, http:// www.testingforpease.com.

347 Hailey Bussey: Kyle Hughes, "Hoosick Falls Residents Urge Action by Lawmakers," **The Record**, June 15, 2016.

348 "That article ran": Jeff McMenemy, "Amico Led Fight on Pease Water Contamination," Seacoast online.com, December 27, 2015.

349 "All of us are guinea pigs": Corinne Roels, Briana Smith, and Adrienne St. Clair, "Military Bases' Contamination Will Affect Water for Generations," News21.com, August 14, 2017.

350 Facebook post: https://www.facebook.com/Erin BrockovichOfficial/posts/10155910934330494.

10. TAKING BACK THE EPA & FLORIDA'S SHORELINES

365 "It's not wrong for Americans": Robison Meyer, "Congress and Trump Won't 'Terminate the EPA,'" **The Atlantic**, February 16, 2017.

366 "little tidbits": Brady Dennis, "Trump Budget Seeks 23 Percent Cut at EPA, Eliminating Dozens of Programs," **The Washington Post**, February 12, 2018.

366 eliminate significant regional water quality programs: Melany Rochester, "Trump Proposes Lowest EPA Budget in 40 Years," Food & Water Watch, June 19, 2017.

366 proposed to significantly cut: "America First: A Budget Blueprint to Make America Great Again," Office of Management and Budget, fiscal year 2018.

367 cost an estimated $1 million: "Initial Report to Congress on the EPA's Capacity to Implement Certain Provisions of the Frank R. Lautenberg Chemical Safety for the 21st Century Act," Office of Chemical Safety and Pollution Prevention, U.S. EPA, January 2017.

367 "The Trump administration currently": Christopher Sellers et al.,"The EPA Under Siege," the Environmental Data & Governance Initiative (EDGI).

368 dropped 69 percent: Amanda Little, "A Look Back at Reagan's Environmental Record, **Grist**, June 11, 2004.

368 the doctrine of Chevron deference: **Chevron U.S.A., Inc. v. NRDC**, 467 U.S. 837 (1984).

370 The bill introduces more than fifty: Lisa Lambert, "Senate Tees Up 'Accountability Act' as Regulation Fight Intensifies," Reuters, May 17, 2017.

371 The Trump administration filed: "Civil Penalties Against Polluters Drop by Half During First Year of Trump Administration," Environmental Integrity Project, February 15, 2018.

371 said in a statement: Ibid.

372 very well known set of tactics: "The Disinformation Playbook," Center for Science and Democracy, Union of Concerned Citizens.

373 new cases of mesothelioma: "Causes, Risk Factors, and Prevention for Malignant Mesothelioma," American Cancer Society.

374 he sued the EPA: "Scott Pruitt's Web of Fundraising and Lawsuits," EDF Action.

374 his secret schedule for private meetings: Justin Wise, "Whistleblower Says Pruitt Kept Secret Calendar to Hide Meetings with Industry Reps: Report," **The Hill**, July 3, 2018.

374 He terminated half of the advisors: Rafi Letzter, "The EPA Just Kicked Half the Scientists Off a Key Board—and May Replace Them with Fossil Fuel Industry Insiders," **Business Insider**, May 8, 2017.

376 in the **EPA Journal**: Gaylord Nelson, "Earth Day '70: What It Meant," **EPA Journal**, April 1980.

377 The EPA has also proposed: Vehicle Emissions California Waivers and Authorizations, U.S. EPA.

377 "For Trump to now destroy": Marissa Papanek, "Gov. Brown Calls Trump Initiative to Roll Back Clean Car Standard 'Reckless Scheme,'" KRCR News, August 2, 2018.

378 According to the EPA's own studies: Regulations for Emissions from Vehicles and Engines, "Draft Technical Assessment Report (TAR)," U.S. EPA.

378 a 2017 report: "Irreplaceable: Why States Can't and Won't Make Up for Inadequate Federal Enforcement of Environmental Laws," Institute for Policy Integrity, New York University School of Law, September 2017.

378 The report discloses: Robert Esworthy, "Federal Pollution Control Laws: How Are They Enforced?" Congressional Research Service, October 7, 2014.

381 Hundreds of tons: Greg Allen, "Tons of Dead Fish Washing Ashore on Florida Beaches," NPR, August 31, 2018.

381 One man became ill: Nestor Montoya, "Fort Myers Beach Clams Send Man to Hospital," WBBH/WZVN (Waterman Broadcasting), August 1, 2018.

381 more than eighty-six people sought treatment: Tyler Treadway, "Blue-Green Algae Bloom in St. Lucie River 10 Times Too Toxic to Touch, DEP Tests Show," TC Palm, August 9, 2018.

381 It's a recurring harmful algal bloom (HAB): R. H. Pierce and M. S. Henry, "Harmful Algal Toxins of the Florida Red Tide (Karenia brevis): Natural Chemical Stressors in South Florida Coastal Ecosystems," Ecotoxicology, October 2008.

382 Scientists believe: Ibid.

383 according to the National Centers for Coastal

Ocean Science (NCCOS): "Harmful Algal Bloom and Hypoxia Research and Control Act," National Centers for Coastal Ocean Science (NCCOS).

383 The EPA says: "Nutrient Pollution, Harmful Algal Blooms," U.S. EPA.

383 Other contributors: Shahram Missaghi and Marte Kitson, "HABs Explained: What, How and What Now?" University of Minnesota Water Resources Center.

384 according to the U.S. Geological Survey: "The Science of Harmful Algal Blooms," USGS, October 24, 2016.

384 it's the Everglades: "About the Florida Everglades," Florida Museum of Natural History.

384 Michael Grunwald writes: Michael Grunwald, **The Swamp: The Everglades, Florida, and the Politics of Paradise** (New York: Simon & Schuster, October 31, 2006).

388 "Hurricanes and major storm events": Florida Waterkeepers Position Statement on Hurricane Irma.

390 a statement on their website: Captains for Clean Water website, https://captainsforcleanwater.org.

390 Tourism: "Florida Quick Facts," State of Florida website, 2018.

390 "This is not the Florida": Jennifer Gray, "Green Slime Oozes into Florida's Primary Elections," CNN, August 28, 2018.

390 Comprehensive Everglades Restoration Plan (CERP): "Comprehensive Everglades Restoration Plan (CERP)," National Park Service, U.S. Department of the Interior.

391 "This is a man-made": Greg Allen, "'A Government-Sponsored Disaster': Florida Asks for Federal Help with Toxic Algae," NPR, July 9, 2016.

392 Mark Perry: Ibid.

392 a 2008 FDEP report: "Integrated Water Quality Assessment for Florida: 2008," Florida Department of Environmental Protection (FDEP), October 2008.

392 "failed to perform": United States District Court, Northern District of Florida Tallahassee Division, Case No. 4:08-cv-00324-RH-WCS.

393 The letter: Julie Hauserman, "Yes, This Really Is Rick Scott, Adam Putnam and Pam Bondi's Fault," **The Phoenix**, August 3, 2018.

393 a high-powered PR firm: Ibid.

393 state leaders wrote in the letter: Bill Kaczor, "Scott Asks EPA to Delay Fla. Water Pollution Rules," CNBC, November 12, 2010.

394 The FDEP: Letter from U.S. EPA to Herschel T. Vinyard Jr., Secretary Florida Department of Environmental Protection, June 13, 2011.

394 letting the state manage: "EPA, Florida Reach Agreement on Reducing Water Pollution," **Southeast Farm Press**, March 25, 2013.

394 In 2011, Scott slashed: Dara Kam, "After $700M in Water District Cuts, Florida Governor Wants $2.4M More," **Palm Beach Post**, December 6, 2011.

394 That same year: Ibid.

394 "Since 2011, when Scott": Dave Conway, "Dead in the Water," **Florida Sportsman**, August 22, 2018.

397 "President Trump's executive order": Brady Dennis and Juliet Eilperin, "Trump Signs Order at the EPA to Dismantle Environmental Protections," **The Washington Post**, March 28, 2017.

398 The EPA has studied: "Cleaning Up Power Plant Water Pollution," Earth Justice.

398 "Thirsty energy sources": Andrew Maddocks,

Robert Samuel Young, and Paul Reig, "The Clean Power Plan: What's Water Got to Do with It?" World Resources Institute, September 8, 2015.

399   The researchers used data: Bryan C. Williamson, "Do Environmental Regulations Really Work?" **The Regulatory Review**, November 24, 2016; Joseph S. Shapiro and Reed Walker, "Why Is Pollution from U.S. Manufacturing Declining? The Roles of Environmental Regulation, Productivity, and Trade," National Bureau of Economic Research, June 2018.

399   One study: Eli Berman and Linda T. M. Bui, "Environmental Regulation and Labor Demand: Evidence from the South Coast Air Basin," **Journal of Public Economics**, October 2, 1999.

400   in his 2013 paper: W. Reed Walker, "The Transitional Costs of Sectoral Reallocation: Evidence from the Clean Air Act and the Workforce," **Quarterly Journal of Economics** 128, no. 4 (November 1, 2013).

400   In 2018, our country experienced: "2018 Was the Hottest Year on Record for the Globe," NOAA press release, February 6, 2019.

401   In Sarasota County: Zac Anderson, "Red Tide Caused Worst Sarasota Hotel Occupancy Dip Since 9/11," **Sarasota Herald-Tribune**, January 28, 2019.

403   To date, the EPA has issued: "EPA Receives Record Number of Letters of Interest for WIFIA Water Infrastructure Loans," U.S. EPA press release, August 16, 2018.

404   lobbying spending totaled $1.45 billion: "Lobbying Database," Center for Responsive Politics, based on data from the Senate Office of Public Records on September 10, 2018.

11. DAY ZERO

409 As one writer: Aryn Baker, "What It's Like to Live Through Cape Town's Massive Water Crisis," **Time**, February 2018.

410 Anthony Turton: Craig Welch, "How Cape Town Is Coping with Its Worst Drought on Record," **National Geographic**, March 5, 2018.

416 Consider the charred wreckage: Andrew Sheeler, "These Three 2018 California Wildfires Caused More Than $9 Billion in Damage," **Sacramento Bee**, December 12, 2018.

416 2018 was the fourth hottest year on record: Christopher Joyce, "2018 Was Earth's Fourth-Hottest Year on Record, Scientists Say," NPR, February 6, 2019.

419 journalist David Wallace-Wells explains: David Wallace-Wells, "UN Says Climate Genocide Is Coming. It's Actually Worse Than That," **New York**, October 10, 2018.

420 As Hans-Otto Pörtner: "Special Climate Report: 1.5°C Is Possible But Requires Unprecedented and Urgent Action," UN press release, October 8, 2018.

421 said Panmao Zhai: Ibid.

421 the report's authors found: IPCC Special Report, "Global Warming of 1.5 °C," chapter 3, p. 177, October 2018.

421 we can expect: Ibid.

423 "Safety nets": Alleen Brown, "Climate Change Refugees Share Stories of Escaping Wildfires, Floods, and Droughts," **The Intercept**, December 29, 2018.

424 The number and scale of droughts: IPCC Special Report, "Global Warming of 1.5 °C," chapter 3, p. 178, October 2018.

425 As **The New York Times** reported: Coral Davenport

and Kendra Pierre-Louis, "U.S. Climate Report Warns of Damaged Environment and Shrinking Economy," **The New York Times**, November 23, 2108.

426 His administration also directed scientists: Scott K. Johnson, "US Tries to Bury Report on Climate Change's Dire Health, Economic Impacts," **Ars Technica**, November 26, 2018.

427 Trump told reporters: Timothy Cama, "Trump on Dire Warnings in Climate Change Report: 'I Don't Believe It,'" **The Hill**, November 26, 2018.

427 "There is a bizarre contrast": Coral Davenport and Kendra Pierre-Louis, "U.S. Climate Report Warns of Damaged Environment and Shrinking Economy," **The New York Times**, November 23, 2108.

427 "More frequent and intense": "Fourth National Climate Assessment," U.S. Global Change Research Program, Volume 2, November 2018.

428 the report is downright bracing: "Fourth National Climate Assessment," U.S. Global Change Research Program, Volume 2, Section 5, November 2018.

428 Estimates show: "2017 Infrastructure Report Card," American Society of Civil Engineers.

429 "Water systems face considerable risk": "Fourth National Climate Assessment," U.S. Global Change Research Program, chapter 3, "Water," November 2018.

430 "Across the Nation," the report finds: Ibid.

433 But, reports **Bloomberg Businessweek**: Christopher Flavelle, "Miami Will Be Underwater Soon. Its Drinking Water Could Go First," **Bloomberg Businessweek**, August 29, 2018.

437 Soon the dishwasher and laundry machine: Noah

Gallagher Shannon, "The Water Wars of Arizona," **The New York Times Magazine**, July 19, 2018.

438 NASA scientists found: Ibid.

446 a team of researchers: Seth Wynes and Kimberly A. Nicholas, "The Climate Mitigation Gap: Education and Government Recommendations Miss the Most Effective Individual Actions," **Environmental Research Letters**, July 12, 2017.

448 A study published in February: P. C. D. Milly and K. A. Dunne, "Colorado River Flow Dwindles as Warming-Driven Loss of Reflective Snow Energizes Evaporation," **Science**, March 13, 2020.

449 In 2015, researchers called: "Reservoir Evaporation a Big Challenge for Water Managers in West," University of Colorado Press Release, Dec. 28, 2015.

449 I even have a study: "Lake Powell Evaporation," Upper Colorado Regional Office, Salt Lake City, Utah, August 1986. www.riversimulator.org

12. TIME TO ACT!

451 water shortages: Ellie Kincaid, "California Isn't the Only State with Water Problems," **Business Insider**, April 21, 2015.

451 More than 60 million Americans: Agnel Philip, Elizabeth Sims, Jordan Houston, and Rachel Konieczny, "Millions Consumed Potentially Unsafe Water in the Last 10 Years," News21.com, August 14, 2017.

452 four hundred coal-fired power plants: "Coal Has an Enormous Environmental Footprint," Environmental Integrity Project.

453 While the EPA did identify: David Andrews, "Report: Up to 110 Million Americans Could Have

PFAS-Contaminated Drinking Water," Environmental Working Group, May 22, 2018.

455 No more mayors: Sara Ganim and Linh Tran, "How Tap Water Became Toxic in Flint, Michigan," CNN, January, 19, 2016.

462 "Perhaps, what is needed": T. Christian Miller, "The Dig: Investigating the Safety of the Water You Drink," ProPublica, June 28, 2016.

466 Text messages: "Text Messaging for Cities and Municipalities," EZ Texting, https://www.eztexting .com/sms-municipalities.

467 a nationwide survey: "Public Willing to Pay to Improve Water Quality, MU Research Finds," University of Missouri press release, March 26, 2018.

469 certified B Corporations: Certified B Corporation website, https://bcorporation.net.

477 Bottled water outsold soda: E. J. Schultz, "There's a Clear Winner in Beverages: Bottled Water Tops Soda," **Ad Age**, March 9, 2017.

477 "When Perrier first entered": "Bottled Water Becomes Number-One Beverage in the U.S., Data from Beverage Marketing Corporation Show," Beverage Marketing Corporation press release, March 9, 2017.

477 Today, Americans spend: Mallory Sofastaii, "Americans Spend $16 Billion a Year on Bottled Water," WMAR-2 News, October 10, 2017.

478 which the EPA defines: "Water Health Series: Bottled Water Basics," U.S. EPA, September 2005.

478 Each bottle of water you buy: G. E. Miller, "The TRUE Cost of Bottled Water Vs. Tap Water (& Comparative Purity & Taste Test Results)," **20 Something Finance**, April 29, 2018.

479 Many of those bottles: Wenonah Hauter, "Bottled

Water, Brought to You by Fracking?" **AlterNet**, March 14, 2018.

479 Plus, plastic manufacturing plants: Elizabeth Glazner, "The Irony of One Polluter's Bottled Water Proffer," Plastic Pollution Coalition, April 15, 2016.

479 free bottled water stations: Ron Fonger, "State Spending on Bottled Water in Flint Averaging $22,000 a Day," MLive.com, March 12, 2018.

482 in a May 2018 campaign email: Sharon Lerner, "Toxic Drinking Water Becomes Top Campaign Issue for Midterm Candidates Across the U.S.," **The Intercept**, June 4, 2018.

482 The forty-seven-year-old did not win: Melissa Nann Burke, "Bergman Defeats Morgan in 1st House District," **Detroit Free Press**, November 7, 2018.

482 she told a local news site: Elisabeth Almekinder, "A Local Woman Doctor in the U.S. House Could Make History," **Politics North Carolina**, January 2, 2018.

483 in a concession message: Dr. Kyle Horton for Congress Facebook page, November 7, 2018, https://www.facebook.com/drkyle4congress.

484 The state is now regularly submitting: Elisabeth Almekinder, "A Local Woman Doctor in the U.S. House Could Make History," **Politics North Carolina**, January 2, 2018.

484 live below the federal poverty level: Julie Mack, "Flint Is Nation's Poorest City, Based on Latest Census Data," MLive.com, September 19, 2017.

485 according to a 2016 study: Mary B. Collins, Ian Munoz, and Joseph JaJa, "Linking 'Toxic Outliers' to Environmental Justice Communities," **IOP Science**, January 26, 2016.

485 Cancer Alley: Tracey Ross and Danyelle Solomon,

"Flint Isn't the Only Place with Racism in the Water," **The Nation**, February 9, 2016.

490 A 2015 study: Judy Woodruff and William Brangham, "New Science Shows Gulf Spill is Still Killing Dolphins," **PBS NewsHour**, May 20, 2015.

INDEX

Page numbers in bold refer to photographs.

ILLUSTRATION CREDITS

5: Courtesy of Erin Brockovich

6: **(top)** NCA (National Climate Assessment) 2018; **(bottom)** User B137, Wikimedia Commons

7: **(top)** © Dow; **(inset)** © The Chemours Company; **(bottom)** U.S. Marine Corps/photo by Cpl. Jonathan Sosner

8: Bob Bowcock

ERIN BROCKOVICH is the president of Brockovich Research & Consulting and the founder of the Erin Brockovich Foundation, a nonprofit organization created to educate and empower communities in their fight for clean water. She is the coauthor of **Take It from Me: Life's a Struggle but You Can Win** and has her own show on PodcastOne. She lives in Southern California.

SUZANNE BOOTHBY is the author of **The After Cancer Diet.** She is a journalist who writes about health, politics, food, and eco-conscious stories and is a graduate of Northwestern University's Medill School of Journalism. She lives in Asheville, North Carolina.